20th Anniversary Edition

SOCIAL SKILLS TRAINING

for Children & Adolescents with Autism & Social-Communication Differences

JED BAKER, PhD

FUTURE HORIZONS

Advanced Praise for *Social Skills Training* 20th Anniversary Edition

"Jed Baker's *Social Skills Training* has always been one of my go-to autism books. And his 20th anniversary edition continues that tradition. This book exceeds my expectations—which are always high! Why? Jed, sums it up in one sentence, 'The model I have used to teach skills has moved from an approach that teaches skills to an approach that teaches children.' His years of teaching and research have coalesced into a wonderful volume of instruction that will benefit any child or adolescent. Jed doesn't just talk about social skills; he uses them in his daily life. He is a lovely person and an excellent role model. This is evidenced on every page of his book."

— Brenda Smith Myles, PhD, autism researcher, consultant, and author of many books including *The Hidden Curriculum* and *Autism and Difficult Moments*

"The 20th anniversary edition of Jed Baker's *Social Skills Training* book provides updated and timely information on a range of topics related to social skills. However, he does not stop there. Jed goes on to provide practical and well thought out lessons on topics ranging from Asking Someone to Play to Dealing with Teasing. Jed is a rare breed the combines both a thorough understanding of the research and practical clinical experience. I cannot recommend this publication highly enough."

— Dr. Cathy Pratt, BCBA-D, Indiana Resource Center for Autism

Praise for the First Edition of *Social Skills Training*

"If you've been searching for a social skills curriculum that really works, you've found it! Jed Baker's long-awaited, much antic¬ipated "how-to" manual is based on his enormously successful social skills training groups. The book covers everything from assessment and strategies for social skills training, to generalization of those skills, to behavior management, to the often-over¬looked importance of promoting peer acceptance through sensitivity training. The core of this book, however, is the inclusion of individual skill lessons and activities that address practically every social situation you can possibly think of. This book is a MUST-READ and should be part of every parent and professional's autism resource library!"

> — Lori Shery, president and cofounder, Asperger Syndrome Education Network (ASPEN®)

"This very user-friendly book provides a wealth of ready-to-use activities for both parents and educators. The centerpiece of the book is a series of 70 specific skills found to cause problems for individuals with autism and other social-communication disorders. Each skill is presented in a handy format, with the skill to be learned on one page and related activities on the facing page. The chapter on sensitivity and awareness training makes this a complete social skills training package."

> — Diane Adreon, associate director, Center for Autism and Related Disabilities, University of Miami

"Dr. Baker's clinical expertise and personal concern for individuals with autism is evident throughout this wonderful book. The chapters contain many easy-to-use strategies to make and keep friends, specific examples for various age groups, and clear direction for assessment and intervention. This book is an essential resource for professionals who want to increase all students' social and coping skills within individual and group sessions and in everyday life."

> — Suzanne Buchanan, Psy.D., BCBA, and Jenna Miller, M.A.T., The New Jersey Center for Outreach and Services for the Autism Community (COSAC)

SOCIAL SKILLS TRAINING:
for Children & Adolescents with Autism & Social-Communication Differences

All marketing and publishing rights guaranteed to and reserved by:

FUTURE **HORIZONS**

(817) 277-0727
(817) 277-2270 (fax)
E-mail: info@fhautism.com
www.fhautism.com

ISBN: 9781957984223

CONTENTS

SKILL LESSONS

CONTENTS   VII

CONTENTS   IX

CHAPTER 1

WHAT'S NEW IN THIS EDITION?

In 2003 I wrote my first social skills training manual based on the groups that I had been running for children with ASD. Back then, I was invested in teaching a curriculum of skills to children based on the evidence at the time for best practices in teaching skills: explanation, modeling, role-play, and practice with feedback and incentives. Now, close to twenty years later with the benefit of more outcome research, we have learned what areas need to be addressed more fully to achieve better outcomes, namely *motivation* and *generalization*.

Without sufficient attention to these issues, skill training efforts do not lead to meaningful outcomes that are sustained outside the training setting. This should come as no surprise; when kids are less motivated and little attention is paid to help them use skills in real settings, skills training effects are diminished (see Bellini et al., 2007).

The model I have used to teach skills has moved from an approach that teaches skills to an approach that teaches children. We don't simply ask how best to teach a set of skills; rather, how do we individualize an approach to maximize a child's motivation and create more lasting impact? To address motivation, it is crucial that children are optimistic enough about themselves that they are willing to work on any challenges. Too often children hear negative information about themselves that simply fosters a sense of hopelessness, resulting in apathy. Then adults may step in to impose behavior plans and skills training that the children do not necessarily accept. It is critical that children are willing participants in establishing goals and ways to solve their own challenges. The chapter on motivation addresses several important ways to create optimism and a willingness to work on skill improvement through self-awareness, collaborative problem-solving, and utilizing the child's own interests.

To address generalization and thus create more lasting changes, it is best to teach and practice a small set of highly relevant skills rather than a large set of skills taught less frequently. This change is reflected in my chapter on generalization of skills, which covers how to help children actually use skills when and where they need them through the systematic use of cues and reminders.

In order to hone in on a small set of relevant skill goals for a child, I have refined my understanding of the assessment process. As is often the case in clinical practice, we continue to modify our approach to get better outcomes. Chapter 6 outlines the assessment process used to target individualized and clinically relevant skill goals in a way that respects the client's wishes and engages them fully in the process.

Though much of the content of this book contains specific skill lessons that could be used as a basic curriculum for classrooms, these lessons are really just one part of entire model of skills training in which lessons are selected to meet the individualized needs of students. This model addresses the crucial issues I have described above, including motivation, targeting relevant skills, and generalization. No matter how one teaches skills (e.g., the structured learning method used in this book, video modeling, live modeling, picture books, cartoons, social stories, play based approaches, ABA approaches), certain key components lead to effective and more lasting learning. That understanding led to my model of **THE KEY COMPONENTS OF SOCIAL SKILLS TRAINING,** which serves as a decision guide to help professionals and parents ensure they are addressing all that is necessary to get better outcomes in social skills training. That model, summarized below, is detailed in Chapter 4.

Key Components of Social Skills Training

1. Establish motivation to participate in learning and using skills

2. Target relevant skills that match the needs of the children

3. Consider how to measures skill performance to assess progress

4. Consider modifications to the environment to improve outcomes

5. Consider the child's cognitive abilities and language comprehension in choosing HOW and WHERE to teach the skills

6. Plan for generalization or transfer of learning by using homework assignments and reminders from key caregivers (like parents and teachers)

7. Consider targeting the peer community to improve socialization and acceptance

To use this book most effectively, one should familiarize themselves with the model outlined in Chapter 4 and then use the SOCIAL SKILL ACTION PLAN (see Chapter 13) to create a specific plan for their child, student or client. One can certainly use the lessons to teach a group or class of students who need some of the same lessons, yet to maximize results for a particular individual, it is crucial to complete the SOCIAL SKILL ACTION PLAN. Once the SOCIAL SKILL ACTION PLAN is created, one can use the skill lessons in Chapter 14 as a reference for teaching specific skills.

Who Should Use This Book?

The lessons in this book are designed primarily, but not entirely for children with ASD, Level 2 and Level 1, which refer to children with enough language comprehension to understand and learn skills introduced through verbal explanation, modeling and role-play. That does not mean they won't also benefit from adding visual supports like pictures and video modeling, but many of the skills involve verbal explanation. Individuals without ASD who also have social challenges will also greatly benefit from the model and lessons in this book. That includes children with ADHD, anxiety and mood disorders, non-verbal learning disabilities, and other social-emotional challenges. **Thus any professionals, teachers or parents that have children with these social challenges and basic receptive language skill can use this book. I have included skill lessons relevant for young children starting in preschool through their teenage years to young adulthood. Where needed, I have indicated the age range for a particular skill.**

The skill lessons have been updated since 2003 to reflect our latest thinking about what skill areas are most relevant and how best to teach skill concepts. In addition, some skills lessons reflect changes in our society since 2003, such as the extensive use of social media to communicate with others.

Individuals with ASD (and many without ASD) often present with communication issues (e.g., nonverbal communication challenges, trouble initiating, responding and managing topics), perspective-taking and empathy difficulties, restricted patterns of play, difficulties maintaining friendships and romantic relationships, and emotional regulation issues. That last issue is the subject of two of my other books called *No More Meltdowns* (2008) and *Overcoming Anxiety in Children and Teens* (2015). Some of the content of those books is reflected in my skill lessons covering emotion management issues, including dealing with frustration, demanding work, handling imperfection (like mistakes or losing a game), not getting desired attention from others, managing upsets over having to wait for desired objects or activities, and handling fears like social anxiety that can become an obstacle to interacting with others. One skill area I have left out is related to employment, as this is well represented in another one of my books, *Preparing for Life* (2006).

CHAPTER 2

WHAT ARE SOCIAL SKILLS, AND WHAT ARE COMMON SOCIAL SKILL CHALLENGES OF INDIVIDUALS WITH ASD?

When I sat down with colleagues over twenty years ago to create a social skill curriculum for students in their school program, we confronted our first obstacle: defining social skills? Another way to ask this question is, "What are **'not'** social skills?" Is doing math work a social skill? It could be, if you do it well and peers think you're smart. Or if you answer every math question in a class, others could think you were bragging. So even doing math work could have social implications, affecting whether peers like you or not.

As we discussed behavioral challenges, friendship problems, manners, and other expected behaviors across settings, we discovered that every behavior is potentially social. Our working definition then was, "Any behavior that has a social impact on others can be considered a social behavior and thus a potential social skill."

Great, then all we had to do was write a curriculum to account for all of human behavior. Not feasible. Rather than giving up, we realized that we did not need a curriculum of all human behavior but a way to figure out, for each student, what specific behaviors were needed to function successfully in a particular social setting.

So instead of teaching a one-size-fits-all curriculum for our students, we developed a process to hone in on relevant skills for each student. That assessment process is outlined in Chapter 6. We still needed a set of ready-to-go skill lessons as a useful reference after we decided what to teach a child. Those particular skill lessons you see in this book were based on the needs of our clients over twenty-five years of working with students with ASD and other social challenges. They fall into categories that are often considered problematic for individuals with ASD, including emotional regulation, communication (verbal and non-verbal), restricted patterns of play, challenges with empathy and perspective taking, and friendship management.

If we look at the current symptoms of Autism Spectrum Disorder, we can see that many of these skill themes are associated with the core symptoms of Autism (see Figure 1).

FIGURE 1: Diagnostic Criteria for Autism Spectrum Disorder (DSM-5, APA)

To meet diagnostic criteria for ASD according to the DSM-5, a child must have persistent deficits in each of three areas of social communication and interaction (see A.1. through A.3. below) plus at least two of four types of restricted, repetitive behaviors (see B.1. through B.4. below). Finally, the level of severity is assessed (C through E).

A. Persistent deficits in social communication and social interaction across multiple contexts, as manifested by the following, currently or by history (examples are illustrative, not exhaustive; see text):

1. Deficits in social-emotional reciprocity, ranging, for example, from abnormal social approach and failure of normal back-and-forth conversation; to reduced sharing of interests, emotions, or affect; to failure to initiate or respond to social interactions.

2. Deficits in nonverbal communicative behaviors used for social interaction, ranging, for example, from poorly integrated verbal and nonverbal communication; to abnormalities in eye contact and body language or deficits in understanding and use of gestures; to a total lack of facial expressions and nonverbal communication.

3. Deficits in developing, maintaining, and understand relationships, ranging, for example, from difficulties adjusting behavior to suit various social contexts; to difficulties in sharing imaginative play or in making friends; to absence of interest in peers.

SOCIAL SKILLS TRAINING

Specify current severity. Severity is based on social communication impairments and restricted, repetitive patterns of behavior.

B. Restricted, repetitive patterns of behavior, interests, or activities, as manifested by at least two of the following, currently or by history (examples are illustrative, not exhaustive; see text):

1. Stereotyped or repetitive motor movements, use of objects, or speech (e.g., simple motor stereotypes, lining up toys or flipping objects, echolalia, idiosyncratic phrases).

2. Insistence on sameness, inflexible adherence to routines, or ritualized patterns of verbal or nonverbal behavior (e.g., extreme distress at small changes, difficulties with transitions, rigid thinking patterns, greeting rituals, need to take same route or eat same food every day).

3. Highly restricted, fixated interests that are abnormal in intensity or focus (e.g., strong attachment to or preoccupation with unusual objects, excessively circumscribed or perseverative interests).

4. Hyper- or hyporeactivity to sensory input or unusual interest in sensory aspects of the environment (e.g., apparent indifference to pain/temperature, adverse response to specific sounds or textures, excessive smelling or touching of objects, visual fascination with lights or movement).

Specify current severity: Level 1, 2, or 3.

C. Symptoms must be present in the early developmental period (but may not become fully manifest until social demands exceed limited capacities, or may be masked by learned strategies in later life). Severity is based on social communication impairments and restricted, repetitive patterns of behavior.

D. Symptoms cause clinically significant impairment in social, occupational, or other important areas of current functioning.

E. These disturbances are not better explained by intellectual disability (intellectual developmental disorder) or global developmental delay. Intellectual disability and autism spectrum disorder frequently co-occur; to make comorbid diagnoses of autism spectrum disorder and intellectual disability, social communication should be below that expected for general developmental level.

(American Psychiatric Association, 2013)

The symptoms described in letter A (Figure 1) highlight the communication challenges as well as difficulties with understanding others' perspectives. The culmination of these symptoms described in letter A leads to difficulties with forming friendships.

The symptoms described in letter B refer to both sensory issues and difficulties regulating emotions when things do not go as expected or change unpredictably. These symptoms describe how many individuals with ASD can have meltdowns when overwhelmed by sensory input (e.g., too many people, sounds, instructions) or when they confront new tasks (e.g., difficult schoolwork) or unexpected changes (e.g., delays or obstacles to doing favored activities). These symptoms point to the need to identify triggers to challenging moments so we can alter those stressors and teach children better ways to manage those stressors. In my book *No More Meltdowns* (2013) I review common triggers to meltdowns and ways to both modify those triggers and teach skills to handle those triggers better. That work is reviewed in Chapter 8 and in the skill lessons on emotional regulation.

Level of Severity and Its Significance to Teaching Social Skills

Across both Letters A and B, the diagnostic system prompts us to rate the severity of symptoms on a three-level system, with Level 3 being most severe, and Level 1 being milder. When it comes to communication skills, Level 3 refers to what we used to call Classic Autism referring to individuals with severe language difficulties. These may be children who do not yet a have symbolic forms of communication. They may be primarily non-verbal. Level 2 refers to what we used to call PDD-NOS (Pervasive Developmental Disorder–Not Otherwise Specified). These are often children who have some symbolic language, yet their language functioning is still very concrete and rudimentary that they may need visual pictures to back up their ability to understand and express themselves with language. For example, I might ask a child what they ate for breakfast, and they may only be able to respond when I show them pictures of the different breakfast items and then they can point to or verbalize what they ate. Here, they are using symbols to communicate but still need a concrete picture symbol of the language. This is different from individuals at Level 1, who can communicate with others without the use of pictures. They are operating completely with language symbols, verbalized sounds and/or the written word. As you might imagine, these are individuals with the ability to converse and often have average to above-average measured intellectual functioning (as many tests rely on verbal comprehension skills to measure intellectual skills). Level 1 individuals often fall into the ASD category formerly referred to as Asperger's Syndrome.

CHAPTER 3

DOES SOCIAL SKILLS TRAINING WORK?

Some of the major approaches to skills training can be categorized into three types as follows:

- **Behavioral Approaches**, such as Applied Behavioral Analysis (ABA), focus on altering observable events in the environment (antecedents and consequences) to increase certain behaviors and decrease undesirable behaviors. For example, an instructor might prompt a student to greet his peers and then reward the student for doing so.

- **Cognitive-Behavioral Approaches** share some of these assumptions about manipulating the environment to change behavior, but they extend the notion to consider how an individual interprets or perceives what happens in the environment. To this end, individuals' thoughts and perceptions become a primary focus in understanding how someone will behave. For example, an instructor might explain to a student how others would think and feel if he did not greet his peers. Structured Learning (see Baker, 2003, 2005) and Social Thinking (see Winner, 2004) fall into this cognitive-behavioral category.

- **Relationship-Based Approaches** posit that developing a trusting and enjoyable relationship is a primary factor in influencing the development of new skills. Through following the lead of the child and respecting his or her preferences, trust and motivation develop so that learning can occur. DIR/Floortime (Greenspan, 2009) and RDI (Gutstein, 2009) are examples of these approaches. Though these models lack the robust outcome studies of other approaches, many well researched approaches have adopted aspects of the relationship-based model (see below).

- **Combined approaches.** Many established skill training approaches have adopted aspects of the relationship-based model. For example, ABA strategies like Pivotal Response Training (Koegel and Koegel, 2018) and cognitive behavior strategies like those described in Baker (2003, 2005) embrace the need for creating joy and fun through social interaction to motivate students to learn. A great example of a combination approach is The Early Start Denver Model (Rogers and Dawson, 2010). This early intervention program (for ages zero to four) combines ABA (Pivotal Response Training in particular) and a relationship-based approach and has proven highly effective in the outcome research.

Deciding whether social skills training works is challenging as the definition of social skills, the type of individuals and social skills targeted, and the ways to teach, generalize and measure progress differ across studies. That being said, there is evidence that a variety of the strategies described above can lead to positive changes. Many of the ABA strategies, which involve modeling, prompting, and reinforcement, have been shown to be effective in teaching a variety of social skills, including attention/eye contact, appropriate content and initiation of conversation, play skills, and frequency and duration of interactions (see Mateson, Mateson, & Rivet 2007, for a review of seventy-nine studies).

With regards to the relationship-based approaches, there has been a paucity of well-designed outcome studies to assess its utility except the Early Start Denver Model (Rogers and Dawson, 2010). I strongly believe that one of the relationship-based tenets is crucial: training should be intrinsically motivating to its participants. However, among popular relationship-based approaches, few, other than the Early Start Denver Model, have been vigorously tested.

On the other hand, cognitive-behavioral approaches have been more widely evaluated. The approach called "structured learning" (explaining, modeling role-playing, practice in real settings) enjoys a large evidence base with varied populations not specific to autism (McGinnis & Goldstein, 1997). Trimarchi (2004) investigated the use of structured learning with those with Asperger's Syndrome using the original version of this book (*Social Skills Training for Children and Teens with Aspergers Syndrome and Related Social-Communication Disorders*, 2003) and found at least minimal improvement on 90 percent of targeted skills compared to a control group. Koning et al. (2013) evaluated the efficacy of a fifteen-week cognitive-behaviorally based social skills intervention for boys aged ten to twelve years diagnosed with ASD. Boys with average or better IQ and receptive language skills were randomly assigned to either a control (n = 8) or intervention condition (n = 7). During intervention, boys attended weekly two-hour-long group sessions focusing on self-monitoring skills, social perception and affective knowledge, conversation skills, social problem-solving, and friendship management skills. Sessions were based on a combination of my work (Baker, 2003), Crick and Dodge (1994), and Garcia-Winner (2002, 2005). Comparison of the outcomes using repeated measures analyses indicated that boys receiving the intervention scored significantly better on measures of social perception, peer interaction, and social knowledge than boys who had not received intervention. There were no differences on generalization measures of socialization; thus the authors concluded *generalization* to new situations needed to be targeted in future work.

Kenworthy et al. (2013) set out to validate the methods used in the manual *Unstuck and On Target* by (Cannon et al., 2011) which targets frustration management skills. The control group used lessons based on the original version of this book (Baker, 2003). The lessons from Baker's manual were not specifically those that target frustration, but instead those that target conversation, turn-taking, and friendship management. Not surprisingly, the Unstuck and On Target group was superior to the control group in frustration measures (remember the control group did not target frustration related skills). What was interesting, though, was that the control group showed extensive improvement in social appropriateness and reciprocity skills, and the lessons were well liked by schools, parents and students. So, although frustration skills were not targeted in the control group, those lessons that were targeted from the Baker (2003) book did in fact lead to large gains in social functioning.

Strategies that involve showing children what to do through video-modeling and Social Stories™ (developed by Carol Gray) also fall into the cognitive-behavioral category and have shown some positive results (Bellini & Akullian, 2007).

Hotton et al. (2015) reviewed outcome studies on group social skills training for individuals with ASD narrowing down 230 articles to thirteen that had some experimental or quasi experimental designs. From their review, the best evidence that group-based social skills training was effective in both improving social skills and mental health outcomes came from those studies that used the PEERS program (see Laugeson, 2013). This program utilizes cognitive-behavioral methods almost identical to Baker (2003). It uses "structured learning" (originally coined by McGinnis and Goldstein, 1997) involving didactic instruction, modeling with feedback, role-play, homework assignments to practice in natural settings, and parent involvement to help with generalization. Though their findings are robust, some shortcomings involve excluding clients who have intellectual disabilities and those who are not motivated to participate. In clinical practice, a high percentage of individuals have intellectual disabilities and/or lack motivation to participate in training. Adjusting the teaching to the child's cognitive level and addressing the issue of motivation to learn and use skills must also be considered to be effective in clinical practice.

In summary, what we know can work well from well-designed studies coming out of university settings are behavioral interventions utilizing ABA techniques, cognitive-behavioral interventions emphasizing "structured learning," and some approaches that combine ABA with relationship-based concepts (e.g., the Early Start Denver Model).

CHAPTER 4

KEY COMPONENTS OF EFFECTIVE SOCIAL SKILL TRAINING FOR INDIVIDUALS WITH SKILL CHALLENGES

Despite the promising outcome studies described in the preceding chapter, there is often a gap between the science of skills training in the lab and the practice of skills training in schools and community settings. In 2007, Bellini, Peters, Benner, and Hopf challenged the social skills world after concluding that most school-based social skills training efforts were minimally effective according to their review of fifty-five outcome studies. They pointed out the problems with many social skills interventions in schools, including failure to match targeted goals to the child's needs, lack of generalization of skills into natural settings, short duration of treatment, and failure to motivate skill performance. Gates et al. (2017), in a more recent review of group social skills training programs, found social skills interventions are modestly effective for youth with ASD but may not generalize to school settings or self-reported social behavior.

One of the issues that can impact generalization of skills is the lack of specific strategies to help students practice skills in natural settings. Systematic cues and reminders to use and practice skills in real life is a critical component of effective skills training.

In addition, even if we teach children skills and manage somehow to get them to use them in natural settings, it does not ensure that peers in the environment will suddenly welcome those peers. Thus, to ensure better outcomes, we must also target the peer community.

Furthermore, when it comes to getting better outcomes with frustration-related problems, research on positive behavioral supports tells us we cannot simply teach replacement skills (i.e., better ways for kids to get what they want). We must also modify the triggers (antecedents in the language of behaviorists) in order to make gains (see www.pbis.org). For example, you cannot simply get a child to calmly ask for help or persuasively negotiate an assignment with a teacher if you always throw overly difficult work at the child. Similarly, you cannot easily teach a child to play with other kids in a loud, overwhelming environment if they have severe sensory issues. You may first need to modify the play environment.

When we take the lessons from well-designed skills training outcome studies and consider the challenges that exist in real community settings, we are left with several key issues that must be addressed for social skills training to be effective. I call these issues "The Key Components of Effective Social Skills Training," outlined below:

The Key Components of Effective Social Skills Training:

1. Establish motivation to participate in learning and using skills

2. Target relevant skills that match the needs of the children

3. Consider how to measures skill performance to assess progress

4. Consider modifications to the environment to improve outcomes

5. Consider the child's cognitive abilities and language comprehension in choosing HOW and WHERE to teach the skills

6. Plan for generalization or transfer of learning by using homework assignments, cues and reminders from key caregivers (like parents and teachers)

7. Consider targeting the peer community to improve socialization and acceptance

Schools do not always address all seven of these components, and sometimes for good reason. There is some research that certain one-size-fits-all curriculums can have positive effects on a school, though they often fall short of addressing the more specific needs of individuals with ASD or other social challenges. This discrepancy can be explained by understanding the tiered approach that schools use to support students.

A Tiered Approach to Social Skill Intervention in Schools

School systems typically offer behavioral, social, and emotional support to students in a multi-tiered prevention model. The National Technical Assistance Center on Positive Behavioral Interventions and Supports (PBIS), which is part of the US Department of Education (www.pbis.org), outlines the following tiered approach:

Tier 1: Usually refers to "Universal Prevention," or what all students receive in a school system. These often include defining and teaching all students about what kinds of behaviors are expected. For example, antibullying programs often begin this way by educating all students about how they are expected to treat others.

Tier 2: "Targeted Prevention" is meant for some students who may need more help improving specific skill deficits. Interventions may include learning and practicing both social and self-regulation skills as well as providing access to greater academic supports to prevent frustration and avoidance behaviors. Often interventions are provided to students in a group format to benefit many children.

Tier 3: "Intensive, Individualized Prevention" is targeted to students who need more individualized help. These services are often, but not always, part of the special education supports a student may receive. Many interventions focus on understanding the function and triggers of challenging behaviors and seek to teach alternative ways for students to handle these triggering situations.

A tiered approach helps us understand the sometimes confusing outcomes in social skills training research. One-size-fits-all curricula have not been terribly effective in teaching skills to special education students, according to some reviews of social skills outcome studies in schools (Bellini et al., 2007; Gresham et al., 2001). Yet at the same time, school-wide interventions have been shown to increase achievement scores, increase prosocial skills and decrease disruptive behaviors, and increase self-esteem (for example, see Payton et al., 2008). How do we square these findings: that some school-wide skill interventions can positively impact the student body, but many of these programs do not do a sufficient job of teaching skills to kids with specific social challenges?

The intensity and specificity of intervention depends on the needs of the students. For many children with typical social skills, school-wide (Tier 1) efforts to increase typically developing skills like empathy and problem-solving can be very helpful. However, for students with specific skill challenges due to ADHD, autism spectrum disorders, or other learning differences, a more targeted skills training intervention (Tier 3) may be needed. The table below summarizes an example of one-tiered approach to Social Skills Training that I developed over the course of a year consulting with a school district in New York:

 ## Tier 1: School-Wide Efforts to Increase Positive Social Functioning

1. Common language and instruction for resolving conflicts

2. Creating more options for play and structure during recess

3. Interest-based clubs available to increase social opportunity

4. Training of aides and other staff on how to facilitate social interaction and resolve conflict rather than relying only on discipline

5. Student sensitivity training that encourages inclusion and discourages teasing/bullying

6. If students are identified as having persistent difficulties interfering with academic/social functioning despite school-wide programs, staff may refer them to Tier 2 intervention (case conference)

Tier 2: Case Conference for Particular Students/Classrooms

1. Push in-class discussions

2. Consultation/observation at lunch/recess

3. Theme-based groups and counseling to teach social skills and create more opportunities for socialization

4. Teacher consultation with specialists

5. If students do not respond successfully to Tier 2 interventions after six to eight weeks or the severity of the problem intensifies, consider Tier 3

Tier 3: Individualized Social Skill Action Plans

Plans must address the following 7 key components:

1. Establish motivation to participate in learning and using skills

2. Target relevant skills that match the needs of the children

3. Consider how to measures skill performance to assess progress

4. Consider modifications to the environment to improve outcome

5. Consider the child's cognitive abilities and language comprehension in choosing HOW and WHERE to teach the skills

6. Plan for generalization or transfer of learning by using homework assignments and reminders from key caregivers (like parents and teachers)

7. Consider targeting the peer community to improve socialization and acceptance

The key components described in Tier 3 in the example above reflect the model utilized in this book for effective social skills training for individuals with social skill challenges. Often these may be students with IEPs or 504 plans (legal documents in US schools that demonstrate a student's eligibility for educational modifications and supports). Often these children have been diagnosed with ASD, ADHD, mood-related disorders, or specific learning disabilities that also impact their social functioning. The next chapters review each of these Tier 3 components in greater detail.

CHAPTER 5

ESTABLISHING MOTIVATION TO LEARN

External versus Intrinsic Motivation

In the world of autism, the traditional way to address motivation is to use rewards after a particular behavior to increase the likelihood that the behavior will occur again (referred to as operant conditioning). In this case the reward is "external" to the behavior. For example, if we wanted to teach a youngster to say hello when they see their friend, we might cue them, say "hello," and then reward them with their favorite food or access to a favored toy after they say hello. Such an approach was embraced early in the autism field for several reasons. There was a rich history in behavioral research with animals whose behaviors we could increase with external reinforcement. Lovaas applied this approach to children with severe autism in one of the first studies to show that kids with autism could in fact learn through systematic reinforcement. As this external reward system was applied to students with greater language functioning, symbolic reinforcement became the favored methodology, where points or tokens were used to reward students in the moment and then later those tokens could be used to purchase more tangible rewards like food, favored objects, or activities.

Some researchers began to notice a phenomenon in which external reinforcement could in fact undermine someone's desire to engage in an activity when the external reinforcement was not provided (Deci et al., 1999). For example, if I get $10 each time I do a math problem, then I no longer get $10 to do math, I may become uninterested in doing math. However, if you make the math fun to do, I might do it even without getting paid. This last notion represents what we call intrinsic motivation, in which the behavior (in this case, doing math) is rewarding in and of itself; that is, the reward is intrinsic to the activity itself.

When there are no intrinsically rewarding reasons to engage in a behavior, one may need to use external rewards to get things started. Yet to help an individual want to behave in a particular positive way when external rewards are no longer provided, it is crucial to transition to an intrinsically rewarding system in which the activity itself becomes naturally rewarding. How can we apply this to the students who walk through our doors because their parents or others have said they need social skill help but the children themselves are not motivated to work on these skills? How can we make working on social skill intrinsically motivating?

Building Positive Self-Awareness

There are plenty of reasons why a child may be against any social skill interventions if they have been told repeatedly that something is not right and they need help. To maintain self-esteem, students may need to deflect any criticisms and instead blame the surrounding social community for being overly harsh, mean, and incompetent. Most students who arrive at my clinic have been worn down by such criticisms (even if constructive) from others, and the last thing they want to hear is more about what's "wrong" with them.

Given the history of criticism many of these students have heard, my starting point when I first meet them is to introduce the idea that all of us have strengths that take us places in the world as well as some challenges that can occasionally interfere with those strengths. Together we then generate a long list of their talents and strengths, and a much shorter list of challenges. In order to accomplish this, I like to be prepared with background information in case the student struggles to come up with strengths. I talk initially with the parents and teachers to get a list of their concerns and a lengthier list of the student's strengths. Typically the student's interests or hobbies represent areas of expertise that can be seen as strengths, along with positive personality characteristics. Keep in mind that challenges associated with certain diagnoses often have an upside. For example, the obsessive interests of those on the spectrum can be areas of expertise that lead to careers. For those with ADHD and bipolar disorder, distractibility and impulsivity are often associated with high energy and an extremely entertaining, interactive style. I typically will list these strengths and challenges on a large white board and give a paper or cell phone photocopy to the student afterwards. Below is a sample list of strengths and challenges for a student who had Autism Level 1 (formerly termed Asperger's Syndrome):

Strengths	Challenges
1. Good memory for facts	1. Organization
2. Good reader	2. Focus and frustration in classes
3. Great at video games	3. Socializing comfortably
4. Expert in Japanese anime	
5. Loves animals	
6. Good singer	
7. Kind and caring	
8. Entertaining	
Can lead to a great academic and work career!	*Possible Supports: HW system, notes for missed info, possible med for focus, teach a few social/frustration-related skills.*

In addition to listing the strengths, I often review **parts** of past testing reports to show the student where their strengths are. Too often students are evaluated and no one reviews with them their particular strengths and challenges. I will cherry-pick the strengths from these reports and summarize some of the challenges so that there are always more strengths than challenges. We then discuss how their strengths can take them places in life, leading to success in both school and work. Finally, I explain to them that no one needs to overcome their challenges; they just need to get to a point where the challenges are small enough not to get in the way of their strengths. We then brainstorm together ways to lessen these challenges, culminating in a list of proposed strategies or supports like those listed in the previous figure.

Use of Diagnostic Labels?

I am not wedded to using diagnostic labels to characterize an individual's pattern of strengths and challenges; however, as children age, there is often practical utility in children knowing labels that can help them obtain desired accommodations. In schools and eventually the workplace, one might need to invoke an official diagnosis to justify getting certain modifications and accommodations. In keeping with a positive self-esteem-enhancing approach, it is critical to convey the growing cultural understanding of autism as a neurological difference rather than as a disability. Some of the characteristics of autism have clear advantages for tasks (especially visual ones) that require attention to detail or collections of factual information. The perseverative interests of those on the spectrum often lead to greater knowledge of a subject area than neurotypicals may possess. There are a variety of biographies of talented autistic individuals that can help inspire and support a strength-based view of autism (see for example, "History's 30 Most Inspiring People on the Autism Spectrum," 2017).

Collaborative and Proactive Solutions (Ross Greene, 2021)

The second key strategy to increase a student's motivation to address challenges: ensure that they are active participants in understanding problems and coming up with potential solutions. All too often, adults create behavior plans without consulting the students, only to find that their efforts to help are rejected. The key to Collaborative and Proactive Solutions (CPS) is to understand and respect the child's view of the challenge and to invite them to solve the problem.

Although Ross Greene was certainly not the first to describe a collaborative process between client and therapist, he has nicely articulated his CPS model in concrete, replicable steps so that others can use it and researchers can evaluate its effectiveness. The interested reader is referred to his website www.livesinthebalance.org for greater detail, current and past research, and additional readings. I will offer a brief overview here of how I adopt his language to collaborate on solutions and skill goals with our clients. Following the outline is an example of a student with whom this collaborative approach was used to pinpoint solutions and skill goals.

CPS General Philosophy

- Understand the problem from the student's point of view

- Respect the student's preferred way to solve life's issues with our guidance

- Don't impose behavior plans on students, create these plans with students

Getting the Child's Perspective on the Issue

- The first step to solving unresolved problems is to explore the **student's perspective**:

  - "I noticed that ... What's up?

  - Explore the student's reasons for the problem

  - Reflective listening: "So let me see if I understand the issues ..."

  - "Is there more?"

  - Validate and Empathize, "It makes sense that you feel that way ... "

Collaborating on Solutions

- Solutions are sought by **inviting** students to solve the identified problems

  - Choose an issue that the student identified and ask, "I wonder if there is a way ..."

  - Solutions must work for both parties and be realistic

  - Consider the probability that it will work

Michael was an eleven-year-old bright, verbal boy with a history of ASD, Level 1 (formerly Asperger's Syndrome). His teachers had reported to his parents that he was frequently disruptive in class, talking with peers to the point of annoying them and not stopping when teachers reminded him to quiet down. Apparently, some of his jokes in class also poked fun at some peers.

I interviewed his parents and the staff at school and discovered that this was a new pattern of behavior; in previous years he had been a very compliant and relatively quiet student. In addition, most of the talkativeness and non-compliance took place in language arts and dedicated reading time. Also, Michael and his peers had only recently come back to school after months of working from home due to the COVID pandemic.

While talking with Michael, we first made a list of all his strengths and talents as described previously in the section on building positive self-awareness. He was certainly a highly intelligent and articulate young man who, despite ASD, had developed friendships and a reputation for being funny. He also had a great deal of knowledge about various sports and could be relied upon by peers for scores and standings for many of the major sport teams. This was certainly an interest that connected him to peers in his school.

Following the enumeration of strengths, I began the CPS steps. Step 1: I asked, "Michael, I heard that your teachers said you sometimes talk in class, especially language arts and reading. What's up with that?" "I am just bored," he said. "And also it's the only time really to talk to my friends." I then went to Step 2: "Let me see if I've got this right so far: you are feeling bored in those classes, plus it feels like the only time you can talk to peers?" He confirmed. I asked, "What makes it boring?" He explained that both those classes involve reading, which he hates. At home he indicated he reads with books on tape, but in school there are no audible books, and he finds it exhausting to read. I checked again to see if I understood his feelings, reflecting what he said. This may seem like rudimentary therapy, and it is, but it sends the message to the student that I am not an adult who is simply going to tell him what not to do or what to do, but rather, I will take the time to understand his point of view.

Finally, after confirming that he hates reading and prefers books on tape and that he has no other time to talk with friends, I asked if there was more to say on this topic. He went on to say that since the pandemic, there had been very few times to talk with peers, and even now that they are back in school, there was no recess or social lunch time due to pandemic restrictions. As such, language arts, which typically involve discussions, felt like the only time to socialize with peers. I asked if he knew that the teachers indicated some peers might be annoyed by his talking and that it also seemed to disrupt the teacher's lesson. He understood but said most of his friends didn't seem to mind his conversations.

We then went on to the problem-solving steps. I started with the issue of being bored and hating reading, and asked, "I wonder if there is a way to make the reading less onerous and boring?" He suggested getting access to books on tape in school. We then planned a time for him to request that from the school staff, who indicated they would be open to any recommendations to help Michael. I then asked him about the next challenge of talking to peers and asked, "I wonder if there is a way for you to socialize with peers at a time that won't annoy the teacher and some of your peers?" This question represents one of the keys of collaborative problem-solving, namely, finding realistic solutions that can work because they work for everyone involved. He suggested that the school should create another social time during the day for kids to just chat. We rehearsed a way to request that from the school administrator, who was open to our suggestions, and she created a home room/social time in the morning and one in the afternoon, which ended up benefiting all the kids. Michael and I also talked about the social skill of picking the right times and ways to be "funny." We carved out some social goals of saving socializing for designated downtimes rather than during a lesson and selecting comments or jokes that do not insult his peers (see chapter 14 lesson on Getting Attention in Positive Ways).

Utilizing the Individual's Interests

Another critical way to motivate involvement in learning skills or anything else is to incorporate the interests of the individual. Brain studies often suggest that those on the spectrum may have different sensitivity in the regions of the brain that control drive and motivation (Kohls et al., 2013). Typical reinforcers that work for neurotypicals may not always work for them. However, the individual on the spectrum may have more brain activity and general responsiveness when engaged with their interests. Thus it is crucial to utilize their interests when teaching social skills. One way to do this is to create social activities related to their interests. Rather than creating formal social skills groups to learn skills (as so often occurs in schools), systematic practice on social skills can occur in the context of theme-based groups related to the child's special interests, such as anime, books, film, robotics, cooking, Legos, or video game clubs. In this context, children can practice talking with each other (about those things that are inherently motivating), learn to compromise, and regulate their comments and other behaviors in order to continue to pursue their interests.

Troubleshooting Resistance: "But I Don't Care What Others Think!"

Creating motivation to work on skills is easier when children recognize that they need to work on a particular skill to reach their own goals. But what if the behavior in question only seems to bother others and the child does not care if it upsets anyone else? How do we help individuals care about others' feelings? Well, they need to see the logical consequences that occur if you do or do not care about others and how it does ultimately impact something they do care about.

For example, I worked with a teenage girl who frequently cursed and used provocative language out in public when shopping with her parents. Her family was quite embarrassed about her behavior, and when she was given feedback how her words might make others feel extremely uncomfortable, she exclaimed that she does not care what others think. However, she soon realized that her parents would no longer take her shopping or to places she wanted to go, and thus she came to realize that she needed to care about what they and others thought in order to go where she wanted. It is important to note that she received the feedback about her behavior much better when she was reminded about how smart and talented she was and that what they were asking her to do was a just a small thing, as she was free to curse if she wanted to in the privacy of her room at home. When she was complimented and their upset over her infraction was downplayed, her defenses lowered, and she was able to take in and use the feedback.

CHAPTER 6

ASSESSMENT OF RELEVANT SKILL GOALS

How do we target relevant skills that match our clients' needs? Although teaching a universal set of skills can benefit a school system, that approach to improving the social skill functioning of individuals with ASD and other specific skill challenges is not usually effective or efficient. Outcome research in the ASD community suggests that we will be better off if we focus on more specific skill issues relevant to our students and practice them for a long period of time. I typically ask that students, caring professionals and family members help prioritize a small set of skills (three to seven) to work on for months at a time across settings. This is a manageable number of goals if we are going to require parents and teachers to consistently prompt these skills to ensure generalization across settings.

In deciding what skills to target, I take a functional approach, asking what skills are necessary for the student to function in a desired setting on a daily basis. Though an older child might one day need to know how to interview for a part-time job, this is not considered a daily priority but rather a skill to learn for an event. However, if a child has his finger up his nose everyday so that neither peers nor educators want to interact with the child, then refraining from nose-picking becomes a social skill priority, as the behavior interferes with successful social functioning.

If a child falls into the ASD, Level 3, category, suggesting significant challenges in receptive language, then the first skill goal is to ensure the child has a consistent system for communicating across settings. Without a way to communicate, many other skills will be difficult to teach. What do we mean by significant receptive language issues?

Receptive Language Ability

Receptive language refers to the ability to comprehend language. Difficulty with language comprehension, often called a semantic language disorder, involves trouble understanding the meaning of words. Many individuals with ASD, Level 1, do not have difficulty comprehending others but have a pragmatic language problem. Pragmatic language refers to the social use of language involved in sustaining or initiating conversation. For example, individuals with what used to be called Asperger's Syndrome may appear to have perfectly intact language based on their ability to express themselves and understand others, yet they may have trouble with social conversation, talking at people instead of with people and relaying factual information without responding to what their listener is saying or doing.

Many individuals with ASD, Level 2 or 3, also have a semantic language problem involving difficulty understanding the meaning of words, certainly for abstract words, metaphors, or sayings, but also sometimes for just basic communicative exchanges.

Individuals with ASD, for example, may hear the abstract saying, "Don't let the cat out of the bag," and search for a cat and bag rather than grasp the symbolic meaning regarding not spoiling a surprise. Those with ASD, Level 3, and to a lesser extent those with Level 2, may not understand more basic words like "up and down," "here or there," "big and small," "on top," and "below." Failure to comprehend what these words refer to means that children are not easily able to follow verbal instructions.

As part of an evaluation for special education supports in public schools, a psychologist may conduct an intellectual evaluation of a student yielding several IQ scores (a full-scale IQ, verbal IQ, and performance IQ). A verbal IQ score along with an interview with the child is often adequate for approximating a child's receptive language ability. Students with a verbal IQ in the average to above-average range and who can follow verbal directions can benefit from a conceptual approach, in which we use words to explain why and how to perform a skill. If a verbal IQ score is not available, an interview with the child can help determine if the child can follow verbal directions.

For example, if Joe can follow directions such as "Walk over to your mother, say hello, and shake her hands," we know he can follow simple verbal directions. We might then ask him to follow more abstract directions like, "Tell us what you ate for breakfast this morning." (This is abstract because breakfast is not right in front of him; he must remember or symbolize breakfast in his mind before he answers the question.) If he is able to respond, we know he can not only follow verbal instructions, but also imagine things that are not right in front of him. This will make it easier to use verbal concepts to teach him social skills, because verbal concepts refer to things that are not right in front of you but must be imagined. For example, asking someone to wait for a "pause" in others' conversations before speaking involves an abstract concept (a pause) that cannot be easily seen. For those who understand what these words refer to, comprehending this skill through verbal instruction is possible.

If, on the other hand, we give verbal instructions to Joe and he repeats them back like an echo without knowing what to do or what we said, he will not easily be able to learn skills from verbal instructions alone. For example, instructions to wait for a pause before interrupting would be challenging for him to understand. He may benefit from an approach that relies on visual aids (e.g., pictures, videos, and direct modeling of how to interrupt) and from methods that help him learn prerequisite language skills (e.g., learning to identify what the word "pause" means).

Initial Skill Goals for those with limited receptive language (ASD, Level 3)

If an individual's receptive language is extremely limited, the first social skill goal that must be prioritized is to develop a reliable system to communicate things like requests for basic needs and responses to requests or directions, and the ability to comment or comprehend the meaning of others' comments. Strategies to accomplish this are beyond the scope of this particular manual. The interested reader might research proven teaching methods for children with Level 3 autism including early intervention ABA strategies, visual supports systems like PECS, those that combine ABA with play-based approaches like The Early Start Denver Model, and strategies that rely on the use of alternative and augmentative communication devices.

Beyond a communication system: Setting individualized social skill goals

For those with ASD Levels 2 and 1 who have relatively intact receptive language, our next assessment task is to identify those social skill goals that will be most relevant to their success in expected settings. To accomplish this task, we (1) send the social skill questionnaire and information-gathering letter (see Appendix 1 at the end of this chapter) to key stakeholders (parents, teachers, caregivers), (2) interview those individuals and the target student to further clarify the skill issues identified by caregivers, (3) observe that student in settings where social problems were identified, and (4) meet with key stakeholders to define and prioritize social skill goals.

Two very practical questions dominate the information-gathering process from the initial letter and throughout the interviews and observation of the student:

- **Question 1 (Behavioral Excesses):** What does the student do too much of that might interfere with social functioning in a desired setting? Examples might include violating others' space, interrupting others, talking at others excessively about their interests, imposing their wishes on others, becoming verbally or physically aggressive in response to work, insulting others, or handling disagreements in aggressive ways. This is often what we call "disruptive behaviors." Often this is the first information we get when a child is referred to us for help. Essentially it is what they did in a setting that upset others.

- **Question 2 (Behavioral Deficits):** What does the student not do enough of that might interfere with social functioning in a desired setting? Examples might include not responding to peers or teachers, not asking for help when needed, not managing their hygiene or attire appropriately, and not initiating interaction with others. Although less noticeable, these behaviors often are reported by parents or teachers when the student tends to isolate from others.

Initial information packet (see Appendix 1 at end of chapter)

The social skill questionnaire asks caregivers to circle specific skill areas that the student may need help with and the letter requests that they prioritize a smaller set of social issues to work on, specifically social challenges that they see on a daily basis. Though we ask caregivers to prioritize three to seven skill areas, some may list many more and others list very few. Often parents and teachers will write skill concerns in broad general terms like they did for one youngster named Charlie: "(1) He gets angry whenever he does not get what he wants, and (2) he does not know how to talk with other kids, and (3) he doesn't play with other kids." These broad areas of concerns can be clarified with examples when we conduct the interviews with parents and teachers or other caregivers. Those examples will help us form more specific skill goals.

Interview with parents/teachers

During the interview process, several goals are accomplished. First is to clarify with caregivers (parents, teachers, and others) what specific social interactions are problematic because of either excesses (doing too much) or deficits (doing too little) in social settings in which they interact.

Let's look at the example of Charlie described earlier, in which parents and teachers said he gets angry when he does not get what he wants and does not know how to talk or play with peers. Our request for providing examples of these issues will help pinpoint more specific issues. We generally ask for "ABCs" of the specific issue: A (antecedent of the situation/setting before the behavior issue), B (the behavioral excess or missing behavior), and C (the consequence, what happened after the behavior). We discovered that getting angry means Charlie becomes verbally or physically aggressive (the behavior) when he must shut down his video games (the antecedent) and then his mom and dad reprimand him and threaten to take his video game away (consequence). In addition, we find out that not knowing how to talk with others means he does not join into conversation (missing behavior) around peers (the antecedent), or if he does talk with peers, he tends to lecture on his own topic of interest: anime (behavioral excess), and not playing with others means he literally does not join in to play (missing behavior) when he is with peers (antecedent). The parents and teachers see these as daily priority issues.

Interview with the child

As described in the chapter on motivation, my first goal in meeting with the child is to review their strengths and their special interests. Then we can begin to look at a shorter list of challenges. Among Charlie's many strengths, it turns out he has an avid interest and knowledge of Japanese anime and related video game content. He can also do some rudimentary programming (at only ten years old). In addressing his challenges, we adopt the Collaborative and Proactive Solutions Model articulated by Ross Greene and reviewed in the chapter on motivation. That model is summarized again below:

Getting the Child's Perspective on the Issue

- The first step to solving unresolved problems is to explore the **student's perspective**

  - "I noticed that ... What's up?"

  - Explore the student's reasons for the problem

  - Reflective listening: "So let me see if I understand the issues ..."

- "Is there more?"

- Validate and Empathize, "It makes sense that you feel that way ... "

Collaborating on Solutions

- Solutions are sought by **inviting** student to solve the identified problems

  - Choose an issue that student identified and ask, "I wonder if there is a way ... "

  - Solutions must work for both parties and be realistic

  - Consider probability that it will work

In going through these steps with the Charlie, I began by telling him that I heard he sometimes does not play or talk with the other kids. I asked, "What's up with that?" I discovered that he was teased in the past for talking too much about anime, so he doesn't like to talk about anything unless he knows the other kids like the same games. He also feels like he is not good at any other games other than the video games he knows, so he prefers to just play his own games. Finally, since these games seem to be his one main pleasure, he becomes upset when his parents tell him to stop, especially in the middle of a mission. Moreover, since they always threaten to take the game from him, he does not trust they will let him go back to play, so he refuses to stop.

When I began to invite Charlie to address these issues, I asked: "I wonder if there is a way to talk and play with kids if it could involve your interests." He said it would be nice if there was an anime or video game club in the school so he could find more kids like him. I also asked, "I wonder if there is any way turning off preferred video games could be easier for you?" He explained it would be easier if he knew he could save his game progress and be guaranteed a time to return to the game sooner than later.

After interviewing him, the next step in the assessment process was to go observe him in the settings where these social challenges occur.

Observation. School and home observation can often be accomplished through videos and/or direct observation. Typically we will observe children in school and receive home videos from parents regarding home-related behaviors. These observations may confirm or further clarify the information received in the interviews. School observations also allow us to see the social setting and understand better what the expected social behaviors are in those settings by observing not only the child but their peers. With regards to Charlie, when we observed him out at recess in school, we confirmed that he indeed did not join into play with other kids. We also saw that he was off in a corner of the recess yard making statue-like poses while other kids were playing tag and football. At lunch, he sat quietly and ate his lunch near other kids without interacting. Home videos confirmed him yelling at his parents for more video game time or ignoring their demands to turn off the video game and come to dinner. He pushed his mom when she went to turn the game off. Eventually he finished what he was doing and angrily came to the dinner table with his head down for the duration of the meal.

Meeting of interested parties. The goal of this meeting is to get all interested parties to prioritize the social skill goals for the individual student. Based on the information gathered previously, we will propose a list of social skill goals to address the social interaction problems reported and then observed by us.

Skill goals should be stated positively, which means problematic behaviors must be converted into skills that can be taught to replace those problem behaviors. Let's look at the following **problem situations** noted in the example of Charlie:

1. The child becomes verbally or physically aggressive when he must shut down his video games.

2. He does not join into conversation, or if he does, he tends to lecture on his own topic of interest.

3. He does not join in to play with peers.

To consider the social skills that will address these problematic situations, we must consider **both** Charlie's perspective about why the problem occurs and what kinds of solutions would work for both Charlie and his parents and others. Take a look at the proposed solutions for each problem and related social skill goals we developed:

1. Angry when shutting down video games at home:

    a. Charlie says he needs to be able to save his progress before shutting down and he would like to complete a mission. Parents say they need to know how long a mission might be before he starts one in case there is not enough time before they have to do something else. They agree they will let him finish a mission as long as he agrees only to start ones that he has time to finish that afternoon.

    b. Charlie says he can stop if he is assured of when he can go back in a reasonable amount of time. Parents agree to a visual schedule with clear times that Charlie can return to the game if he leaves at scheduled times.

    c. The social skill Charlie will work on is: **Accept no when it is time to shut down video games (and other favored activities) because stopping on time guarantees that he can return at the next scheduled time.**

2. Doesn't initiate or join into conversation or play:

    a. Charlie suggested the school start an anime and video game club. After assessing interest from peers, we developed a lunch time anime/video game club involving discussions of characters and games, a designated time to play a video game, and some physical games such as "guess the anime character." That last game was inspired by Charlie's statue-like poses we had observed at recess, which turned out to be imitations of his favorite anime characters.

    b. In the context of these preferred social activities, Charlie agreed to work on the following social skills: **initiating play for desired games; initiating conversation using on-topic and relevant questions and comments, and maintaining a reciprocal conversation rather than lecturing at others.**

As you can see, the plans above involved both modifications from the school and parents as well as skills Charlie will work on. Once we have identified social skill goals, we can then break those skills down into teachable components (referred to as task analysis). The skill lessons you see in Chapter 14 represent task-analyzed ways in which individuals can successfully carry out particular skills.

Though there may be many other skills from time to time we might want to address with an individual as they progress through life, we often want to begin with a small set of daily priority skills so that we can focus our efforts. The skill goals above (written in bold) represent daily issues this child needs to address in order to successfully manage daily social situations. We may add a skill when new critical situations emerge. For example, if the child develops a new challenge, like handling correction from teachers, that might be a skill we add to the list. If we become aware of peer pressure to engage in risky behavior, we may then add that to the list as well. If after measuring the child's progress we find that he consistently uses a skill without our prompting or cuing, we may remove that skill from our list of daily priorities.

Appendix 1: Initial Information Packet

Dear Parent(s) or Teacher(s):

Your child/student will be receiving social skills training. Skill lessons will be targeted based specifically on the needs of your child/student. To better serve your youngster, we ask that you share your thoughts about what skill challenges you feel are priorities for your child/student this year. Please see the attached Social Skill Menu and circle the items you feel your child needs help with. Though you may circle many items on the menu, help us prioritize a smaller set of skill challenges that occur on a daily basis.

TO HELP YOU PRIORITIZE IMPORTANT SKILL CHALLENGES, WE ASK THAT YOU CONSIDER THE FOLLOWING TWO QUESTIONS:

1. **What does my child/student do *too much* of on a *daily* basis that might interfere with social functioning?** Examples might include interrupting others, talking at others about their interests, imposing their wishes on others, avoiding work in an aggressive manner, insulting others, or handling disagreements in aggressive ways.

2. **What does my child/student *not do enough* of on a *daily* basis that might interfere with social functioning?** Examples might include not responding to peers, not asking for help when needed, not managing their hygiene or attire appropriately, and not initiating interaction with others.

Please select no more than 7 skill challenges to work on. Research shows that if we work on a small set of goals for a long period of time, we will get better results than trying to work on too many goals in a short period of time. Thank you for taking the time to help us serve your child better.

Thank You,

_____

Name of student: _____

Please list the skill challenge and provide an example of the challenge or problem.

1. _____

   _____

2. _____

   _____

3. _____

   _____

4. _____

   _____

5. _____

   _____

6. _____

   _____

7. _____

   _____

Social Skill Menu

Name of student: _____

Date: _____

Please circle the items that your child/student may need to learn

EMOTION REGULATION ISSUES

1. Recognizing Emotions

2. Discriminating the Size of Emotions

3. Understanding the Connection between Events, Thoughts, and Emotions

4. Understanding Our Alarm System: Hulk versus Dr. Banner

5. Keeping Calm

6. Problem-Solving

7. Talking versus Acting Out Feelings

Frustration/Anger

8. Understanding Your Anger: Using the Daily Anger Record

9. Using a Growth Mindset to Manage Frustration

10. Trying When Work Is Hard

COMMUNICATION

PLAY/GROUP ACTIVITIES

Conflict Management

Dating

CHAPTER 7

MEASURING SOCIAL SKILL CHANGES

There are four main ways to measure skill changes before, during, and after training: (1) Measures of an individual's social skill knowledge, (2) objective/observable measures of social skill performance, (3) subjective ratings of social skill targets, and (4) standardized/normed measures of social skills. Each have their own advantages and disadvantages.

Measures of knowledge might include open-ended interviews or a structured questionnaire to determine whether the individual knows how to engage in the targeted skills. These can be good measures of the individual's knowledge of skill steps, but they tend to be poor predictors of skill performance. Knowing what to do does not guarantee one will do it. I know I should stick to a Mediterranean diet to ward off chronic illnesses, yet if someone puts a pizza followed by chocolate cookies in front of me, I will eat them. I certainly use measures of knowledge to determine if my client has learned the steps of a skill, but I do not use these measures to see if they are actually using the skills outside of my office.

Observable measures allow us to see whether a skill was performed correctly. Using Charlie from the previous chapter as an example, we might observe how many times he asks others to join into play out at recess or "accepted no" when asked to turn off his video games without verbal or physical aggression. These kind of measures are the most objective way to indicate whether an individual can and does perform a skill. However, observable measures are time-consuming in that they require us to create our own measurement tool (e.g., a data collection card like the one below) where we clearly define the behavior to observe (called operational definition); decide whether to measure the frequency, percentage of correct versus incorrect responses, or duration of a particular behavior; and then allocate the personnel to observe the individual in a particular setting. Though I always want to use these kinds of measures, it is not always realistic to expect parents and teachers to track behaviors on a data sheet that I create for them.

Data Collection Card

SETTING: Recess

Date and Time of Observation: _____

Did the child join into a game with peers?   YES or NO

Did the child use the correct steps to join in?

    Walk near them and wait without intruding into their personal space?   Y / N

    Ask to join in or accept an invitation?   Y / N

    Did the peers allow the child to join?   Y / N

How long did the child sustain play with peers? _____ minutes

SETTING: Lunch

Date and Time of Observation: _____

Did the child join or start a conversation with peers?   YES or NO

Did the child use the correct steps to join or initiate conversation?   YES or NO

    Ask a question or comment on topic?   Y / N

    Initiate by asking about the others or a common interest?   Y / N

Did the child maintain the conversation appropriately?   YES or NO

    Did not monopolize or lecture?   Y / N

Ask on-topic questions or comments?   Y / N

How long did the child sustain conversation with peers? _____ minutes

SETTING: Home

Date and Time of Observation: _____

Did the child accept stopping a video game time without being aggressive?   YES or NO

Without verbal aggression?   Y / N

Without physical aggression?   Y / N

How long did it take the child to stop playing once instructed to do so? _____ min

Subjective ratings refer to measures that involve an observer's rating of a behavior often from memory rather than while directly observing. A good example of this might involve using a "Likert Rating Scale" where we would ask parents and teachers to rate a child on how often or well they engage in a particular skill: (see below):

1. Rate how often the child appropriately accepts when it is time to stop playing video games without becoming verbally or physically aggressive (Circle one)

never	rarely	sometimes	usually	always
1	2	3	4	5

2. Rate how often the child initiates or joins into play with peers (Circle one)

never	rarely	sometimes	usually	always
1	2	3	4	5

3. Rate how often the child appropriately intiates or joins into conversation using relevant conversation starters (Circle one)

never	rarely	sometimes	usually	always
1	2	3	4	5

4. Rate how often the child maintains a conversation with peers without monopolizing or lecturing (Circle one)

never	rarely	sometimes	usually	always
1	2	3	4	5

Although this is a subjective measure of skill performance, these kinds of ratings are considered good measures of social competence. One's competence is not necessarily tied to the exact behavior they engage in but rather how it is perceived by others. When it comes to social skills, how you are perceived is often more important than what you actually do. For example, growing up in New York City, I took the subway to school every day and learned to never make eye contact with strangers on the train as that frequently resulted in older kids demanding I give them money. In contrast, I flew down to Atlanta as an adult to do a talk and went to a restaurant where the hostess greeted me with direct eye contact and a hug! As a New Yorker I quickly checked my pocket to see if she stole my wallet but soon realized she was just showing me southern hospitality. The point of the story is that socially expected behavior changes from context to context, so direct measures of how one performs a skill are not always perfect correlates of whether one is seen as competent. Subjective measures may in fact be more accurate reflections of whether one is doing what is expected in that situation, even though it may not be as accurate a reflection of the exact behavior one engages in.

An important advantage of subjective ratings is the ease with which they can be gathered. Rather than allocate personnel to directly observe an individual, one can send out a Likert Rating Scale, like the one in the example above, through email to parents, teachers, and the targeted student. Working in the school systems for over twenty-five years, I frequently relied on these subjective ratings, along with any direct observational measures I could gather, before writing periodic progress reports.

Subjective ratings should be created for the particular skill goals that have been targeted for an individual, but one can also use my social menu as a rating measure of all the skills covered in this book. Since parents and teachers are asked to fill this out menu prior to treatment, they can fill it out periodically to measure progress as well, rating the particular skills that they endorsed. However, as the assessment chapter described, we create our own set of skill targets for an individual that may not directly match skills in the book. These individualized sets of skills are the ones for which we need to get observational data and subjective ratings to track progress from social skills training.

The last measure of social skills involves **standardized measures** that have normative data. Questionnaires like Constantino's Social Responsiveness Scale (SRS, 2013) or Gresham & Elliott's Social Skills Improvement System (SSIS, 2008) are examples of questionnaires that yield scores in relation to normative samples, allowing one to compare children's scores to the average scores of those of the same age and gender. These measures are quite useful in validating the results of social skill outcome studies where one can indicate that training altered social skill scores compared to a control group. They might also be useful for a school to answer the question about whether students' social skills look similar to those of their peers. However, I do not rely on these measures in my clinical work focused on specific individuals; for outcomes with individuals, I usually design my own set of social skill goals, which may or may not be represented in the standardized questionnaires.

CHAPTER 8

COMMON MODIFICATIONS TO THE ENVIRONMENT TO IMPROVE SOCIAL FUNCTIONING

According to a recent review on autistics transitioning to adulthood, the key to successful adult outcomes was creating a good environment/person fit (Anderson et al., 2018). That means, our focus cannot simply be on teaching skills, but also on creating an environment that allows for success. The following sections list a variety of environmental modifications for common challenging situations faced by individuals on the spectrum as well as many others. Much of the information below comes from the prevention plans outlined in greater detail in my book *No More Meltdowns* (Baker, 2008).

Frustration with Difficult Academic Work

Chapter 14 includes a variety of skills like handling academic frustrations and mistakes, asking for help, negotiating work demands, and taking temporary breaks. One of the most important skills is learning about Carol Dweck's "growth mindset" (Haimovitz and Dweck, 2017).

Essentially Dweck and her colleagues have shown that if individuals believe that difficulties with work are a sign that they are learning something new (growing their intelligence) rather than a sign of mental deficiency, they end up with more successful outcomes than those who believe their intelligence cannot change over time. The critical skills that Carol Dweck's growth mindset teaches us are to *persevere* after mistakes and *seek help* to achieve better outcomes.

In practice, these skills alone may not always help if individuals have a long history of insecurity about their competence. As such, work tasks also need to be modified in order to plan for success and help individuals begin to see that they can be successful with perseverance and assistance. The following is a short list of common academic work modifications and accommodations that can help increase the student's opportunity for success:

Challenge	Modification/Accommodation
Limited language comprehension	Add visual supports to make the task clearer. Examples: use pictures/cartoons to back up words to understand a story. Use labels to indicate place value for numbers. Use photos to indicate multi-step directions to complete a task.
Limited patience with larger assignments	Break up assignments into less intimidating tasks with breaks in between. Use timers to work for short periods of time before breaks.
History of frustration/lack of confidence	First model how to do all the work before requiring a student to try it by themselves. Use the 80/20 rule; provide 80% of work the individual can do first, followed by the 20% of work that might require assistance.
Boring or tedious work	Incorporate the student's interests into the work. Math could be a cooking lesson. Practice calculating numbers using a favored game. Writing and reading assignments can focus on the child's interests.

SOCIAL SKILLS TRAINING

| Specific reading and writing challenges | Allow the individual to fulfill the task with alternative ways to receive information (e.g., instructional videos, books on tape, graphic novels) and alternative ways to demonstrate knowledge (e.g., PowerPoint demonstration, a video or graphic representation). If student is open to writing but has graphomotor challenges, use keyboarding and speech-to-text software programs. |
| Trouble remembering homework assignments and having materials necessary to complete | Use a homework journal or post assignments on the web or email them to the individual. Provide extra copies of needed materials for home, perhaps utilizing digital copies of books and articles. |

Fears and Phobias

The treatment of choice for most "irrational" fears and phobias is gradual exposure to the feared situation until the individual realizes it does not pose a threat. The trick is how to convince individuals to gradually face their fears. In my book *Overcoming Anxiety in Children and Teens* (Baker, 2015), I describe a variety of strategies to help clients face fears for a variety of anxiety disorders. Strategies described include educating them about false alarms in their body, using a fear ladder to break down exposure into small steps, creating incentives to face fears, implementing user-friendly cognitive-behavioral therapy to challenge fearful thoughts, and using physical tools like exercise, meditation, neurofeedback, and medication. Some of the common environmental modifications are listed below:

Challenge	Modification/Accommodation
Fears related to overwhelming sensory input such as fire alarms	Evidence for those with sound sensitivities show they do not habituate the way others do to sound. If possible, it may be better to allow the individual to avoid these sensory violations altogether rather than attempting a program of gradual exposure.

Feared situation is too threatening	Break down the exposure to the fear into easier steps (create a Fear Ladder). For example, a child afraid of a swimming pool might be taught to first watch others in the water, then dip his feet into the water, go into shallow water, and eventually submerge. Rewards can be given for participating in each step of the ladder. A collaborative approach is crucial so that the child does not feel forced but instead chooses when they are ready to try each step.
Fear is supported by non-scientific/false beliefs	Use cognitive-behavioral therapy to challenge false beliefs. Ask the individual: 1. Are you overestimating the probability of a something bad happening? 2. Are you overestimating how bad it would be if it did happen? Create a "think like a scientist" cue card to record the scientific gathering of evidence to combat the false beliefs (see example in Chapter 14).
Child's arousal is so high that they cannot begin to face their fears	Consider physical strategies that reduce anxiety, like deep breathing, meditation (which could include engaging in the child's passions or listening to meditation guides), aerobic exercise, neurofeedback, and possible anti-anxiety medications (see Baker 2015 for a full description of these strategies).

Delayed Gratification/Disappointments/Changes in Schedule

The skill of delaying gratification is critical in order to manage one's emotions and reach longer-term goals. However, unexpected delays and disappointments are often difficult for our clients. In addition to teaching them the value of patience and waiting (that they will eventually get more of what they want if they can wait or accept a change), it is equally important that we modify the environment to make this easier to learn. The following are common modifications to help individuals wait and deal with unexpected delays or changes in schedule:

Challenge	Modification/Accommodation
Delays in getting a desired object or activity	Use a visual timer for children who cannot tell time using clocks. There are many excellent apps like the "time timer" that allow individuals to see a shape shrinking and thus see progress in their waiting. Start with small amounts of time (5 sec, then 30 sec, then a minute and so on) and say "wait" before giving the reward. Gradually increase the wait time to help individuals understand that "wait" does not mean "never," it just means until the shape on the timer disappears.
Not getting a particular desired object or activity because it is forbidden	Create a visual schedule to show other desired objects and activities the individual can have in place of the forbidden one.
Not getting a particular desired object or activity because the schedule changed	Create a visual schedule to show other desired objects and activities the individual can have in place of the rescheduled one, and show when the date/day/time the individual can have the originally desired object or activity.
Stopping a favored activity	Create a visual schedule to show that if the individuals stop an activity on time, they will get to do it again (for a longer period) at the next scheduled time. It is easier to stop something if they know when they can go back to it.

Lack of Attention from Others

Some children tend to crave attention from teachers and parents all the time, interrupting their activities. Other children crave attention from their peers and may do it in inappropriate ways, failing to discriminate "attention" from "being liked." For example, saying provocative comments often works to get others' attention but not necessarily to make others like them. The following is a list of modifications and accommodations that may help youngsters learn to wait for adult attention and find positive ways to get attention from peers.

Challenge	Modification/Accommodation
Delays in getting attention from teachers, parents or others	Use a visual timer and/or visual schedule to indicate when the desired person will be available. Red (means stop) versus green (means go) cards can also be posted on doors to indicate when a person is available.
Individual engages in provocative or undesirable ways to get attention	Create a visual list showing positive versus negative ways to get attention and the consequences of both (see Getting attention in Positive Ways in Chapter 14).
Some peers laugh or provide other social reinforcement for inappropriate ways to get attention	Teach peers to redirect the individual to positive ways to get attention and ignore inappropriate ways to get attention. A reward program can be used in a classroom or home where tokens are received by the group for either (a) avoiding inappropriate comments or (b) ignoring those moments when others make inappropriate comments.

Over-or Under-whelming Sensory Stimulation

Individuals on the spectrum often have sensitivities to too much stimulation, engage in repetitive self-stimulating behaviors to soothe or entertain themselves, and at times seek more stimulation when bored (especially for those with ADHD-like symptoms). The following is a short list of potential environmental modifications to address these broad categories of challenges. A more comprehensive list can be found in books like *Sensory Issues and High-Functioning Autism Spectrum and Related Disorders* (Myles and Mahler, 2014), *Raising a Sensory Smart Child: The Definitive Handbook for Helping Your Child with Sensory Processing Issues* (Biel and Pesk, 2009), and *The Out-of-Sync Child* (Kranowitz, 2022).

Challenge	Modification/Accommodation
Overwhelming stimulation	Provide the individual with a quieter/safe area to retreat from sensory stimulation. This could be a room in a house or school or the car when on outings. Individuals can also be given headphones and music or videos to temporarily escape into a virtual world.
Under stimulation/boredom	Provide the individual with more engaging activities or frequent breaks from tedious tasks. In academic settings, this often means including the child's interests in the academic task or using more hands-on activities and movement opportunities during the lesson. For those with limited receptive language, visual supports of material will also allow for greater engagement.
Individual engages in repetitive self-stimulation such as rocking, flapping or scripting from favored TV shows	Consider that the individual may be over-stimulated or under-stimulated and use the suggestions above. In either case, the individual is likely not engaged in the task offered by the teacher or parent during times of high self-stim. So, rather than trying to get the individual to stop self-stimming, seek to make the task at hand more interesting, using visual supports or movement opportunities.

Threats to Self-Esteem

Many of our youngsters have a history of frustration and teasing, culminating in very tenuous self-esteem. As a result, any mistake, corrective feedback, criticism, or further teasing can result in a larger upset for them than for others. These are some ways to modify the environment to help youngsters manage threats to self-esteem:

Challenge	Modification/Accommodation
Feedback that the individual has made a mistake with an academic task	During academic instruction: Provide the individual with tasks they can easily succeed with 80% of the time before introducing the 20% of work that they may find challenging. Earlier success can inoculate students against upset from later mistakes.
Criticism over a particular behavior	Before providing criticism, ask the individual if they would like to receive feedback to "do even better." Use the sandwich technique: say something positive, then provide corrective feedback, then reiterate the positive.
Individual is teased by peers or siblings	In addition to teaching an individual how to respond to teasing (see Chapter 14), we must also protect individuals from teasing. Adult supervision should be in place for teasing hot spots (buses, locker rooms, gatherings just before or after school). In addition, consider creating a peer buddy program in which positive peer influencers support and/or protect the individual from other peers (see Chapter 12 on Peer Sensitivity Training).

Overly Demanding Social Situations

Sometimes individuals on the spectrum will not socialize with others not only because they do not know what to do or say, but also because they find it uninteresting and/or they anticipate rejection. How can we make socializing easier and more enjoyable for those individuals?

Challenge	Modification/Accommodation
Individual finds socializing with others uninteresting	Utilize the individual's interests to motivate desire to socialize. For example, find peers with similar interests for a club or discussion group.

SOCIAL SKILLS TRAINING

Student does not know how to play or interact with others	Modify the games and activities to be within the capability and interest of the targeted student. For example, with students who have limited language and attention, identify activities that do not require language or waiting time (e.g., follow the leader, hide and seek, catch, tabletop games such as Go Fish or Hungry Hungry Hippos, charade games where individuals can act out an activity or an animal shown on picture cards and others must point to the card to indicate what their peer is demonstrating).
Individuals anticipate rejection from peers	Consider creating a peer buddy program in which positive peers volunteer to participate in a discussion group or club with targeted students (see Chapter 12 on Peer Sensitivity Training). Use gradual exposure to help individuals learn that they can interact with select peers who will not tease them. For example, ask them to just watch the group once without participating. Then come participate for five minutes, then ten minutes and so on.

CHAPTER 9

HOW AND WHERE TO TEACH SOCIAL SKILLS

How to Teach Skills

Chapter 3 mapped out some of the various skill-training strategies that have proven effective, including ABA, ABA combined with play-based strategies for early intervention, and cognitive-behavioral strategies like structured learning (explanation, modeling, role-play, and practice). When considering which strategies to use, one must consider the symbolic language and cognitive skills of the students. For students who have great deficits in symbolic and receptive language (ASD, Level 3), one cannot simply "talk about" how to perform a skill; instead, the instructor must model and prompt the skill in the actual situation and perhaps supplement this process with pictures or videos of skill steps (see, for example, my Social Skills Picture Books: Baker, 2001; 2006).

Those with adequate receptive language (e.g., ASD, Level 1 and Level 2) can benefit from strategies in which skill steps are explained verbally in addition to being modeled and prompted. Many cognitive-behavioral strategies can be used with such students who are capable of understanding explanations about others' perspectives and social cues when they are described concretely. Structured learning is the technique used in my previously published social skill manuals (Baker, 2003; Baker 2005) and has been shown to be effective in numerous studies (see Chapter 3). This strategy typically involves the following steps: (1) explanation of the skill steps, (2) modeling, (3) role-playing with corrective feedback, and (4) assigning practice activities. In this revised social skill manual, I have elaborated on the explanation step to include an additional strategy, providing a clear **rationale** for learning a skill, thus embracing the need to better capture students' motivation. We must explain not only what to do, but why (the rationale for learning a skill). We are trying to increase individuals' understanding of how their behavior impacts others and how that, in turn, impacts goals that are important to them. For example, before teaching the steps of the skill "compromising," we would explain how this skill relates to one of the student's own goals of being included in play with others. When you compromise, others will like being around you and thus include you when playing.

The following section outlines five steps for teaching using the structured learning method.

1. *Rationale*

In Chapter 5 we discussed collaborating with the student to come up with solutions to their own challenges, which might involve agreeing to learn certain skills. If our work was done well, we can then remind them of their proposed solution as a way to introduce why we would learn a particular skill. Recall our student, Charlie, from Chapter 6. After our collaborative problem-solving session with Charlie, he came up with some solutions that involved (a) modifications that the school and his parents would embrace (creating an anime/video game club and parents agreeing to give him regular video game time in a scheduled way) and (b) certain skills Charlie would learn like "accept no when it is time to shut down video games" and "initiate conversations and play with peers" who share his interests and "talk reciprocally rather than lecturing others." Before teaching these skills, we must remind him why we were learning these skills and how it fits into his own goals. The rationales for each of his skill areas are listed below:

a. **Accepting no or stopping a fun activity on time** makes his parents feel better, and when they are happy, they are willing to let him return to the video game at the scheduled time (and maybe even give him more video game time).

b. **Initiating conversation and play** focused on shared interests, like anime and video games, allows him to have fun, learn from others, and make friends.

c. **Talking reciprocally** rather than lecturing about his interests decreases the likelihood of being rejected or teased by others since that was reportedly something he was teased about in the past.

2. *Didactic Instruction and/or Video Modeling*

Didactic instruction involves the instructor (teacher, aide, or parent) explaining the steps of a particular skill, often with the skill steps written on a poster or black board as a visual aid. The key to this approach, or any other approach that relies partially on verbal and written instruction, is to engage the child's attention. Explanation of a skill is inherently "dry" and needs to be spiced up with game formats and lively presentations. For example, many of the children I have worked with are game-show fans (often because they excel in memorizing facts). Thus, discussing and reviewing the steps in the form of shows like *Jeopardy!* or *Who Wants to Be a Millionaire?* is usually well-received. When explaining the skill steps, I might say, "Listen carefully to these skill steps because afterward we will play a game to see how well you remember them, and if you get enough questions right, I will give you a prize."

I find *Who Wants to Be a Millionaire?* to be the easiest game-show format to use as you can ask the questions in a straightforward manner. To play this game, I pretend to be the host and invite students to sit across from me to answer one question at a time. I ask, "Where are you from? Who did you bring with you to the show today?" Then I say, "Are you ready to go for a million dollars?" (as they would say in the show). Unlike the real game show, where only one contestant answers a series of questions until he or she reaches the million-dollar question, I have members of a group or a class take turns answering questions, and collectively they can reach the million-dollar question. Also, as a group they share the following three lifelines (i.e., three opportunities to receive help with a question): (a) let the group vote on which answer is correct, (b) ask one person in the room for the answer, or (c) fifty/fifty—where two of four multiple-choice responses are removed, leaving just two from which to choose.

Starting at $2000, I ask the first student a question about the skill lesson we just had. Then, taking turns with all the students, we work through the $4000, $8000, $16,000, $32,000, $64,000, $125,000, $250,000, $500,000, and then the $1,000,000 question. As in the show, after each contestant responds, I ask, "Are you confident? Final answer? You're right." We can use rewards to increase participation, telling them that if they get to $30,000, they all get a snack, and if they get to a million dollars, they all get a prize.

Although I encourage the use of lifelines, I always make sure the students can get to a million dollars. I give hints so that they will not fail but still have to think about the answer. The goal, of course, is just that: to keep them thinking about the skill.

Sometimes it is helpful to write down the "game-show" questions ahead of time (see activity sheet for "Sensitive Topics" or for "Starting a Conversation"), but you can easily improvise the questions by using the skill lesson sheets (in Chapter 14) as your guide. Each step on a skill lesson sheet can be turned into a question. Often each step has several parts that can also be converted into questions. It is often easier to create questions without providing four multiple-choice responses, thus requiring students to recall the answer rather than recognize the answer from several choices. For example, when discussing the skill "Complimenting Others," we can ask a question about Step 1: "Why is it important to compliment others?" A second question could be, "Name another reason why it is important to compliment others." Step 2 can be another set of questions regarding what to compliment others about: "What kinds of things can you compliment others about? Name another thing you can compliment someone about." Step 3 can yield another set of questions, like, "What is a nice tone of voice? Why is it important to use a nice tone when complimenting others? What would be a nice tone of voice to use when complimenting others about their looks? What would not be a nice tone of voice to use when complimenting others about their looks?"

3. **Modeling the Skill Steps (Live or Through Video)**
   Once the skill steps have been explained, it is important to model them before asking students to carry them out. To do this, the facilitator needs (a) a situation to act out and (b) co-actors. Students, teachers, or parents can serve as co-actors to help model the skills. Ideas for situations to act out are provided for most skill lessons in Chapter 14. In addition to modeling the skill steps live in front of students, video lessons can also be used to depict the steps of a skill. Although some of my skill lessons are on YouTube already (see Jed Baker, "No More Meltdowns" on YouTube), I often invite students to make their own videos with me of the skill steps as a way to learn the skill. This can be done very simply using a smart phone. There is no need to be perfect and edit the videos, as mistakes can be utilized for learning purposes to discuss what went right and what went wrong, just as we do when we role-play.

SOCIAL SKILLS TRAINING

Before the skill is modeled, it is important to give any students who are observing the lesson very specific instructions on what to look for to maintain their attention. Say, "Watch what we do and, at the end, tell us if we did Step 1, which is … and Step 2, which is … and Step 3, which is … Give us a 'thumbs up' if we did it right or a 'thumbs down' if we did it incorrectly." Giving the observers a physical action to do, such as a thumbs up or down gesture, often helps to keep their attention on the skills.

After modeling the skill, ask the observers whether each step was performed. "Did we do Step 1, which is …? Thumbs up or down? Did we do Step 2, which is …? Thumbs up or down? Did we do Step 3, which is …? Thumbs up or down?" We can model several more times to help students understand the nuances of the skill. Each time, we will ask observers to notice whether each step was performed correctly and to provide a "thumbs up or down." Each demonstration can involve doing one step incorrectly in order to highlight the importance of each step. For example, when modeling "How and When to Interrupt," we can say, "Excuse me" correctly but forget to wait for a pause. Then we can ask the observers about how each step was performed, highlighting the step that was modeled incorrectly and why it is important to perform correctly. Depending on the student's personality and nature, the instructor may choose not to explain nor show the wrong way to enact a skill step and instead just focus on the right way to engage in the skill. The potential disadvantage of reviewing the wrong way is that some students are so entertained by inappropriate behavior that they may continually perform the skill the wrong way for their own or others' amusement. On the other hand, the advantage of demonstrating the wrong way is twofold: (a) certain skills will be much better understood when both the right and wrong way are shown, and (b) students who are reluctant to role-play may be more likely to try if the person modeling also does things incorrectly sometimes. The bottom line is "know your student." Youngsters who show a lot of "silly" attention-seeking behaviors may not be good candidates for having the opportunity to observe or role-play a skill the wrong way.

4. *Role-Playing the Skill/Providing Corrective Feedback*
   During role-plays, the student is asked to act out the skill steps in the right order. Role-playing is often more effective when done with two instructors or with one instructor and two students. This way, an instructor can avoid participating in the role-play directly and act as a coach to help the students through the skill steps. Just as described in the modeling situation, the observers of the role-play should be given instructions to see if each step is done correctly. If children are reluctant to role-play for fear of making a mistake, we can ask them to do something the wrong way and then we can guess what it was. This will relieve some anxiety

about performing in front of others. Ideas for role-plays are provided on the activity sheets that accompany most skill lessons in Chapter 14.

After each role-play, the instructor provides feedback about how each step was enacted. Feedback should always begin by noting what was performed correctly and should include ample praise. Observing students are asked to name what the role-playing student did well.

Avoid directly telling students that they performed a skill or step incorrectly. Instead, give corrective feedback, saying something like, "In this step, here is what I want you to do to perform the step even better." Observers can also be asked what they would do to make the role-play "even better" rather than what was done poorly. If needed, model the correct way to perform the skill. Corrective feedback and practice should continue until the student can demonstrate the step correctly. The process of teaching a particular skill—reviewing the steps, role-playing the skill, and providing corrective feedback—should be repeated until the student is able to demonstrate the skill with minimal prompting. At this point we can begin to promote generalization of the skill by assigning practice assignments.

5. *Practicing the Skills*

Ideally, before the students leave the session, we want them to decide with whom and when they will practice the skill. The activity sheets in Chapter 14 have suggested activities to practice each skill. In addition, there is a practice area at the bottom of each skill lesson sheet in which the student can indicate with whom they will practice and when. We can tell students that if they return the assignment sheet and indicate how they practiced the skill, they can receive a bonus prize at the next session/lesson. Chapter 11 provides more details on how to encourage practice and promote skill generalization.

Where to Conduct Skill Lessons

Though we may want to generalize the skills in many places, this question is about where we do our initial teaching of skills. Skills are generally taught in three venues: a classroom, small group in or out of school, or individually.

Why might we teach skills in a **classroom**? First, there is evidence that teaching in a classroom can increase generalization (Bellini et al., 2007). Because the skills training is completed in front of the teachers and typical peers, it is easier for the skills to become part of classroom expectations and routines. Moreover, for many younger children, it often makes sense to teach the skill in class because most peers will benefit from the same targeted skill lessons. Lots of young children struggle with things like compromising, sharing, and dealing with frustration, anger, and anxiety. Therefore, when targeting skills for an individual, we may find that most of the classmates also struggle with those same issues, so it would be beneficial to teach the whole class.

However, a large class is typically not as conducive to building close friendships. Besides, the skills to be taught may not be relevant to all the students in the class. This is particularly the case in middle and high school, where students with ASD and related issues often have greater needs for conversation skills than their typical peers. Another practical problem in middle and high school is that the students routinely switch from class to class, making scheduling of a large skills-training class difficult. By comparison, the **small-group** setting is ideal for developing close friendships among the members and allows the facilitator to group students with similar skill-training needs and interests. Moreover, students might be highly motivated to attend a group centered around their special interest, such as a gaming, anime, film, or book club.

If students have significant behavioral challenges and difficulties attending in group settings, it may be best to begin with individual treatment prior to considering a group. In this setting we can ensure students hear and understand the lesson, and we can work more on motivating them to learn those skills to reach their own goals. Individual lessons can also be offered by parents prior to playdates.

Playdates are perhaps the most ideal setting for developing the closest friendships. It is in the context of one-on-one play that young children typically find their "best friends." Parents can try to encourage and arrange playdates for their children throughout their childhood. Much of the time, this occurs through parents meeting other amenable parents and arranging for their families to get together, thus bringing the children together. One way to find other families is through local support groups of parents whose children have ASD and/or learning disabilities. Also, parents who have children participating in after-school social skill groups often get to know each other while waiting for the children to finish their session. The instructor for the children's group can encourage the parents to arrange playdates outside of the group meetings to continue the children's socialization.

Let's take a look at both the common elements and the unique features of the various settings for social skills training—classrooms, small groups, and individual sessions. In all settings, we should allow time for a formal lesson as outlined in the previous chapter, followed by less structured times to practice the skills in a more spontaneous fashion. In the classroom, the formal skill lesson may be conducted early in the week and the less structured practice times spread out during the rest of the week through specific conversation and play activities organized by the classroom teacher. For example, the teacher may use a daily "show and tell" or "morning meetings" to work on conversation skills like staying on topic and starting a conversation. In the small group, both structured and spontaneous activities occur within an hour-long session. Typically a ten- to twenty-minute skill lesson is embedded into the group along with less structured activities.

Classroom Skills Training

A thirty- to forty-minute structured skill lesson (i.e., explanation, modeling, and role-plays) should be done in class as early as possible during the week. For example, each Monday, one can review or introduce a new skill lesson. That leaves the rest of the week for practicing the skills. Ideally, social skills training should occur on a daily basis, but it is not necessary for a formal skill lesson to take place daily as long as the students have a chance to practice the skills each day as described below.

The job of a facilitator of classroom skills training is to (a) conduct the skills training lesson that introduces the skill concept, and (b) consult with the classroom teacher and aides to conduct daily activities to practice the skills. Even if the classroom teacher will not be not the one teaching the skill lessons, it is important for the teacher to take ownership of the program in both selecting and practicing skills. One way to approach a busy teacher who may not always be open to yet another "nonacademic" activity in the classroom is to explain how social skills training will eventually reduce social conflicts in class, allowing more time for academic teaching. In other words, although the teacher will have to put some time and energy into practicing the skills, this will later free up more time when they are no longer constantly addressing peer conflicts in class. At a minimum, teachers should be present for the lessons so that they know what the students are learning. In addition, the classroom teacher may be requested to reward children for demonstrating the skills and to conduct daily activities to practice the skills.

The activity pages in Chapter 14 describe a variety of ways to practice each skill. Two examples of practicing conversation skills are described below. In "show and tell," students take turns bringing in an item or pictures of something they want to share or somewhere they have been (particularly if it is known to be a common interest among classmates). Other students are prompted by the teacher to make on-topic comments or ask follow-up questions. The "poster summary of starting and maintaining conversations" (see Skill #39 in Chapter 14) should be present in the classroom as a visual aid to this activity. For example, the teacher may direct a student to stand in front of the class and describe what he brought. Then the teacher will ask, "Does anyone have a question or comment about what he brought in?" The teacher can point to the conversation poster and say, "Does anyone have a 'Where' question like 'Where did you get it?' or a 'Who' question like 'Who got it for you?' or a comment like 'I like it' or 'I have one too'?"

In the "morning meeting" activity, students are split up into dyads or groups of three to four and told to ask each other a series of conversation-starter questions like, "What did you do yesterday?" or "What are you going to do after school today?" Questions are usually pulled from the conversation poster. One fun way to do this is to ask the students to walk around the room until the teacher says, "freeze." At that point the students are instructed to turn to the nearest person and ask a particular conversation starter like, "How was your weekend?" Other questions might involve students' plans for the upcoming weekend, after-school activities, or a special interest. Students are instructed to ask follow-up questions and make on-topic comments to keep the conversation going. Then they are free to walk around again until the teacher calls "freeze." Again, they must pick the closest (but a different) person and ask another question the teacher calls out, such as "What are you going to do for the upcoming vacation?" Each student is asked to report what they learned about their classmates. This activity promotes listening, starting conversations, staying on-topic, and using general conversational skills.

Prior to conducting skill lessons, the teacher and the skills facilitator can decide what activities they will use to practice the skill during the week and whether to use incentives to reward students for demonstrating the skills. One of the most user-friendly ways to reward students in a large classroom is the marble jar system used by Lee Canter (1987). A marble or token is put into a jar every time a student exhibits the target skills. When the class accumulates enough marbles (typically twenty to fifty), the whole class receives a reward (e.g., a party, extra art period). So as not to overwhelm the students and the teacher, it is wise to focus on no more than two or three skills at a time. In addition, avoid removing marbles for misbehavior so that students can maintain a positive attitude about the incentive system.

Small Group Setting

The small group can take place in school (perhaps at lunch or after school) or in a private setting (clinic or someone's home). Though some students might seek out the opportunity to learn social skills, most kids are more likely motivated to come to group if the activity in group appeals to them. Rather than calling it a "social skill" group, I prefer to label the group based on children's special interests and open up the group to so-called "typically developing peers" who also have those interests. I have created clubs centered around books or films, games (video, card, or board games), cooking, robotics, Legos®, music appreciation, musical bands, and more.

Our groups generally meet once per week all year long with meetings every twelve weeks with parents to review progress. For after-school groups and those in private settings, parents typically pick up their children, allowing us to tell them what we worked on, review any skill assignments, and possibly arrange playdates with other kids' parents. Details for running sessions in a small group are provided in the next chapter.

Individual Sessions and Playdates

Individual treatment is often a good first start when students do not yet have any motivation to work on social skills and/or have significant behavioral challenges (such as high levels of physical aggression with peers) that preclude participation in a group. Individual sessions can help prepare students to eventually be in a group with peers.

Sessions can initially focus on the motivational work described in Chapter 5 to build a collaborative relationship to work on problems. The goal is to use the child's perspective to understand problem situations and invite the child to offer ways to solve those problems. In this setting we can establish a rationale for working on certain skills to reach their own goals.

Even if students never join a social skill group, social skills can be taught individually through explanation, modeling, and role-play, with practice being assigned to situations outside the session when they interact with others. One situation where children can practice skills that were initially taught in an individual session is on a playdate. In fact, parents can teach and review critical skills just before a play date.

The first step in conducting playdates is to arrange for one! This is not always easy for children with ASD and related issues, who may be isolated from peers. Often, teachers can be a great resource in helping to determine which classmates might be open to a playdate. In addition to asking the student's teacher, parents can seek out local support groups for parents of children with ASD or learning disabilities. Parents of children attending the same social skills group in school or in a private clinic are another option.

Once a playdate has been arranged, it is recommended that parents consider a couple of practical issues to increase the chances of a successful get-together. First, consider having the playdate

    SOCIAL SKILLS TRAINING

at your house so that you can be on hand to coach and guide the activities. In addition, arrange to pick up and drop off your guest so that you can end the playdate early if the children begin to have conflicts they cannot resolve. (Warn the other parents that this may happen, so arrangements can be made to ensure they are available to receive their child early.) Parents of multiple children may want to send their "neurotypical" children to the neighbors prior to the playdate to avoid a common problem whereby the invited guest ends up ignoring the neurodiverse child to play with his or her siblings. Consider having short (e.g., thirty-minute) playdates at first, then gradually increasing to longer social times after having a chance to see how the children interact. Finally, parents may want to collect "cool" toys and games like a trampoline in the front yard, great video games, and fun art project materials to increase motivation for peers to return.

Formal skill lessons can be conducted any time prior to the playdate. But the skill steps needed for the playdate should be reviewed just prior to the guests' arrival as well. Some of the more important rules and skills to consider teaching are to play with the guest rather than separately, play what the guest wants to play (or at least a shared interest), compromise, take turns, deal with losing, and avoid sensitive topics (see Chapter 14 for these skill lessons). Parents can use the structured learning approach described in this chapter to explain, model, and role-play the steps for these and other skills. Parents may negotiate a reward for their child for complying with the rules and skills steps if the interaction with the peer is not yet rewarding. For example, parents may agree to buy the children ice cream (if that is rewarding for their child) after their child plays what the guest wants to play for the first ten minutes and for the remaining time, works to compromise with the guest on what else to play.

For children who have great difficulty taking turns and/or losing, it makes sense to initially avoid games and activities that require waiting for a turn and have a winner or loser. Most board games, video games, and outdoor competitive games fall into this category. Only after the child has had many chances to practice these activities with parents should they be introduced with peers. Instead, initial playdates can focus on activities that students can do in parallel without any wait time and with no winner or losers. Art and cooking projects fall into this category, with each child getting his or her own materials and putting the projects together side by side. Materials might include Play-Doh®, building materials (Legos®, blocks), paper-maché, and ingredients for making food. Older children can create model ships, cars, and other hobby items, sitting side by side with little interaction.

As children get accustomed to each other, you can progress to more interactive activities. For younger children, these might include pretend play with kitchen items, cars, building materials, and puzzles. Parents may facilitate this by helping their child notice what their guest is doing and trying to imitate it. For example, the parent might say, "Look at Sam; he is pretending to put out a fire with the fire truck. Can you put out the fire too?"

Younger children can also learn to take turns by sharing materials. For example, children can be directed to take turns using a trampoline, going down a slide, or playing dress-up with a particular hat. For elementary-aged children, board and video games require more social interaction, patience, and the ability to tolerate frustration. Parents may decide to start with games with which the child already feels very competent so that she can tolerate taking turns and losing. New games that require great skill are not the best choice to introduce into a playdate for a child who gets frustrated easily. Instead, let the child learn the game ahead of time with her parent, and then when some level of comfort is established, incorporate the game into a playdate.

CHAPTER 10

FACILITATING GROUP SESSIONS

In order to facilitate group sessions, you will need the following materials: a board to write on, copies of the skill handouts (see Chapter 14), possibly a token system for younger kids (e.g., play money), snack items, and three posters. One poster lists the rules so they are visible during all sessions. Another poster is a visual cue for maintaining conversations (see "Keeping the Conversation Going" at the end of this chapter and #39 in Chapter 14). The poster below lists the schedule of activities for the group.

SCHEDULE FOR EACH SESSION

1. Talk Time

2. Skill Time

3. Activity Time

4. Snack

As in the classroom, the schedule reflects time for a formal lesson (skill time) and less structured times (activity time) to practice skills. In addition, there is an opportunity at the outset of each session for members to converse with each other to practice conversational skills. The first session, however, has a slightly different schedule than subsequent sessions (see below).

The First Session

The first session generally entails four components:

- Review the purpose of the group and establish group rules
- Get to know each other through discussion of interests
- Activity
- Snack time

The following contains transcripts from a first session with a group of seven-year-olds with ASD whom we will call Sam, Joe, Jenna, and Tommy. They all enjoy building things with Legos®, Kinex®, and other similar materials, so the group was labelled as a "Building" group. In preparation for the group, I asked each child to bring in a picture or an object that represents one of their special interests, related either to the group theme of building or to another interest they have so that the other kids can learn about them.

Review the purpose of the group
Here we open the group and remind everyone why we are meeting. We need to establish motivation to learn new skills. For some children, the motivation is not to make friends, but to participate in their shared interest (in this case, building). We must then link learning the skills as a means to getting what you want, as we did for Sam in the following transcript. (The group leader bases his comments on information gathered from an initial intake session where he met with the student and explained the group.)

> GROUP LEADER: Welcome to the group, ladies and gentlemen. Let me introduce you to each other. This is Joe, Sam, Jenna, Tommy, and you know me, my name is Dr. Baker.
>
> SAM: *(looking at Joe, who is carrying some special Lego® pieces)* Can I see it?
>
> GROUP LEADER: Guys, we can see what everyone brought in just a moment, but first I want to ask you if you remember what this group is about. Why are we here?

JENNA:	*(shouting out)* To build stuff and maybe make friends!
GROUP LEADER:	That's right. We have some very cool building projects we can make. If we can get along with each other, we can build things that would be harder to do alone, and also we can make friends.
SAM:	But I do not want any more friends. I just want to build.
GROUP LEADER:	Didn't you tell me when we met that you wanted to get new things to build?
SAM:	Yeah.
GROUP LEADER:	Well, by working with the other kids, you get to build new stuff here and maybe get to learn about other projects they are doing at home. Plus, you can make bigger things when we can all work together. So before we do our projects, we will go over a couple things to make sure we can get along, okay?
SAM:	Okay.

Establishing group rules

The members are encouraged to develop their own group rules. However, I guide their choices so that we will at least include the following rules:

- Listen to each other (wait for a pause to talk during conversation time, raise your hand and wait to be called on during skill time)
- Talk nicely to each other (do not yell, tease or insult others)
- Keep hands and feet to yourself (do not push, hit, kick, pinch, or grab others)

Most of the time these are the rules, in one form or another, that are suggested by the students themselves. Three to four rules are satisfactory, as more would be overly complicated to remember.

GROUP LEADER:	Okay, eyes up here. Thanks for listening. Guys, this is your group, so you should decide what rules you might need so we can all get along. What rules would you like in this group?
TOMMY:	Don't yell at each other.
GROUP LEADER:	Okay. That sounds good. Does everyone agree with that rule? Sam, Joe, Jenna, what do you think?
SAM, JENNA, JOE:	Okay.
GROUP LEADER:	Let's call that rule, "Talk nicely to others." I will write it on this poster.
JENNA:	How about no put-downs?

GROUP LEADER: Sounds great to me. Guys, what do you think? *(The other students look around the room.)* Look up here. Thanks for listening. Jenna suggested no put-downs. Do you guys agree?

TOMMY, SAM, JOE: Yeah, and no teasing.

GROUP LEADER: Okay. I think these are all ways of saying "Talk nicely to each other, so I will write under "Talk nicely," "No yelling, put-downs, or teasing." (Teasing is a subject that can help the group begin to bond around their similarities. So when someone brings it up, I use it to help the group feel connected and safe.)

I know I have been teased. Most everyone I know has been teased. How many people here have ever been teased? It's okay if you do not want to say anything about it, but I think we can all raise our hands."

(They all raise their hands.)

TOMMY: This kid called me a geek when I was in gym because I couldn't kick the soccer ball.

GROUP LEADER: It is not nice or fair to be teased like that. Plus, you are totally an expert in soccer. I remember you telling me all about soccer when we met. I know I have been teased like that a lot of times. Has that happened to anyone else? Does anyone else want to tell a time they were teased?

JENNA: This boy called me stupid because I did not get my math problems right.

GROUP LEADER: Well, I know you are not at all stupid. In fact, you are quite intelligent, like the rest of you guys. I am sorry that happened to you. You know, Albert Einstein, who was considered one of the smartest people ever, failed math when he was a kid. So just because you missed a math problem doesn't mean you are not smart. Does anyone else want to tell a time they were teased?

SAM: I was, but I do not want to talk about it.

GROUP LEADER: You don't have to. But I think we can all understand how it feels to be teased, and it's not fun. We all have something in common. We are all very smart and we all have felt what it's like to be teased. Can we all agree not to tease each other here?

GROUP MEMBERS: Yeah.

GROUP LEADER: That's great. We will be like a family here and try to make each other feel better. Now, what other rules might we need?

GROUP RULES

- Listen to each other (wait for a pause to talk during conversation time, raise your hand and wait to be called on during skill time).

- Talk nicely to each other (do not yell, tease or insult others).

- Keep hands and feet to yourself (do not push, hit, kick, pinch, or grab others).

At this point we elicited the two other rules: "Listen" (wait for a pause during talk time, and raising your hand during a skill lesson) and "Keep hands and feet to ourselves" (no hitting, pushing, kicking, or grabbing).

I then describe any behavioral management system we may use for following rules—such as a reward system. I have rarely needed a behavioral management system with teens. But with younger groups, I have used a token system with play money earned towards a previously described incentive. I find the play money to be an effective, concrete, visual incentive, quieter than coins (which can sometimes disrupt conversation when students clang them together) and somewhat reinforcing by association. I say to the students the following about the token system:

GROUP LEADER: Now that you guys came up with the rules, I will help you to follow them by giving you these dollars (play money) as you listen to each other, talk nicely, and keep hands and feet to yourselves *(pointing to the rules listed on a poster board)*. When you guys get enough dollars, we will get a snack or a prize.

I usually do not tell them how many dollars they need during the first session because I do not know how many they will earn. I want them all to earn enough for a snack the first session to help them feel successful and motivated to continue the "dollar" system. If, for example, they have each earned nine dollars by the end of the session, I will tell them they need ten dollars for their snack or prize and then offer the last dollar in exchange for cleaning up and getting ready to leave.

Getting to know each other

Since most members are quite nervous entering the first session, we usually spend most of the time in familiar territory. Each member has the opportunity to tell about his current interest during a "Getting to Know You" period. This usually breaks the ice, allows members to identify with each other further, and sets the stage for conversation skills we will be working on. My comments as the group leader first center on getting the members to listen to each member as they discuss their interests. I direct them to the poster "Keeping the Conversation Going" and instruct them that they can make comments or ask questions about what others say. Depending on the members' age and language ability, I may give a minimal prompt like, "Does anyone have a question or a comment about what Joe is saying?" For students who need more help, I might give a more intensive prompt like, "Can you ask Joe a 'where' question, like 'Where did you get that?'"

KEEP CONVERSATIONS GOING

ASK	TELL
Who	I like _____
What	I also _____
When	I never _____
Where	My _____
Why	
How	
What else	

The following excerpt is from the first session with Joe, Sam, Jenna, and Tommy:

GROUP LEADER: Okay, ladies and gentlemen, we usually have a talk time, skill time, building activity, and snack time in each session (pointing at the schedule poster). But since this is our first session, instead of learning a skill, we are going to get to know each other. I know everyone here likes to build, but does anyone want to say a little about what else they like to do or what they are interested in? Did anyone bring something in to show the others to help explain what they are interested in?

TOMMY: Yeah, I did. I have my *Pokémon* card collection. I have—

JENNA I brought in my roller skates because—

GROUP LEADER: Okay, we need to take turns talking. Jenna and Tommy both want to talk. Can one of you let the other go first?

TOMMY: Okay, Jenna can go first. Ladies first.

GROUP LEADER: That was very nice of you. Letting others go first can help make friends. *(The leader hands Tommy play money.)* Here is a dollar for letting others go first. *(Sam and Joe begin to lose their attention.)* Eyes up here, everyone. I like the way Sam, Joe, and Jenna are listening now; you can get dollars too. *(Leader hands the others a dollar.)* Okay, we are listening to Jenna now. As we listen, you can ask Jenna questions or say something about what she is saying *(Leader points to the poster "Keep the Conversation Going").* Let's all look at Jenna. Go ahead, Jenna.

JENNA: These are my roller skates.

GROUP LEADER: Do you want to say something about why you brought them?

JENNA: I love roller skating. I go really fast and can beat my brother in a race.

GROUP LEADER: *(Leader hands Joe, Sam, and Tommy a dollar and whispers)* Good listening, guys. *(In a louder voice)* Does anyone have any questions or comments for Jenna?

TOMMY: What are the wheels made of?

GROUP LEADER: *(Although this is not a totally relevant question in terms of Jenna's interests, it is on the topic of roller skates, so it should be supported in this first session.)* Tommy, that's a good on-topic question *(handing a dollar to Tommy).*

JENNA: I don't know what they are made of.

JOE: Where did you get them? *(Leader hands Joe a dollar.)*

GROUP LEADER: *(Leader also hands Sam a dollar, whispering.)* I like the way you were listening to Jenna also.

JENNA: At the skating shop.

GROUP LEADER: Does anyone else like to skate?

SAM I like to watch skating.

GROUP LEADER: *(In an attempt to bring the group together, the leader points out similarities in interests.)* So it looks like you have something else in common. Besides all agreeing that you like building things, it looks like some of you like to skate, and others like to watch skating. Maybe sometime you might all go skating or watch skating together. Does anyone else have a question or comment for Jenna? *(No response.)* Jenna, did you want to say more about what you like, or should we go on to someone else?

JENNA: I'm done.

GROUP LEADER: Tommy, I think you wanted to tell us about your *Pokémon* card collection. Everyone, let's look and listen to Tommy.

TOMMY I have 150 *Pokémon* cards that I brought in, including this rare 'Charizard' card. *(All the students gather to see the card.)*

JOE: Can I see it? *(Reaching out to touch it.)*

GROUP LEADER: Joe, you have to wait for Tommy's permission to touch the card. Tommy, what do you want Joe to do, look at or touch the card?

TOMMY I think just look at it right now.

JOE: *(looking at the card)* I have a lot of *Pokémon* cards too.

GROUP LEADER: *(handing Joe a dollar and whispering to Joe)* That's a good on-topic comment that really shows you are listening to Tommy.

SAM: I do not love *Pokémon*. I like *Digimon* better. *(Leader hands Sam a dollar and whispers that it was a good on-topic comment.)*

GROUP LEADER: What about you, Jenna, do you like *Pokémon* or *Digimon* or any animated cartoon shows?

JENNA I like a lot of the shows, like *SpongeBob*. *(Leader hands Jenna a dollar and whispers to her that her comment was on-topic.)*

GROUP LEADER: Wow, you all have something else in common: you all like animated cartoon shows. Does anyone else have a question or comment for Tommy? No response. How about a 'where' question ... where did you? ... *(waiting for the group members to respond)*

JOE: Where did you get the cards, Tommy? *(Leader hands Joe a dollar and whispers that Joe asked a good follow-up question.)*

SOCIAL SKILLS TRAINING

The group continues with each member getting a turn to discuss his or her interests, after which the group leader makes more comments to try to point out the members' similarities and ignore some of the differences. For example, if they all like different TV shows, the leader points out that they all like TV rather than highlighting the differences in the shows they like. Early on, it is important for the members to see how they can relate to each other.

Subsequent Sessions

Subsequent sessions follow the format described earlier: conversation time, skill time, activity time, and snacktime.

Conversation time

This part of the session resembles any typical therapy group in which members discuss their week, including problematic situations, and gain support and advice from other members. However, the difference is that I am as concerned about *how* the group participants are conversing as I am about *what* they are saying. My main job as facilitator is to coach, prompt, praise, and highlight the social environment as it unfolds during group.

At least two conversation skills typically need to be taught before conversation time can run smoothly. These are:

1. Maintaining a Conversation
2. Starting a Conversation

Given that these skills will not have been taught formally prior to the group, I do not expect conversation time to flow smoothly for some time. I coach the students through these skills during conversation time by prompting them on what to say and do in the moment. Then during the skill time of each session, we might have a formal lesson on one of these skills (if that was one of the targeted skills for the group members). Often in the first two sessions, skill time actually precedes conversation time. This allows two skills—maintaining and starting a conversation—to be taught so that the group members have some idea of what to say during conversation time. In subsequent sessions, the conversation time can precede skill time.

To prompt *starting a conversation* (see "Poster summary of starting and maintaining conversations," #39 in Chapter 14), I will tell them to ask each other questions about the past (e.g., "How was your week?"), present (e.g., "What are you doing?"), future (e.g., "What are you going to do this weekend?"), and the others' interests (e.g., "Have you been skating recently?" posed to a member who is known to skate). Then to prompt maintaining a conversation, I remind them to ask follow-up questions and make on-topic comments (see "Maintaining a Conversation" in Chapter 14).

To address members who are *talking incessantly*, I prompt them to talk briefly and check if others want to hear more: "Look at the other guys; do they seem interested? Why don't you ask them if they want to hear more?" In addition, I remind them to take turns talking, wait for a pause (which is typically part of the rules of the group), make eye contact (at least sporadic gazes in the direction of the speaker), keep an appropriate distance from each other, and modulate their volume and tone of voice as necessary.

Topic management is a major issue in conversation time as members may stray from the topic quite rapidly. For example, two members may be discussing a video game, and a third member asks, "What are you going to have for dinner today?" I respond to this abrupt shift in topics by saying something like, "Was that on-topic? They were talking about video games, and you asked about dinner. Wait until they are done talking about the video game and then say, 'Can I talk about something else?'"

I also prompt them to edit *sensitive remarks* (see "Sensitive Topics" in Chapter 14). Sensitive topics are words that insult, embarrass, or otherwise make others uncomfortable. For example, a student might say to another student, "Why do you talk with a lisp?" I would explain, "That is a sensitive topic that might make someone upset, especially if other kids have teased him about it. Even though there is nothing wrong with talking with a lisp, it might make him upset when you point that out. So you can think it, but do not say it." To prompt the members to show understanding when someone is upset, I might say, "He looks upset; what can you say?" If there is no response, I say, "Ask him if he is okay or if you can help him."

As seen in the transcript of the first session, I often use play money with younger students to reward them as they spontaneously or, with some prompting, demonstrate a skill. You must train yourself to watch for and praise the use of these skills as they occur in order to shape more appropriate conversation. For example, we may not notice when someone is sitting quietly, listening, and making eye contact while another member is talking. That is the time to go over to the quiet student and whisper, "Nice listening," and hand them a dollar. The youngster who asks a good follow-up question can also be given a dollar. The student who, with my prompting, asks the other members if they want to hear more rather than going on about his special interests also receives a dollar. The student who says, "Can I talk about something else?" rather than just changing the topic can get a dollar. In this way, the dollars highlight the positive conversation skills the members are demonstrating and encourage more prosocial behaviors.

Skill Time

I typically allot no more than fifteen to twenty minutes of direct teaching of skill lessons as this can be the least interesting part of group for kids. For students with average or above-average receptive language, I follow the model described for teaching skills outlined in Chapter 9: Provide a rationale for why we want to learn the skill, explain the skill steps, model the skill steps, role-play the skill providing corrective feedback, and plan for practicing the skill in real life. For example, if I was introducing the skill "compromising in a group" to help group members get along in doing activities together, the skill lesson might go as follows:

Rationale. Explain how compromising helps us to get along so that we can build great projects together. "Together we can make bigger, more complicated things than we could by ourselves. Yet when people disagree about what the group should make, it becomes impossible to let everyone build everything they want. We have to compromise."

Explanation of steps. We can write these steps on a poster or white board and hand out the skill sheet from Chapter 14 to each child. I might say, "Compromising in a group means we try to give everyone at least some of what they want, and then vote on what to do as a group."

Compromising in a Group

1. Find out what everyone wants to build.

2. Discuss how to try to give everyone some of what they want (for example, by putting people's ideas together).

3. Take a vote on what to build.

4. Go with the majority vote.

Modeling. "Let's say we have three possible projects from this Kinex Amusement Park set: We can build a Spinning Ferris Wheel, Twirling Boom Ride, or Spinning Swing Ride.

Step 1: Let's find out what each person wants to build. Let's say we find out that Jenna and Sam want to build the Ferris Wheel, and Tommy wants to build the Boom Ride, but Joe wants to build the Spinning Ride.

Step 2, then, is we discuss if we can do a little bit of what everyone wants. We consider combining projects, but we agree that would mean we won't have enough pieces to really make any of them work. So we consider just doing one project at a time, which would mean some of us would have to wait longer to do the projects we want.

Step 3 is to take a vote. We already decided to do one at a time, so now we vote on which project we should do first. Let's say that we vote on the Ferris wheel first, but then we cannot decide on the second one because no one wants their favorite project to be last. What could we do to compromise so everyone gets a turn at deciding what to do first? We could say whoever is willing to let their project go last can be the one to choose which project we do when we are done with these three projects. So if you get last pick on this set, you get first pick on the next set we do. So let's say Tommy says he will let the Boom Ride be the last one, so he gets first choice on the next set of projects we do. So did we do the steps correctly here?" The group agrees we did. "Now let's say Tommy and Joe both insist their project goes second and cannot agree. What happens now?" The group members respond, saying we cannot move forward as there are not enough pieces for both of them to do their projects at the same time. Someone has to compromise. "Exactly. If we compromise, everyone eventually gets to do their project!"

Role-play: "Now you guys try it for real. Here is the Kinex Amusement Park set where we can build a Spinning Ferris Wheel, Twirling Boom Ride, or Spinning Swing Ride. What is the first step, everyone?" The group goes through each step with my coaching. I provide feedback along the way if anyone is unwilling to compromise. Sometimes one member may be inflexible and then we ask the other members to compromise, offering them first pick on the next project. I provide ample praise to those who do compromise and tell the one who refused to compromise that it is okay if they cannot compromise yet; maybe they will be ready next time. I remind them that if they can, others will be more willing to work with them. As they see the praise go towards those who compromise, eventually even the more inflexible kids come around when doing future projects.

SOCIAL SKILLS TRAINING

Plan out practice: After we role-play, I ask the members to consider where else they will practice this skill and fill that in on the practice section of the skill sheet. I point out that we are about to actually build these projects, and this is a perfect time to practice compromising as they will have to decide on who builds what parts of the project and who gets what pieces. We might also ask about any group decisions that might be made at home later that night, like what to get for dinner or what show to watch on TV. They can write into the practice section whom they will try this with and report back to us in the next group session on how it went.

Activity Time

The group leader's role during activity time is similar to that during conversation time: highlight for members how others are feeling, and prompt and reward the use of appropriate skills (e.g., compromising, sharing, taking turns, deciding who will go first, dealing with mistakes). For example, if members have a conflict about who will build a particular part of a project, I prompt them to use a skill they have just learned. I might say, "You guys both want to build the same part. What can we do to decide who will build that?" If members do not offer a solution, I will try to reintroduce the notion of compromise, where each member is asked to flex a little to let the others build some of what they wanted.

If members still are unable to solve the problem with this minimal prompting by me, and they begin to raise their voices or position to fight each other, I will step in quickly to solve the problem for them. I get between them to prevent any physical confrontation and then offer my own solution, such as, "Sam, you build this, and Tommy, you can build this part. Next time we can switch parts. I will give you each an extra dollar if you can accept this." If tempers continue to flare despite my efforts to solve the problem, I try to use a distraction to calm the students. For example, I might say, "Hey, who wants some of this clay? Why don't you guys create your Pokémon and Digimon characters using this clay?" Using the members' interests (in this case, Pokémon and Digimon), I try to get their minds off the conflict at hand. In a later group, I return to the problem of deciding who gets to build what part and incorporate it into a social skills lesson or problem-solving discussion to prepare the students for similar situations in the future. This way of handling temper flare-ups in group is summarized below:

Rule of Thumb for Temper Outbursts

- try to get students to solve the problem if they have been taught the skills ahead of time

- offer your own solution if they cannot work it out, and use an incentive to follow the plan

- during moments of intense anger, use distraction as a calming technique

- after the individual is calm, try to prevent future temper outbursts by modifying the triggers for the outburst and reviewing a skill that prepares the individual for handling the problematic situation (see Chapter 8 on Modifications)

CHAPTER 11

GENERALIZATION STRATEGIES: PRIME, COACH, AND REVIEW

One of the goals of skills training is to improve social functioning outside the skill training session (whether in class, group, or individual therapy). This is referred to as **generalization**, using the skill across settings and time. It is the constant repetition of a skill in real situations that facilitates learning in a meaningful way. High repetition rates may eventually allow a skill to become second nature rather than effortful.

A good metaphor for this process is learning a new musical piece. When learning a new tune, most musicians have to consciously think about the notes they are playing. After many repetitions of practicing the piece, however, they no longer have to think about the notes, and everything just seems to flow. To speed up the process of learning, one can systematize practice sessions by specifically *priming* the musical tune ahead of time (e.g., listening to the tune and looking at the sheet music before trying to play it), getting active *coaching* from a teacher while playing, and *reviewing* the performance afterwards.

In many ways, these three processes for generalization (prime, coach, review) are the same steps taken in the initial learning of a skill. The process of structured learning when initially learning a skill (as discussed in Chapter 9) involves explaining skill steps along with modeling, much like *priming* the skill ahead of time. The next part of structured learning is conducting role-plays with feedback, akin to getting active *coaching* and *reviewing* performance. Thus, practicing a skill to generalize it is essentially a less intense version of the initial lesson. Over time, as kids learn the skill, less and less direct priming, coaching, and reviewing will be necessary as kids begin to demonstrate a skill without direction from others. Of course, this entire process of systematically practicing a skill is more likely to happen when individuals are motivated, so we must first revisit how to motivate individuals to use skills.

Motivation to Practice

To use the musical analogy again, if a student likes a song, they are more likely to practice it. When it comes to social skills, if a child likes interacting with others or likes the activity they are doing together, they are more likely to practice skills with others. As described in the chapter on motivation, social interaction will happen more frequently when individuals are doing things they enjoy. Thus, setting up social activities that appeal to students will help ensure there are opportunities to use skills. This is why many of my social skill groups are no longer called "social skill" groups but are labelled by the activity that draws students to the group. Thus, we may have a group centered on robotics, music, gaming, film, books, role-play games, cooking, art, or other interest-based activities.

Sometimes a student has such narrow interests that it is difficult to attract them to a social interaction based on a shared interest. When there is no intrinsic motivation to interact with others, we can jumpstart the process with external rewards. For example, skills like joining in or compromising with others could be tied to powerful external reinforcers like video game time, snacks, or even money. In these instances, the use of a reward chart, as shown in the next section, can be useful. Eventually, for skills to generalize more naturally, we will need to shift from these external motivators to more natural reinforcement, like social activities that the individual will eventually enjoy. External motivators can sometimes help youngsters gain exposure to different activities until one actually appeals to them.

Prime Skills Use

Priming ultimately means preparing someone to act in a certain way. We are trying to get the brain ready to execute a particular behavior. Just like a musician who looks at sheet music and listens to a song before playing, children learning social skills benefit from seeing the skill steps and watching how something is done before they do it.

Getting children to use skills outside of the training session starts with how we teach skills in the first place. Role-plays conducted in training sessions should resemble, as best as possible, the actual situations that children will confront outside the group. For example, to role-play joining into play at recess in school, one can play the actual recess games.

After a skill lesson is completed, students are asked to consider with whom and when they will practice the skill, and they can fill out this information at the bottom of each skill lesson in Chapter 14. If needed, we can offer rewards to children for following through with practicing a skill.

To prime the skill adequately before practicing it, children may need a visual cue, much like musicians need their sheet music. The actual skill lesson sheets can serve as a visual reminder of the skill steps outside of the skill-training session. However, eventually kids may be trying to practice several high-priority skills each day (see Chapter 6 on targeting skill goals). I find it useful to create a *Cue Card Summary* of several key skills for a youngster on a one-page reminder. This might be depicted on a regular sheet of paper, a smaller cue card, a digital reminder on their smart phone, or a behavior chart linked to rewards (for those who need more incentive to practice skills). An example of a *Cue Card Summary* is shown below for our student Charlie (mentioned in the assessment chapter), who had difficulty with stopping video games and joining conversations and play with peers. Also depicted is a *Sample Behavior Chart* for a student who had difficulty managing difficult work, handling mistakes, and accepting no for an answer. The behavior chart was used for this child because he was not motivated to work on these skills without some incentives.

Cue card summaries or behavior charts should be shared with the child, parents, teachers, or other caregivers who can prime the skills each morning and just before situations in which the skills may be needed. When using behavior charts to help students use skills, it is critical to go over the skills prior to situations where they are needed rather than simply filling out the behavior chart after the child uses or fails to use the skills. It is the priming of skills just before they need it that allows students to remember what to do.

SAMPLE CUE CARD SUMMARY (for Charlie)		
SITUATION	**Wrong Way**	**Right Way**
1. Stop doing something fun	Yelling or hitting will mean others cannot give you the fun thing again for a while	Accept no when it is time to shut down video games (and other favored activities) because stopping on time guarantees that you can return at the next scheduled time

2. Talking with people you like	Ignore others or lecture at them	Initiate conversation:
		    Shared interests: How is ____?
		    Present: What are you guys _____?
		    Past: How was your _____?
		    Future: What are you going to do_____?
		
		Keeps it going using on-topic WH questions and comments

3. Joining into play	Ignore others or tell others what to play	Ask to play with others who share your interest. Be willing to compromise on exactly what to play

SOCIAL SKILLS TRAINING

Name: _____   **Date:** _____

Please rate this student in each target area for each period using the following scale:

1 = try harder   2 = good   3 = excellent

TARGET BEHAVIORS	Period 1	Period 2	Period 3	Period 4	Period 5	Period 6	Period 7	Period 8
Tries When It's Hard Tries it, asks to watch or for help, asks for three-minute break, tries again								
Accepts Imperfection Does not get mad if corrected or gets something wrong								
Accepts No and Goes with the Flow Gets some of what they wanted later								

Average daily points earned during baseline: ____

Points needed to earn basic privileges: ____

Points in savings needed to earn special privileges: ____

Instructions for Using an Individual Behavior Chart

1. Each student has a daily behavior chart and gets rated for each period on three different target behaviors.

2. This chart follows the student from class to class and must be filled out by the student's teacher or their aide each period.

3. During the first week of classes, the chart is to be filled out each day to get a one-week baseline. We can then determine the average daily points each student gets.

4. Based on the average daily points students receive, we can determine how many points to expect students to get each day. The average daily point value, or five points less, can be set as the "points needed to get daily privileges." The point value may need to be adjusted to ensure that the child can succeed most days.

5. When a student gets the "points needed to get daily privileges," he may receive daily privileges in school or at home. Daily privileges in school may include a homework pass, snack, and free time during the last period. At-home daily privileges may include TV, computer, and video game time.

6. Any points in excess of "points needed to get daily privileges" can go into savings for special privileges. Savings can be accumulated over weeks and months and might be recorded by a number posted on the refrigerator at home, a jar filled with pennies, or any other means the student and parent may desire. Special privileges might include material items like video games or going to movies or other outings.

7. If possible, this program should be coordinated with parents so students receive their daily and special privileges at home for points earned in school. If parents are willing to participate, the daily student rating must go home every day and be presented to parents for the child to receive their privileges. For children who forget or hide the ratings from parents, the rating sheet should be emailed to parents.

Coach the Skills in Real Situations

Coaching of skills in actual situations is not much different from role-playing the skill in the initial training session. We go over the skill ahead of time (priming), then cue the youngster through the skill steps as needed, providing redirection to the appropriate skill steps if they veer off course. The key to this work is to (1) create opportunities to practice and (2) keep the coaching/feedback positive to keep the student motivated.

Create opportunities to practice

This might include parents and/or teachers scheduling activities to practice as suggested on the activity pages of each skill lesson. For example, parents can set up playdates to practice conversation and play skills. Teachers can set up conversation times (e.g., during snack or downtimes) or group projects where students may have to learn to compromise with one or more peers. Sometimes the daily routine allows for practice without adults going out of their way to set up activities. However, we can also create more opportunities by a process we call *baiting* the skills.

Baiting skills

Both teachers and parents must be vigilant to praise (and maybe reward) any positive demonstration of the skills. In many instances, adults must learn how to draw the skills out of their children and not just wait for them to display the skills. As teachers, parents, facilitators, and aides, it is our job to create situations so that students must use the skills and can then be rewarded for doing so.

To do this, we may "bait" the skill. This means doing something that requires the student to show how to use the skill. For example, with the skill "Accepting No for an Answer," you might tell students that they will be tested on their ability to accept no. Show them a favorite food, game, or toy and wait for them to ask for it. Then say, "No, you cannot have it now." If they accept no, then say, "Great job, you accepted no, so you can have a point on your chart." With the skill "Showing Understanding for Others' Feelings," you might fall down and loudly pretend to be hurt in front of a child, then wait for him or her to say, "Are you okay?" If the child does not, you might say, "What can you say if I look hurt?" For conversation skills, we can direct them to start conversations with each other by breaking them up into pairs and giving them a conversation starter to use (see "Starting a Conversation" and "Maintaining a Conversation," Chapter 14). Then we can give them praise or points on a reward chart for starting the conversation.

At first, students may not be able to demonstrate the skill in its complete form, but we can reward approximations of the skill. We can *shape* the skill performance to help students progress.

In *shaping* behavior, we may not see a complete demonstration of the skill. We may have to prompt a student to engage in part of the skill and then reward this partial demonstration. For example, a child may forget a couple of steps when introducing himself to someone new and will need a reminder of the missing steps. Perhaps he told the person his name but forgot to make eye contact when doing so. Nevertheless, we may praise and reward this behavior because it demonstrates progress for this student and remind him to make at least sporadic eye contact next time.

Reviewing Skill Performance

The last critical component in generalization of skills is to review skill performance with individuals after an activity to help correct or further guide their interactions. When using a reward chart, the time for skill review is built in as an adult provides points on the chart. When showing the child how many points they received, one can say why they got the points and what they might need to do to get even more points.

When using cue card summaries, teachers and parents can review how a child did with the skills on the card after activities or at the end of the day. One can ask the child questions such as, "Were you able to [fill in the skill] today?" "How well do you think you were able to [fill in the skill] today?"

At the beginning of a group, I will often post the key skills for members on a white board and remind them to try to do these skills as we do our activity. I will also refer back to the white board to coach skills as necessary during the group. Then at the end of a group session, I will often review with each member how they did with their personal targeted skills.

As a rule of thumb, when giving feedback, use the **Sandwich Method**:
Say something they did well, provide any correction on what "they could do even better next time," and end with the thing they did well again.

For example: "Johnny, I really liked how you asked your partner what they wanted to do today [positive statement]. It would have been even better if you were willing to do some of what they wanted to do in order to compromise [corrective feedback]. But it was really a great start to at least ask them what they wanted to do [reiterate positive part]."

Involving Parents and Teachers

If generalization of skills depends on adequate priming, coaching, and reviewing of skills, then it is crucial to involve the adults in children's lives to help those processes occur. Adults can *prime* kids each morning using the Cue Card Summaries or Behavior Charts, *coach* as needed if they are observing the child interacting with others, and *review* after key activities or at the end of the day. Adults can also help to arrange opportunities to practice, teachers can set up group activities, and parents can set up get-togethers or sign their children up for activities that interest them.

As a rule, in my clinic-based groups, I include parents of children eight years old and younger. In schools, I often invite parents to come and observe any new skill that we are working on. This means that the parents may come for the twenty minutes or so of skill time and then leave so as not to disrupt their children in their other school activities. Alternatively, I can video the skill lesson and send a copy to all the parents. This allows me to model for parents how to prompt their children at home.

Prior to the start of skills training, parents and educators (teachers, aides etc.) receive instructions on how to practice with their students (see sample emails to parents and teachers at the end of this chapter). Adults can engage in five key actions to encourage generalization in their students:

- Set up enjoyable activities to practice skills (e.g., interest-based groups, playdates, in school group projects or brief opportunities for play/conversation).

- Prime the skills early in the day and before activities by going over the Cue Card Summary or Behavior Chart:
  – Review the skill steps with the child.
  – Model and role-play the steps.

- Coach skill performance: prompt the child to enact the skill if you are present when they are interacting with others.

- Review skill performance after activities or at the end of the day using the **Sandwich Method** (positive statement, corrective feedback, positive statement). Provide points towards rewards if using a behavior chart.

Limits to Generalization

It is important to remember that not all problems can be addressed through social skills training. Teaching students what to do and why does not guarantee that they will be able to perform the skills. Individuals with extreme impulsivity may need a good behavioral management program and/or medication to allow them to implement the skills they have learned. For example, an individual with ADHD may learn how and why to wait for a pause before interrupting but nevertheless be unable to wait consistently because of attention and impulse control problems. Providing a reward for waiting or possibly medication to control impulsivity may help. Similarly, some individuals are too anxious to implement the skills they have learned. Despite learning how to start and maintain conversations, they may be too frightened to do so, anticipating rejection or humiliation. Such individuals may need therapy to address and combat their self-defeating beliefs and possibly medication to reduce their anxiety (see managing anxiety skills in Chapter 14 and my book *Overcoming Anxiety in Children and Teens*, Baker, 2015).

Lastly, abstract thinking ability also impacts the trajectory of generalizing skills. A student who is very concrete and has limited abstract thinking ability may not see how to adapt a skill to varying situations. For example, a more concrete-thinking student might have learned to ask another student, "How is your bowling club?" because the other student regularly goes bowling. That student may then ask everyone, "How is your bowling club?" even if others do not attend a bowling club. The student may have failed to understand the more abstract concept: to ask about others' particular interests rather than simply apply the same word-for-word script to everyone. This child will take longer to learn how to ask about others' interests, as he may need to learn a different memorized script for different people. In contrast, those with more abstract thinking can learn a general concept, like "Ask about how the other's interest is going," that can immediately generalize to multiple situations. Thus, in many ways, a youngster's language and conceptual development will partially determine their ease with learning and generalizing social skills.

Sample Email to Parent

Dear Parent(s):

Based on your input, teacher feedback, and our observations, we have prioritized a small set of social skills for YOUR STUDENT to work on during social settings. They have been learning these skills in our group. The social skills are summarized below:

Sample Cue Card Summary of Skills (for Charlie)

Accept no when it is time to stop preferred games (remind when they can return)

Initiate play and conversation with peers who share similar interests (anime, video games)

Take turns talking and listening (make on-topic questions and comments)

To help STUDENT generalize these skills, we ask that you do the following:

- Set up enjoyable activities to practice skills (e.g., interest-based groups, playdates)
- Prime the skills early in the day and before activities by going over the *Cue Card Summary* or Behavior Chart:
  - Review the skill steps with the child
  - Model and role-play the steps
- Coach skill performance: prompt the child to enact the skill if you are present when they are interacting with others
- Review skill performance after activities or by the end of the day using the Sandwich Method (say something positive about what they did, give any corrective feedback about what they could have done better, then reiterate what they did well). Provide points towards rewards if using a behavior chart.

Thank you for taking the time to help us serve your child better. If you have any questions, you can email me at jandbbaker@aol.com.

Thank You,
Jed Baker, Ph.D.

Sample Email to Teacher

Dear Teacher:

Based on your input, parent feedback, and our observations, we have prioritized a small set of social skills for STUDENT to work on during social settings. They have been learning these skills in our lunch bunch. The social skills are listed below:

Sample Cue Card Summary of Skills (for Sam)

Don't be the Rule Police, unless someone is doing something dangerous

Respect others' space and belongings (i.e., ask before you touch)

Be sensitive to listeners' interests (ask about others or discuss common interests rather than only self-interest)

To help STUDENT generalize these skills, we ask that you do the following:

- Set up enjoyable activities to practice skills (e.g., interest-based groups, opportunities for play/conversation)
- Prime the skills early in the day and before activities like recess/lunch by going over the Cue Card Summary or behavior chart:
  - Review the skill steps with the child
  - Model and role-play the steps
- Coach skill performance: prompt the child to enact the skill if you are present when they are interacting with others. Redirect the student to the appropriate skill as needed.
- Review skill performance after activities or by the end of the day using the Sandwich Method (say something positive about what they did, give any corrective feedback about what they could have done better, then reiterate what they did well). Provide points towards rewards if using a behavior chart.

Thank you for taking the time to help us serve your student better. If you have any questions, you can email me at jandbbaker@aol.com.

Thank You,
Jed Baker, Ph.D.

CHAPTER 12

PEER SENSITIVITY TRAINING

Training of "typical" peers is a crucial element of a comprehensive social skills training program. Social difficulties can be defined as both a challenge for the students with social differences and a problem of acceptance of those students by their peers. Thus, intervention must also focus on teaching typical peers how to be more accepting. In my experience, including typical peers as a focus for intervention yields better results, as neurotypical peers can learn to be understanding of a student while a neurodiverse student learns to interact more effectively with peers.

A growing body of evidence also demonstrates that educating peers about their classmates' differences and having them participate as peer mentors yields positive effects for both the neurodiverse students and their neurotypical peers (Dunn, 2005; Twemlow et al., 2001; Haring & Breen, 1992). For neurodiverse students, involving peers seems to increase positive social interactions and generalization of skills. Moreover, peers who become peer mentors demonstrate increased achievement test scores and self-esteem (Twemlow et al., 2001). Research also suggests that without ongoing support, peers may not maintain a high level of interactions with targeted peers (Odom & Watts, 1991). Thus, just as it is important to plan for generalization of skills for neurodiverse students, it is equally important to plan for generalization for typical peers.

When targeted students have little opportunity to interact with peers or, worse yet, are being teased, it is crucial that training of "typical" peers become part of the social skills intervention. Peers can be taught to be "helpers" or coaches to neurodiverse students during play or work. They can also be taught to be good "bystanders" by taking a protective role if their neurodiverse peers are teased or bullied (see Baker, 2003, 2005). In addition, they can participate in social skills groups with their neurodiverse peers to find opportunities to interact in conversation and play.

Training of typical peers involves at least two components: (a) sensitivity training lessons for typical peers to be more accepting, engaging, and helpful to students with unmet social needs, and (b) activities and incentive programs to promote generalization of sensitivity skills in the situations where they are needed.

Sensitivity Training Lessons

Training of peers can involve **generic** lessons to help a particular group or classroom of children be more accepting of everyone despite their differences; alternatively, sensitivity lessons can be more **specific**, focused on helping typical peers better understand and accept a particular child or special group of children.

With generic lessons, no particular student's personal information is being shared, so no special releases of information or permissions are needed. However, when conducting specific lessons about a particular student, such permission and releases must be obtained. In that case I would meet with the child and family to discuss exactly what information they are comfortable discussing with peers. I usually write up a script (see sample scripts below) so that the student and family can know precisely what will be said.

Why would one want to conduct a lesson about a specific individual? For many youngsters with a social challenge related to ASD, the typical peers already know that the student's behavior is different, and some may have begun to tease, ignore, or reject the student. At this time, it is crucial to conduct a sensitivity lesson to help change the negative perceptions that peers may have and to explain that the child's behaviors are NOT meant to bother others. In addition, it is important to highlight the neurodiverse youngster's talents and abilities so that the typical peers can value that student and consider ways they can be helpful. Teaching a specific sensitivity lesson involves talking to the peers about a neurodiverse students' strengths and challenges and how peers can be helpful.

The following are some guidelines for conducting sensitivity lessons. At the end of this chapter are sample lessons that can be used generically or about a specific student. One is for younger students; the other two are for older students with optional usage of the student's diagnostic information.

Guidelines for Specific Sensitivity Training

1. Get permission from the target student's parents to talk about their child to the class. Discuss the advantages and disadvantages. If the child has noticeable behavioral differences, particularly those that upset the other children, then the sensitivity training can only help. If there are no noticeable behavioral differences, then there may be no need to do a specific sensitivity training. Instead, make sure the student has opportunities to socialize (e.g., create a social skill/interest-based group or generic peer program for the entire classroom).

2. Have sessions with the target student about his or her strengths and challenges (see Chapter 5 on building self-awareness). It is important that students understand these things about themselves before information is shared with peers.

3. Get permission from the student to talk to his or her peers. I usually ask the student, "Would it be okay to talk with your classmates so they can be more friendly or helpful to you?" If they say no, I say, "Well, I won't if you do not want me to, but can I just show you what I would say if you decide to allow it?" Then most students will say yes when they see the positive information I will be presenting about them. If they still say no, many will come back months later and ask for me to do it because they realize that their peers have continued to tease or reject them. Ideally, the content that will be presented to peers should be created in cooperation with the student. I usually show them an outline of a presentation (see sample lessons below) and have them add or make changes. The presented information should contain a list of the student's strengths and some of their challenges, the reason for any misunderstood behaviors, famous people who have had similar patterns of strengths and challenges, and how peers can help.

4. Select the peers for the sensitivity lesson. Usually we want to pick students with whom our targeted student interacts (e.g., everyone in his or her class). For those in older grades, we might select one or two students from each of the student's classes. The ideal peers will be students who are "caring" individuals and who would use the information wisely to help the student rather than use the information against the student. Guidance counselors, teachers, and the targeted student are usually the best sources of information for good peer candidates. Peers who do much of the teasing are not good candidates to help the student, but they need to be spoken to about their behavior by administrators who can let them know the consequences for continued teasing.

5. Send a letter home to the parents of the selected peers informing them that you would like to have them participate in a peer leadership program (see sample letters at end of this chapter).

6. Conduct a specific sensitivity training lesson, preferably without the target student there if we want peers to be open about their concerns, so that we can correct any misperceptions about the targeted student. That being said, the targeted student has the right to be there if they prefer, so give them the choice, explaining the pros and cons.

7. Create ways to follow up on this session by developing incentives for peers to stand up for the student if teased, engage the student at lunch or other social times, or volunteer to work with the student on group projects.

8. Arrange times to meet with peer leaders to follow their progress in helping the targeted student(s). This might be weekly sessions to begin, followed by monthly follow-ups.

Activities and Incentive Programs to Promote Peer Kindness

Several activities have been developed that can promote peer acceptance and reinforce skills taught during a sensitivity training (see Wagner, 1998, 2009). The following is a description of three such programs.

Lunch Buddy Program

In this program, students are asked to volunteer to eat lunch and interact at recess with the target student. After the sensitivity training is completed, the teacher asks for volunteers to help the target student or students. Then, on a rotating basis, volunteers are randomly selected to be a special lunch buddy to the target child that day. The peer volunteer's job is to engage and coach the target student in conversation and age-appropriate recreation. The volunteers need to be instructed on how best to engage the student and what skills to coach the target student on (these skills are the ones we have selected to generalize for the target student and may be written on a cue card for the student and his assigned peers).

Lunch buddies can then be rewarded for their participation with letters of recognition sent home to parents, the opportunity to put their participation down on resumes for college applications, and possible course credit.

Peer Buddy Program

This is similar to the Lunch Buddy Program, but rather than targeting lunch and recess time, this program focuses on helping the peer during class with work or other responsibilities. Again students are asked to volunteer on a rotating basis and recognized for their efforts.

Class-Wide Incentive Program

This program is useful for younger grades or for self-contained classes where the students generally stay in the same classroom for most of the day. The teacher is encouraged to create an incentive system to reward all students for being helpful and kind towards each other. A user-friendly version of this system is modeled after the "Marble Jar" used by Lee Cantor (1987). In this system, a marble or token is put into a jar every time any student exhibits the target skills. When the class accumulates enough marbles (typically twenty to fifty), the whole class gets a reward (e.g., a party, extra art period). It is wise to focus on no more than two or three skills at a time and to avoid removing marbles for misbehavior. I typically target three "kind" behaviors: (a) include others who appear left out, (b) stand up for others who are teased (directly or by anonymously getting help for the victim), and (c) help others (e.g., if they are upset, hurt, need help with work, or need encouragement). See the poster of **Be a Hero Not a Bully** below.

1. Include others in conversation and play

2. Stand up for others who are teased (tell teaser to stop or go get help)

3. Help others in need

Artist: Justin Canha

SAMPLE LESSONS

Sensitivity Training for K-5
(Generic or Specific to an Individual)

1. What would it be like if everyone in the world were exactly the same? The world would be a boring place if everyone were the same.

2. We are all the same and different in some ways.
    a. How are we all the same? Discuss physical attributes like arms and legs.
    b. How are we different? Discuss physical attributes like hair color, eye color, etc.

3. We have other interesting differences besides how we look.
    a. READING. Some people read very quickly. Others might find it hard to read but easier to throw or catch a ball.
    b. ATTENTION AND SITTING STILL. For some people, it is easy to sit still for a long time and listen, while others like to get up and move and get distracted by other things.
    c. PLAYING. Some children have an easy time playing with others, and other children may be a little shy to play with others.
    d. TALKING TO OTHERS. Some children love to talk to their classmates, while other children may be shy to talk with others.

If sensitivity training is about a particular student, then discuss how that student is the same as everyone else in the class and how that student is different as well. Be sure to include both the student's talents and difficulties. If there are any behaviors that annoy other students, make sure you explain how these behaviors are not done intentionally to bother the other children.

4. Sometimes children tease or don't play with children who they think are different. Is this fair? How would you feel if you were left out because you were different in some way?

5. What is it like to feel left out? A sample EXERCISE:

    a. Ask the children to stand if they want to play the game "**Simon Says**." Tell anyone with white sneakers that they must sit down and cannot play yet. Then tell anyone with brown hair that they too must sit down and cannot play yet. Continue telling students with various attributes to sit down until no one is allowed to play.

    b. Then discuss how it felt to be left out of play because you have different-colored sneakers or hair or eyes. Discuss how much worse this would be if others teased those who were left out. Explain this is how it is for children who may feel left out because they do not know how to play or are shy. Tell the students how they can help by asking those who might be left out to play.

6. HOW CAN WE HELP?

    a. If you see students being left out, ask them to talk and play with you. Try three times, and if they do not want to play or talk, then do not force them.

    b. If you see students getting teased, tell the teaser to leave the other person alone.

    c. If someone looks upset, ask if you can help.

If the sensitivity training is about a particular student, then discuss concrete ways to help that student. For example, if the student does not respond to questions, explain to the peers how to get his or her attention or how to rephrase a question.

7. REWARDS FOR KIND BEHAVIOR

    a. When students are observed being kind in any of the ways described above, they will receive a _____. When the class gets _____ number of _____, they will get _____.

Sensitivity Training 6ᵗʰ-12ᵗʰ Grades
(Generic or Specific to an Individual;
Diagnosis Not Mentioned)

1. The trainer says, "I am here to ask for your help with a classmate (or classmates) of yours. They are the same as you and different in some ways. How are we all the same? How are we different?

2. We are also different in our senses. What are the five senses? Hearing, Seeing, Taste, Smell, and Touch. Some of us differ in how we see, hear, taste, or smell things, or in our sensitivity to touch.

3. Does anyone know what the 'sixth sense' is? The sixth sense is the 'social or friend' sense." (This notion was adapted from Carol Gray, 2004). "The friend sense has to do with:
    a. Knowing how to talk to other kids.
    b. Knowing how to play with other kids.
    c. Understanding how other people feel.

4. Some of us have trouble with our 'friend sense.' We might have trouble:
    a. Knowing how to talk to other kids.
    b. Knowing how to play with other kids.
    c. Understanding how other people feel."

5. If the sensitivity training is about a particular student, then discuss how that student has trouble with their friend sense despite their special talents and abilities. Discuss the student's intellectual strengths as well as their difficulties with socializing. If there are any behaviors that annoy other students, make sure you explain that these behaviors are not done intentionally to bother the other children. For example, say:
    a. "John has trouble with his 'friend sense' despite being so bright and intelligent. He has some difficulty knowing what to say to talk with others. Some of you have complained that John sometimes annoys you ... what does he do that upsets you?"

(As students relay information about what the student does, be ready to explain why he does it, assuring them he does not do it purposely to annoy them. Also, explain how they can help the situation rather than create more problems). For example, "Some of you have complained that John talks about topics you do not want to hear even after you have asked him to stop. John explained that sometimes the thoughts rush in his head and he is unable to stop from talking about it. He does not do it purposely to annoy you. If that happens, you can tell him that you do not want to hear about that now and will return to talk with him later when he is done. Don't tell him to 'shut up' or insult him; this will only upset him, and *then* he might want to purposely annoy you."

b. Point out the student's strengths (often associated with the student's particular interests). "John also has some extraordinary talents. He is an avid reader and expert mathematician and has a wealth of information about transportation systems throughout history. If you ever need to know anything about transportation, he knows more than anyone. He also happens to be an expert on weather systems, so if you ever need to know what the weather is here or in other parts of the country, he is the resident expert."

6. Discuss how talented and valuable individuals can be despite any difficulties with their "friend sense." Review famous people who have had trouble with their friend sense despite their terrific talents and successes. These individuals (who have been described as having symptoms of autism) might include Albert Einstein, Bill Gates, Amadeus Mozart, Thomas Edison, Thomas Jefferson, Marie Curie, and Temple Grandin. Review these individuals' special gifts and talents as well as their social difficulties.

7. "What is it like to have trouble with the friend sense?" Explain that you want the students to understand what it is like for people with these difficulties (or for your targeted student). Explain that you will conduct an exercise so they can experience what it might be like not to know how to join a social group.

    a. Tell all the students they can be part of a special club if they figure out how to join in. In the club, you get one homework free pass (if you can arrange for them to be excused from one homework assignment that night). All they have to do is join in.

    b. Before explaining how to join in, ask for three students to volunteer to leave the room while you explain to the remaining students how to join the club. (Consider pre-selecting volunteers who are resilient and unlikely to be embarrassed in front of the other students.)

    c. Tell all the remaining students how they can join the club. They just have to say, "Can I join in?" while showing three "secret" behaviors (scratching their heads, pulling their ear and coughing, in any order). Practice for three minutes with three or four new volunteers until the students can do these secret behaviors subtly.

    d. Ask the three students who left the room to return and have them try to join the group. Tell them to ask if they can join. After the first student asks, turn to the entire group and say, "Did he do it right, can he join?" The students, seeing that he did not pull his ear, scratch his head, or cough, will say "No, he cannot join." Then ask one of the volunteers who knows the secret to ask to join in. After the student successfully joins in and receives a homework free pass or some other privilege, ask the whole group, "Did he do it right?" They will say "Yes," as he will demonstrate the secret behaviors. Then ask another one of the three students who left the room to try to join in again. Take turns between the students who do and do not know the secret behaviors, rewarding those who successfully join in.

    e. Before the three students catch on to the secret behaviors, ask them how it felt not to know how to join in. Discuss the feelings of anger, unfairness that others were being rewarded (e.g., with a homework free pass), and the embarrassment at not knowing what to do. Then discuss how students who have trouble with their "friend sense" often do not know how to join in, and this is the way they feel: angry, embarrassed, anxious.

    f. Make sure all the students are told how to join in, and everyone gets rewarded. Then give ample praise and applause for the courage of the three students who were not originally told the secret of how to join in.

8. "How can we help?"

    a. For generic lessons (not about a particular student):

        i. "If you see students being left out, ask them to talk and play with you. Try three times, and if they do not want to play or talk, then do not force them.

        ii. If you see students getting teased, tell the teaser to leave the other person alone.

        iii. If someone looks upset, ask if you can help."

    b. If the sensitivity training is about particular students, then discuss ways to help them. Ask who among them would like to be a PEER LEADER to help coach the students at lunch and/or during class. Try to get five volunteers for each targeted student so that each peer only helps the targeted student one day per week. Peer leaders can help at lunch or during class.

        i. At lunch, peer leaders engage and coach the student. They may coach them to start and maintain conversations and avoid certain topics. They may help protect the students from conflicts with others.

        ii. During class, peer leaders might help the student with their class and homework and coach them on working cooperatively with others during group projects. They may also continue to protect them from conflicts with others.

9. If peers are helping specific targeted students, then schedule follow-up meetings with peer volunteers (all meetings are facilitated by a staff member).

    a. Peers are asked to participate in several weekly meetings, followed by monthly follow-ups to help them effectively coach the targeted students.

Sample Sensitivity Training
6ᵗʰ-12ᵗʰ Grades
(Generic or Specific to an Individual; Diagnosis Mentioned)

This presentation is identical to the one above, but instead of introducing the concept of "the sixth sense," students are taught about the student's particular diagnosis and the strengths inherent in that diagnosis as well as the challenges. Then the profile of those particular students is highlighted. The discussion of famous individuals is the same, but students are told that the individuals may have had an autistic spectrum disorder. The joining-in exercise is also the same.

1. Trainer begins by saying, "I am here to ask for your help with a classmate (or classmates) of yours. They are the same as you and different in some ways. How are we all the same? How are we different?

2. We are also different in our pattern of strengths and challenges. For example, some of us may be great with one area but need some help with other areas. For example, some might be great at athletics and socializing but have a difficult time with schoolwork. Some might be great actors or entertainers but have difficulty with athletics.

3. One pattern of strengths and challenges is when individuals are good with academic work but have difficulty socializing. This pattern resembles those with something we used to call Asperger's Syndrome but that we now call Autism Spectrum Disorder. People with ASD may have excellent intellectual ability and a wealth of knowledge about certain subject areas but have difficulty socializing. They may have trouble with:
   a. Knowing how to talk to others.
   b. Understanding how other people feel.
   c. Managing their feelings when overwhelmed.
   d. Making friends.
   e. Sensitivity to sounds, light or touch.

4. If you have permission, mention the name of the student(s) you are targeting for help. "John is someone with an Autism Spectrum Disorder. He is very bright but has difficulty with socializing.

   a. John has trouble making friends despite being so bright and intelligent. He has some difficulty with knowing what to say to talk with others. Some of you have complained that John sometimes annoys you. What does he do that upsets you?" (As students relay information about what the student does, be ready to explain why he does it, assuring them he does not do it purposely to annoy them. Also, explain how they can help the situation rather than create more problems). "For example, some of you have complained that John talks about topics you do not want to hear even after you have asked him to stop. John explained that sometimes the thoughts rush in his head and he is unable to stop from talking about it. He does not do it purposely to annoy you. If that happens, you can tell him that you do not want to hear about that now and will return to talk with him later when he is done. Don't tell him to 'shut up' or insult him; this will only upset him, and *then* he might want to purposely annoy you.

   b. John also has a number of great strengths. He is an avid reader and expert mathematician and has a wealth of information about transportation systems throughout history. If you ever need to know anything about transportation, he knows more than anyone. He also happens to be an expert on weather systems, so if you ever need to know what the weather is here or in other parts of the country, he is the resident expert."

5. Discuss how talented and valuable individuals with autism can be. Review famous people who may have had autism or a related difficulty. These individuals (who have been described as having symptoms of autism) might include Albert Einstein, Bill Gates, Amadeus Mozart, Thomas Edison, Thomas Jefferson, Marie Curie, and Temple Grandin, among others. Review these individuals' special gifts and talents as well as their social difficulties.

   a. "What is it like to have autism and to have difficulty socializing with others?" Explain that you want the students to understand what it is like for students with these difficulties (or for your targeted student). Explain that you will conduct an exercise so they can experience what it might be like not to know how to join a social group. Tell all the students they can be part of a special club if they figure out how to join in. In the club, you get one homework assignment free pass (if you can arrange for them to be excused from one homework assignment that night). All they have to do is join in.

b. Before explaining how to join in, ask for three students to volunteer to leave the room while you explain to the remaining students how to join in the club. (Consider pre-selecting volunteers who are resilient and unlikely to be embarrassed in front of the other students.)

c. Tell all the remaining students how they can join in the club. They just have to say, "Can I join in?" while showing three "secret" behaviors (scratching their heads, pulling their ear and coughing, in any order). Practice for three minutes with three or four new volunteers until the students can do these secret behaviors subtly.

d. Ask the three students who left the room to return and have them try to join the group. Tell them to ask if they can join in. After the first student asks, turn to the entire group and say, "Did he do it right, can he join in?" The students, seeing that he did not pull his ear, scratch his head, or cough, will say "No, he cannot join." Then ask one of the volunteers who knows the secret to ask to join in. After the student successfully joins and receives a homework free pass or some other privilege, ask the whole group, "Did he do it right?" They will say "Yes," as he will demonstrate the secret behaviors. Then ask another one of the three students who left the room to try to join in again. Take turns between the students who do and do not know the secret behaviors, rewarding those who successfully join in.

e. Before the three students catch on to the secret behaviors, ask them how it felt not to know how to join. Discuss the feelings of anger, unfairness that others were being rewarded (e.g., with a homework free pass), and the embarrassment at not knowing what to do. Then discuss how students who have autism sometimes do not know how to join in, and this is the way they feel: angry, embarrassed, anxious.

f. Make sure all the students are told how to join in and everyone gets rewarded. Then give ample praise and applause for the courage of the three students who were not originally told the secret of how to join in.

6. "How can we help?"
    a. General ways to help
        i. "If you see students being left out, ask them to talk or interact with you. Try three times, and if they do not want to, then do not force them.
        ii. If you see these students getting teased, tell the teaser to leave the other person alone.
        iii. If someone looks upset, ask if you can help."
    b. Discuss specific ways to help targeted students. Ask who among them would like to be a PEER LEADER to help coach the student(s) at lunch and/or during class. Try to get five volunteers for each targeted student so that each peer only helps the targeted student one day per week. Peer leaders can help at lunch or during class.
        i. At lunch, peer leaders engage and coach the students. They may coach them to start and maintain conversations and avoid certain topics. They may help protect students from conflicts with others.
        ii. During class, peer leaders might help students with their class and homework and coach them on working cooperatively with others during group projects. They may also continue to protect them from conflicts with others.

7. If peers are helping specific targeted students, then schedule follow-up meetings with peer volunteers (all meetings are facilitated by a staff member).
    a. Peers are asked to participate in several weekly meetings, followed by monthly follow-ups to help them effectively coach the targeted students.

SOCIAL SKILLS TRAINING

Content of Subsequent Meetings with Peer Leaders

1. In the first follow-up meetings, peers are taught how to protect their targeted students from others by (a) explaining to others the unintentional nature of any provocative social mistakes the student made and (b) standing up for them if they are teased, either directly or by getting help from an adult. Rules are reviewed with peers, such as keeping private information about their targeted student confidential and the consequences of violating those rules (they will no longer be allowed to be a peer leader). They are also praised and given letters to take home to their parents about being selected to be a peer leader. If possible, serve special food at these meetings if during lunch time to honor these peer leaders.

2. In the next two or more sessions, peers are taught the skills that their assigned students are working on generalizing. They are also taught how to coach their assigned students on these skills.

3. In subsequent meetings, peers meet to bring up any difficulties they are having with their assigned student(s) or other peers, and together, the group tries to solve the problems.

Sample Letter to Parents of Children Targeted to Receive Help from Peers

Dear Parent(s) or Guardian(s):

We are creating a peer buddy program to increase opportunities for peers to play and converse with children in _____ 's class at lunch and recess. In order to get peers to volunteer, we will be doing a sensitivity lesson in the regular _____ grade class about the importance of including all children despite our differences. We will ask for peers to take turns being lunch/recess buddies to children in _____ class who may be "shy and need some help to talk and play with others." Other than indicating that children in _____'s class may need some help to talk and play with others, we will not be providing any other specific information about your child without your permission.

Peers will learn about some of the games that children in _____'s class enjoy and so that they can successfully engage in play.

Please feel free to call us or ask your child's teacher if you have any questions.

Sincerely,

_____

Sample Permission Letter to Parents of Peer Volunteers

Dear Parent(s) or Guardian(s):

We are offering students in your class the opportunity to be a special peer buddy in their school. Peer buddies will talk and play with other students who may be shy or need help learning to converse and play with peers. Your child's participation would involve, once per week, acting as a coach or buddy during lunch/playtime for other students.

The benefit to your child may include enhanced self-esteem and social skill development. We find that most students who take an active role in helping to teach social skills become more socially skilled themselves.

Participation is voluntary and space is limited, so students will have to take turns being a peer buddy. If you *do not* want your child to participate, please sign the form below. If we do not hear back, we will assume you are okay with having your child participate.

Please feel free to call me at _____ if you have questions.

Sincerely,

_____

Form If You Do Not Want Your Child to Participate

I do not want my child _____ to participate in the peer leader program during the _____ school year.

_____   _____
Date   Signature

CHAPTER 13

PUTTING IT ALL TOGETHER

In order to organize the information you have gathered about a particular student or group of students, it is helpful to create a Social Skills Action Plan (see below) that ensures you have addressed each critical element of social skills training. The following form prompts you to fill in information about each key component of skills training that was reviewed in the previous chapters. Reminders of the kinds of questions that need to be asked and possible treatment suggestions are indicated on the form. It is best to consider this action plan a work in progress, as new social challenges may emerge or previously targeted skills may no longer be relevant. Thus, revisiting this form at least once a month to make any updates is recommended.

As skills are articulated in Step 1, one can then use Chapter 14 as a reference tool to see if there are appropriate skill lessons to address the student's goals. Chapter 14 is not likely to be an exhaustive list of every skill you may want to target, but it can act as a template to build your own skill lessons as needed. You may need to write up your own skill lessons, breaking down the skill into smaller components and creating scenarios to role-play and practice. Hopefully, after seeing the lessons in Chapter 14, you will be able to follow a similar format to break down new skills and teach your students.

Social Skills Action Plan

(Prepared by Jed Baker, PhD)

Student: _____ Date: _____

Step 1: Target relevant social skills (See Chapter 6)

- Consider the settings in which we hope the student will function successfully.
- Have parents and teachers consider what the student does too much of or too little of on a daily basis that interferes with social functioning in those settings.
- Understand the student's point of view and preferred ways to solve problems in those settings.
- Use the social skill menu as a guide to identify critical skills that may be part of the solution.
- Articulate a user-friendly number of skill goals (three to seven) to work on at a time. Do lessons for these skills appear in Chapter 14?

Step 2: Is the student motivated to learn or use new skills? (See Chapter 5)

- Need a better rationale that fits with the student's perspective of the problem?
- Need more intrinsically motivating activities to practice skills?
- Need external rewards to jumpstart the student to begin using the skills?

Step 3: Measurable objectives/how will we measure progress? (See Chapter 7)

- Are there staff who can take observable data?
- Can we create a Likert Rating Scale for teachers, parents, and the student?
- Is normative data needed? Use standardized rating scales?

Step 4: Are modifications necessary to be successful? (See Chapter 8)

- Simplify task demands?
- Use gradual exposure for feared situations?
- Modify sensory environment?
- Shorten wait times?
- Use visual supports to increase predictability and understanding?

Step 5: How will skills be taught? Consider symbolic language ability (See Chapter 9)

- Less receptive language ability: Use methods that rely on prompting behavior in actual situations (e.g., ABA, ABA combined with play therapy) or those that rely on visual supports (e.g., picture books, video modeling)
- Adequate receptive language: Use methods that incorporate verbal explanation such as Structured Learning (explanation, modeling, role-play, and practice). Visual supports can also be used here and can include information about how others think and feel.

Step 6: Where will skills be taught? (See Chapter 9)

- In the classroom if applicable to all students?
- In a pull-out group if applicable to only some students? (See Chapter 10)
- Individually if student resists group instruction or cannot attend in group setting?

Step 7: How will skills be generalized? (See Chapter 11)

- Prime through Cue Card Summary or behavior charts
- Use a digital format like smart phone reminders?
- Coach at what point during the day? What are practice activities?
- Review through charts, cue cards, or self-monitoring?
- Is a reinforcement system needed?

Step 8: Is peer sensitivity a part of the plan because they are isolated or teased? (See Chapter 12)

- Generic lesson or one that names a particular child?
- Create a Lunch or Recess Buddy Program?
- Create a Class or Homework Buddy Program?
- Create an Extracurricular Buddy Program?

CHAPTER 14

SKILL LESSONS

Each lesson is set up so that there is a **lesson page** and an **activity page**. The lesson page explains the rationale for the lesson and details each step of the skill to be learned. The activity page explains how to introduce the skill to students, ideas for how to model, role-play, and practice the skill, and any important tips related to that skill.

Although the book is set up for you to go to any skill lesson that is relevant to a student, there is logic to the way the skills are ordered. In many ways, emotion regulation skills are key to all the other skills. Non-verbal skills might need to be considered before conversation skills. Conversation and play skills are required for friendship skills, and friendship skills may help with dating skills.

The skill lessons alone are just one tool to effectively improve social skills. Remember that for real learning to occur, students must be motivated, and steps to systematically practice and generalize skills must also be addressed.

Rationale: In order to manage our own feelings and help others with theirs, we first need to be able to recognize various feelings.

1.   Below are facial expressions and body sensations that go with different feelings.

HAPPY
Smiling, voice is upbeat, body feels energetic

SAD
Frowning, voice is quiet, may cry, body feels tired

ANGRY
Scowling, voice is growling, body feels tight, heart pounding

SCARED
Eyes wide open, voice is shaky, body feels tight, heart pounding

DISGUSTED
Feel nauseous, voice growly

SURPRISED
Eyes wide open, may gasp, body feels energetic

Write the name of the emotion under each face below:

_____   _____

_____   _____

_____   _____

#2. CATEGORIZING THE SIZE OF EMOTIONS

1. Label each main group of feelings.

2. Write the feelings that belong in this group in order from the least amount of feeling to the most amount of feeling.

3. See "happy" as an example. Fill in the words for sad, angry, and scared.

HAPPY		SAD	ANGRY	SCARED
Elated	_____	_____	_____	_____
Joyful	_____	_____	_____	_____
Delighted	_____	_____	_____	_____
Excited	_____	_____	_____	_____
Pleased	_____	_____	_____	_____

4. We might react differently when emotions are smaller than when they are big. Big emotions may require help, while small ones may go away without too much help.

#1 and #2. RECOGNIZING FEELINGS (BUILDING AWARENESS OF FEELINGS) Activity Page

Some children have difficulty recognizing the facial expressions, tone of voice, and situations that may be associated with different feelings or moods. For those youngsters, direct instruction and practice in recognizing these cues for different feelings is imperative. They can work through all the activities described below until they can consistently identify feelings.

1. Look through photos of people showing basic emotions like happy, sad, mad, and scared.

   a. Show and explain to the student how shape of mouth, eyes, eyebrows, and body position correspond to different feelings.
   b. After you have taught the student what to look for in the pictures, have him or her try to pick out pictures corresponding to happy, sad, mad, and scared feelings.
   c. After you have worked with these basic feelings, try to expand to less obvious feelings like being proud, nervous, guilty, confused, disgusted, surprised, and bigger versus smaller emotions (e.g., annoyed versus furious).
   d. Engage the student in a discussion of what makes the people in the pictures feel the way they do.

2. Watch clips of video or TV without sound and guess feelings. (Video is easier, as it can be paused to highlight facial expressions and body position.)

   a. Discuss why the people in the video feel the way they do.

3. Use a mirror or video to help the students watch themselves as they try to enact different feelings. Children often think they are accurately portraying a feeling even when their faces and bodies do not correspond to the intended feeling. Give them feedback until they can accurately display the feelings.

4. Play "counting to 10" feeling charades:

   a. Take turns counting to 10 while enacting different feelings. See if the others can guess what feeling it is. Since you will only count to 10, there are no words that indicate the feelings. One can only guess by attending to nonverbal cues and tone of voice.
   b. Repeat this activity while hiding your face so observers can only use your tone of voice to guess.

5. Play activity charades:

   a. Use two sets of cards—one with feeling words and one with various activities (e.g., bowling, eating, writing, watching TV).
   b. Each person takes a feeling and an activity card and tries to act out the activity while feeling as indicated on the card.
   c. Observers must guess what the person is doing, what he is feeling, and why he feels that way.

6. Play the game "hot and cold" without words.

   a. Hide an object (e.g., snack, special treat) in the room while the student(s) are not there. When they return, instruct them that they must look at your face to see where the object is. You will make an increasingly happy face when they are close to the treat, and an increasingly sad or angry face when they are far from the treat.
   b. Coach them to keep checking your face for clues as to how close they are rather than searching the room without referencing your face.

7. Play any board game and give extra points or turns if they can correctly identify your feelings and intentions during the game.

   a. For example, while playing a board game, steal the student's game piece when they are not looking and demonstrate a mad or playful (happy) face. When they notice, ask them whether they think you are kidding (happy face) or trying to annoy them (mad face). Make sure that they look at your face to decide rather than guessing. If they can correctly identify your feeling, give them an extra turn or point. Remind them how important this is during games with other children to determine when others are just being playful versus trying to upset you.

b. Periodically get upset during a game when you are losing or miss a turn. If the students can recognize your feeling, then give them an extra point or turn. If they can also say something positive like "You will do better next time" or "You can go again" then give them another extra point or turn. Remind them that this is how they win the friendship game: by recognizing others' feelings and trying to make them feel better.

8. Help the student keep a journal of what makes him happy, mad, sad, scared, and other feelings. This can later serve as topics to discuss during talk-time of a small group for elementary-aged children through adulthood.

a. Using the structure on the following page (see Journal Page) to make entries in the journal.

b. Use the journal entries as topics of conversation during small-group talk-time. Encourage group members to show understanding for another member's journal entry (see skill Showing Understanding for Others' Feelings). Also encourage members to help each other brainstorm coping strategies to deal with situations reviewed in journals.

#3. UNDERSTANDING THE CONNECTION BETWEEN EVENTS, THOUGHTS, AND EMOTIONS (JOURNAL PAGE)

1. We feel emotions because some event happened to us. We may think the event was good or bad, which will then lead to positive or negative emotions (see below):

TRIGGER

(Something that happens to you. For example: someone wants to be your friend, you get a good grade, you are teased, make a mistake, or do not get something you want. Other triggers might be related to internal conditions like lack of sleep, physical pain, going without food.)

THOUGHTS

(We think about how good or bad the event was. For example, if someone bumps into us, we might think it was on purpose because they do not like us; or we might think it was an accident and it didn't really hurt anyway.)

FEELINGS

(Angry, not angry, sad, scared, happy)

2. Keep a journal of the events that make you feel good or bad (see next page).

Journal Page

Date: _____

What happened (draw or write):

```



```

What I felt when this happened (draw or write):

```



```

What I thought when this happened:

Examples: Thoughts about others: They did not mean it. It was on purpose. They like me. They do not like me. They are just tired or cranky. Thoughts about me: I am okay. Something is wrong with me. I am successful. I am a failure.

How I tried to deal with this feeling:

Examples: I tried to talk to a friend. I tried to talk to the person bothering me. I asked for help. I did something fun until I felt better. I tried to change my thoughts.

#3. UNDERSTANDING THE CONNECTION BETWEEN EVENTS, THOUGHTS AND EMOTIONS Activity Page

1. Help the student keep a journal of what makes them happy, mad, sad, scared, and other feelings using the Journal Page.

   a. Use the journal entries as topics of conversation with parents or during small-group talk-time. Encourage group members to show understanding for another member's journal entry (see skill Showing Understanding for Others' Feelings). Also encourage members to help each other brainstorm coping strategies to deal with situations reviewed in journals.

2. As parents or teachers notice events that elicit feelings in their students, they can suggest the student keep track in their journal, or they can write it in with the student for those who do not want to write themselves.

3. Whenever the child is upset, parents and teachers can help the youngster understand the event that upset them.

   a. Reflect to the youngster the feeling they seem to be showing, pointing out their face or body language that suggests they feel that particular emotion.
   b. Ask, "I wonder if something happened that made you feel that way?"
   c. If the child cannot identify anything that triggered the emotion, you can then offer possibilities based on your observations, saying things like, "I wonder if _____ happened?" or "I wonder if someone said something to you?"

SOCIAL SKILLS TRAINING

#4. UNDERSTANDING OUR ALARM SYSTEM

Rationale: Learning about our alarm system can explain why sometimes
we have big emotional reactions

1. A part of our brain called the limbic system is like an alarm system that responds quickly to danger by readying us for fight, flight, or freeze. Adrenaline pumps and we are ready to run, hide, or if there is no escape, fight. This causes our heart to pound, our brow to sweat, our breathing to become rapid, and our muscles to tense, among other things. We call this the Incredible Hulk state.

2. Another part of our brain is called the forebrain, which responds slowly and carefully to solve problems. It's like the scientist part of our brain and I call it Dr. Banner. We need it too to solve problems like schoolwork or solve problems we have with others.

3. When we feel like something will hurt us, the limbic system (The Incredible Hulk) can take over the brain and shut down Dr. Banner so we cannot think logically anymore to solve problems and we just start to fight, flee or freeze up.

4. We need the Incredible Hulk if there is a **TRUE ALARM** like a car coming to hit us and we need to run out of the way quickly. But mostly we have **FALSE ALARMS**. A **FALSE ALARM** is when there is no real life-or-death danger (like someone just insults you), but we perceive there to be one and react as if our life were in danger. It would be better to use our Dr. Banner forebrain for false alarms so we can think like scientists to solve the problem.

1. When other people, including characters from shows get upset, discuss how they may be in an Incredible Hulk state. Point out how they may not be thinking like a scientist to solve the problem, but instead just fighting, fleeing, or freezing up. Ask them:

   a. "Do you think it was a true alarm (real life-or-death danger) or false alarm?"
   b. "What else could they have done to solve the problem if they were still in Dr. Banner scientist mode?"

2. When your child is starting to get upset or after they have calmed down, you can ask your child the following questions:

   a. "Do you think it is/was a true alarm (real life-or-death danger) or false alarm?"
   b. "What else could they have done to solve the problem if they were still in Dr. Banner scientist mode?"

#5. KEEPING CALM

Rationale: When we are in the Hulk state, it is hard to think logically to solve the problem; in these moments it's better to distract ourselves from the problem.

1. Stop and count to 10 before you do something you will regret.

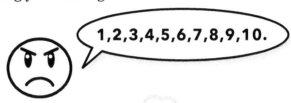

2. Take three deep breaths, and breathe out slowly.

3. Tell someone how you feel or write it down.

4. Do something you enjoy to feel better.
   What's your hobby? Music, gaming, videos, exercise?

Practice

Who will I try this with? _____

When? _____

What happened? _____.

#5. KEEPING CALM Activity Page

1. This skill is about calming after becoming the Hulk. It's an emergency tool when we are already upset. Ultimately, we will *also* want to identify repeat triggers for getting upset so we can get ahead of these problems. To prevent getting upset after certain triggering situations, we can review the following skills in this manual:

    a. Understanding your repeat triggers, growth mindset, trying when it's hard, dealing with mistakes, dealing with losing, handling delays and disappointments, dealing with teasing, accepting criticism, dealing with anxieties, and dealing with depression.

2. Role-play the steps for KEEPING CALM. These practice sessions must occur frequently (e.g., daily) when the student is not upset to ensure the student will actually be able to use a calming routine when upset. Suggested role-plays:

    a. Pretend the student cannot get something they want (e.g., toy, treat, privilege).
    b. Pretend the student must stop playing with a favored activity (e.g., must stop the computer or TV to come to dinner).
    c. Pretend the student broke a favored object (e.g., a toy, game, video device).
    d. Pretend the student loses when playing a game.

3. Bait the skill. This means doing something that requires the student to show how to calm down. For example, purposely frustrate your child by refusing to give them something. Prompt or wait for them to calm down. Do this only after they have learned to calm down and *pick situations that will only mildly frustrate* the student. For example, if the student does not usually get upset over being told they cannot watch TV, choose this situation to practice. As they get more adept with the calming procedure, choose a slightly more frustrating situation.

4. Try to distract students when they are too upset to listen to you. Do not give in to what they want if they are tantruming because they want a particular toy or activity.

SOCIAL SKILLS TRAINING

Instead, try to distract them by another activity and change in the physical environment (e.g., take them out of the sight from the person or thing that is upsetting them).

5. Provide rewards for appropriately KEEPING CALM (i.e., using the skill or not needing the skill because they did not get upset).

   a. Give verbal praise for correct or partially correct use of KEEPING CALM.
   b. Give tokens, pennies, or points every time the student keeps calm or for periods in which they do not get upset. When they get an agreed-upon number of tokens (e.g., five tokens), give a special reward (e.g., snack, stickers, privileges to play special game).

#6. PROBLEM-SOLVING

Rationale: If one uses their scientific brain (Dr. Banner), almost all problems can be solved or at least greatly improved.

1. Use Keeping Calm to try to get back to a Dr. Banner state.

2. Tell yourself, **"All problems can be solved if I can WAIT and TALK to the right person."**

3. You might be able to solve it yourself if you stay calm. Try these steps.

   a. Say what the problem is. Can't figure something out? Can't have something?
   b. Brainstorm possible ways to get what you need.
   c. Think about the consequences of each solution and pick one that will likely help but not worsen the situation.

4. There is always someone who knows how to fix, or at least help, solve the problem.

5. Be willing to WAIT for the RIGHT person. If you wait, it will get better!

Practice

Who will I try this with? _____

When? _____

What happened? _____.

#6. PROBLEM-SOLVING Activity Page

1. Teaching problem-solving involves two key ideas: (1) instill hope that things will get better because someone out there can help: (2) realize that out-of-control emotions get in the way of good problem-solving. The activities below may help make these points:

   a. Review times when their emotions delayed the solution of a problem. Also point out how they did eventually solve the problem.

   b. Review and role-play the following scenarios that show how big emotions can delay problem-solving:

      i. You lose something, like a card from a game or another special item. In anger, you break other special items, compounding the problem and not leading to finding the original item. Or you are so sad that you don't even look for it when it might be right next to you.

      ii. You can't go to the movies because your parents have to stay home and wait for a repair person. If you have a tantrum, your parents ground you from all activities. If you stay calm, your parents will let you do something else you want to do or you may suggest that a friend's parent drive you to the movies. (See "Accepting No for an Answer" for similar role-plays).

      iii. You make one mistake with homework and in anger you rip up all your homework, leaving you much more to do. Alternatively, you make a mistake, stay calm, ask for help and correct the problem. Now you go play because you are done with your work. (See "Dealing with Mistakes" for similar role-play ideas).

2. Some students with abstract thinking difficulties will have a harder time using the steps of problem-solving on their own. They may do better reaching out to trusted individuals for help as well as learning more concrete steps to solve specific problems. The following is a list of other skills in this manual that relate to specific problem areas: Dealing with Mistakes, Dealing with Losing, Compromising, Getting Attention in Positive Ways, Dealing with Family Problems, Accepting No, Accepting Criticism,

Asserting Yourself, Dealing with Being Left Out, Trying When Work is Hard, Trying Something New, Dealing with Peer Pressure, Dealing with Rumors, and Don't Be the Rule Police.

3. Bait the skill. This means doing something that requires the student to solve a problem.

    a. For example, tell them you will test their ability to problem-solve, and make sure they are in an okay enough mood to try this. Then use one of the following scenarios to see if they will problem-solve: cheat in a game you are playing, tell them they cannot have something, give them a very challenging math problem, or hide something they want. Remind them that if they stay calm, they can solve the problem, and then coach them through a solution.

4. Provide ample praise or rewards for appropriate problem-solving.

#7. TALKING VERSUS ACTING OUT YOUR FEELINGS

Rationale: Acting out feelings can mean yelling, threatening or causing physical harm to yourself or others, or refusing to talk or listen to others at all. Such displays frighten people and don't help you solve the problem. **Talking about the problem** calmly means telling someone how you feel in a calm way. You have a much better chance of getting what you want when you talk out your problems calmly.

1. **Get Calm first.** To talk to someone calmly, you may first have to use one of the calming strategies from the previous skill (#5). Often, we have to take time to calm down before we can approach someone to talk about it.

2. **Schedule a time to talk.** Sometimes people are not ready to listen if they are busy or very angry. Thus, it is important to schedule a time to speak rather than just insist on talking when you want to. Say, "Can I speak to you privately for a moment?" If they say no, ask when you can schedule a time to talk. If they still say no, ask to talk with someone else you trust.

3. **Use an "I" Message.** This is a calm way to tell people what upset you without scaring, accusing, or blaming others. In a pleasant voice, let the person know how you feel using an "I" message (see below).

I feel _____ (Feeling word)

when you _____ (Describe their actions. Don't insult them.)

because _____. (Describe why you feel that way)

What I want you to do is _____.

1. Explain the difference between acting out and talking out feelings.

2. Explain the steps for talking calmly to others using an "I" message.

    a. Give examples of what is and is not a feeling word. The sentence: "I feel you are stupid" is not using a feeling word. "I feel upset" is using a feeling word.
    b. Show examples of the difference between "action" words and insults. "I feel upset when you are a mean and horrible person" is just using insulting words. It would be better to say, "I felt upset when you shouted at me."

3. Model and role-play how to talk calmly to others. Use situations that really happened to the students to model or role-play the following situations:

    a. You get together with your friends and you are angry about an interaction you just had with your family. You are snickering and turning away from your friends as if you are angry with them. What could you say to talk instead of act out your feelings? (Answer: You could say "It's not you guys; I am just mad about an argument I had with my parents.")
    b. You heard that a friend of yours said you were a mean person. How could you talk to the person rather than act out your feelings? (Answer: remember to schedule a time, and calmly use an "I" message).
    c. Your teacher or parent told you that you did something totally wrong. How can you talk to them about this? (Answer: remember to schedule a time, and calmly use an "I" message).

4. Whenever students are upset, they can be reminded to schedule a time to talk about their feelings with a trusted person. Remind them they can talk about it when they are ready rather than act it out. Respect the fact that it may take some time for a youngster to be calm enough to talk about the problem.

5. Provide praise and even a reward when students talk about their feelings rather than acting them out.

#8. UNDERSTANDING YOUR ANGER

Rationale: Being angry in a controlled manner can be productive when it helps you reach your goals. Being angry in an "out-of-control" way is rarely productive because you may make things much worse by saying or doing something that creates more problems. It's easier to solve problems when you are calmer.

1. **What makes us angry?** People get angry for a reason. Usually something happens (a trigger) that makes you think something (your perception and thoughts about what happened) that leads to certain feelings (sometimes anger). See diagram below:

TRIGGER
(Something that happens to you. For example, teasing, losing, making a mistake, not getting what we want, waiting too long for things. Other triggers might be related to internal conditions like lack of sleep, physical pain, other physiological conditions that make one more irritable.)

THOUGHTS
(How we understand what happened. For example, if someone bumps into us, we might think it was on purpose, leading to more angry feelings, or we may think it was accidental, leading to less angry feelings.)

FEELINGS
(Angry, not angry, sad, scared, happy)

2. **Know your triggers.** When you know the triggers, you can either avoid them or plan how to deal better with them. For example, if certain schoolwork makes you angry, you can ask that they simplify the work or make a plan to get help with that work.

3. **Change your thoughts** about the trigger. For example, if mistakes upset you because they make you feel like you are not smart, you can learn to change how you think about making mistakes and see them as opportunities to learn more.

4. **Use the Calming the Hulk skill.** If you cannot avoid getting angry, then it might be better to find a distraction from the angry outbursts through a calming activity, like reading, watching TV, listening to music, taking a walk, playing a game, or another activity.

5. **Talking versus acting out your angry feelings** involves using the problem-solving approach to talk calmly to the person you are angry at or to someone else who can help you figure out what to do about the situation.

Practice by Keeping a Daily Anger Record (see next page)

Who will I try this with? _____

When? _____

What happened? _____.

Keeping a Daily Anger Record

Rationale: Keeping track of instances in which you were angry can help you identify your triggers so you can prepare for them. The Record can also serve as a visual reminder of how to respond to these situations.

FILLING OUT THE RECORD

Each time you get angry, fill out a record following these steps. You might want to do this with a parent, counselor, or other helper.

1. On Page 1, indicate what happened that made you angry, what you thought, how you felt and reacted, and how others reacted.

2. Then on Page 2, think about how you could solve the problem. Fill out each section on:

    a. Changing or avoiding the triggering situation.
    b. Learning a skill to change how you think about and deal with the trigger.
    c. Finding ways to calm down.
    d. Talking out the problem with someone you trust or the person who upset you.

Daily Anger Record
(Page 1: What Upset Me)

Name: _____ Date: _____

TRIGGER:
What happened prior to getting angry? Was it demanding work, making a mistake, being corrected, stopping a favored activity to do something less interesting, getting criticized, being teased, losing a game, having to wait or not getting what you want, sensory triggers (e.g., loud noise, distracting lights, uncomfortable touches, repulsive smells), physical illness (e.g., allergies, infections), certain foods, interrupted sleep, or possible medication side effects?

THOUGHTS (the way you perceived the situation):

HOW YOU REACTED (what you felt and what you did):

HOW OTHERS REACTED (what others said or did after you got mad):

SOCIAL SKILLS TRAINING

Daily Anger Record
(Page 2: Plan of Action)

WAYS TO CHANGE OR AVOID THE TRIGGER:
(change work demands; alter sensory issues like noise, smells, lights; avoid those who tease; get more sleep, eat better or explore possible medications changes)

Change my thoughts: (Use the thoughts below as a guide or create your own.)	
Dealing with frustrating work	It's okay not to know what to do. You can ask to watch others first, get help (the smartest people ask for help), or negotiate doing part of the work.
Dealing with mistakes	It's okay to make mistakes; that's how we learn. The smartest people make mistakes.
Dealing with correction	Correction makes you better. The quicker you correct, the sooner you can do other things.
Dealing with losing	If you lose a game, you may win a friend if you do not get mad.
Accepting criticism	Constructive criticism is made to help you, not hurt you. Accepting criticism helps you grow.
Responding to a complaint	Calmly considering the validity of a complaint may help you improve. Calmly disputing false complaints helps others respect you.
Dealing with teasing	Don't give others the power to control your feelings. Were they kidding? Their teasing may have more to do with their problems than anything you did.
Accept no or waiting for things	If you don't get what you want and you don't get mad, you may get something else you want later.
Your trigger and new thoughts	_____ _____

WAYS TO CALM MYSELF: (Use self-talk, count to 10, take deep breaths, think of pleasant images, listen to music, watch TV, play a game, read, talk to a friend, write or draw ways to get your mind off what is bothering you.)

PLANS TO TALK OUT PROBLEMS: (Schedule a time to talk, then use an "I" message.)

I feel _____

when you _____

because _____.

I want _____.

#8. UNDERSTANDING YOUR ANGER Activity Page

1. Explain the rationale for controlling anger and present the model of how anger is triggered by events and thoughts. Explain that in subsequent skill lessons they will learn more ways to identify triggers and learn ways to prevent or control anger.

2. Have students fill out page 1 of the Anger Record, recording the events that upset them.

3. To help them identify **triggers**, consider the following:

   a. External triggers: demanding work, making a mistake, being corrected, stopping a favored activity to do something less interesting (e.g., from a computer game to homework), getting criticized, being teased, losing a game, having to wait or not getting to have or do something they want, sensory triggers (e.g., loud noise, distracting lights, uncomfortable touches, repulsive smells).
   b. Internal triggers: physical illness (e.g., viral or bacterial infections), certain foods, sleep patterns, certain medications that can lead to feeling sick, tired, or agitated. These make it more likely for external triggers to upset you.

4. Help them figure out what they were thinking that upset them. Here is a list of the types of thoughts that usually upset students.

   a. The other person did something on purpose to upset me.
   b. I am stupid or a failure if I cannot do something or make a mistake or am criticized. Taking things personally and feeling ashamed is at the root of a lot of anger.
   c. I will never get what I want when there is a delay or obstacle to getting something.

5. Look at Chapter 8 for ways to modify common triggers to reduce upsets

6. Chapter 8 also lists ways to think differently about situations to reduce upsets. Here is a short list of ways to think differently for a variety of triggers:

Trigger	Name of skill to deal with trigger	Thoughts that help you deal with the trigger (Better ways to think about the triggering situation)
	Table of Skills to Deal with Different Triggers	
Demanding work	Dealing with frustrating work	It's okay not to know what to do. You can ask to watch others first, get help (the smartest people ask for help), or negotiate doing only part of the work.
Making mistakes	Dealing with mistakes	It's okay to make mistakes; that's how we learn. The smartest people make mistakes.
Getting corrected	Dealing with correction	Correction makes you better. The quicker you correct, the sooner you can do other things.
Losing a game	Dealing with losing	If you lose a game, you may win a friend if you do not get mad.
Getting criticized	Accepting criticism	Constructive criticism is made to help you, not hurt you. Accepting criticism helps you grow.
People complaining about you	Responding to a complaint	Calmly considering the validity of a complaint may help you improve. Calmly disputing false complaints helps others respect you.
Being teased	Dealing with teasing	Don't give others the power to control your feelings. Maybe they were kidding. Their teasing may have more to do with their problems than anything you did.
Not getting what you want, having to wait for what you want, or having to stop doing what you like to do	Accepting no and waiting for what you want	If you don't get what you want and you don't get mad, you may get something else you want later.

SOCIAL SKILLS TRAINING

7. Role-play using the following situations and ask how we can change the trigger or our thoughts about these events to solve the problem:

    a. Pretend the student cannot get something they want (e.g., toy, treat, privilege). Could we schedule a later time to get it? Could the student think that if they are calm they will get it later?

    b. Pretend the student broke a favored object (e.g., a toy, game, video device). Could the student think they will get it fixed or find a replacement if they stay calm?

    c. Pretend the student keeps losing when playing a game. Could the student pick an easier level to start or think that they will eventually improve?

    d. They got a bad grade from a teacher, and they think the teacher misgraded them.

    e. They were teased by another student. Could they think the teaser is the one with the problem instead of taking it personally?

8. After an angry outburst, the student can get feedback on the skill they can use next time to deal more effectively with the triggering situation. If the student is reluctant to talk about the past outburst (e.g., because it embarrasses them) then do not review what happened. Instead, focus only on preparing before the next possible trigger. The Daily Anger Record is an ideal way to review how a student handled a trigger. The record can be used for both individual and group counseling. For counseling situations, students can fill out the first half about what happened to upset them, and then the second half related to how to handle the trigger can be saved for the counseling session.

#9. USING A GROWTH MINDSET TO MANAGE FRUSTRATION

Rationale: Sometimes we think we are not smart if we cannot understand something at first or we make a mistake. Understanding that this is just part of learning can help us feel better and allow us to keep learning more.

1. Carol Dweck, PhD, from Stanford University has shown us that the way we think about our intelligence can affect how motivated we are in the face of frustrating work, which affects how successful we are in school, work and other areas:

   a. **Fixed Mindset** leads to worse outcomes. Fixed mindset is the belief that you are born with a fixed, unchanging amount of intelligence. In other words, it's the belief that you cannot get smarter over time.
   b. **Growth Mindset** leads to better outcomes. Growth mindset is the belief that you can get smarter over time by trying new things, making mistakes and learning from them, and getting help from others.

2. The following chart shows the consequences of both types of mindsets. People with a **fixed mindset** prefer easy tasks because they do not want to make any mistakes for fear others will think they are not smart. They think they are not capable if they make a mistake or need help, so they quit trying. People with a **growth mindset** try hard work, expect mistakes, and understand one needs help to learn new things.

Mindset	Preferred tasks	Response to mistakes	Acceptance of help	Learning outcomes
Fixed	Easy	Lose motivation	Avoid	Lower
Growth	Hard	Stay motivated	Welcome	Higher

3. Growth Mindset suggests two keys to success: **(1) persistence** with hard work and **(2) willingness to get help!** Her research shows people who do this achieve more.

SOCIAL SKILLS TRAINING

#10. TRYING WHEN WORK IS HARD (APPLYING GROWTH MINDSET)

Rationale: If we only approached work that was easy and familiar, we would rarely be able to grow and learn new things. The only way to develop new skills is to challenge ourselves with difficult work, keep trying if we make a mistake, and get help when needed.

1. Try it first to see if you know how to do it.

2. Ask to watch so you can see how to do it.

3. Ask for help so someone can explain it to you.

4. Ask to do a smaller amount. Maybe someone can help you by doing some of the other parts.

5. If you are still frustrated, take a short break. It is difficult to think when one is angry. After a break, you may feel calm enough to try again.

Practice

Who will I try this with? _____

When? _____

What happened? _____.

1. Modify work in addition to teaching this skill. Students often refuse to try work because it really is too hard or they have developed anxiety about certain kinds of work due to past struggles.

    a. Break down work into simpler steps and/or reduce the amount of work. See Chapter 8 for specific ways to modify difficult work.
    b. For students who have developed fears about inabilities to do certain kinds of work, build their confidence by starting with work they definitely can do and showing tremendous encouragement and praise when they try it.

2. **Explain the rationale and skills steps.** Then when **modeling** the skills, consider showing the right and wrong way to handle frustrating work. In modeling the wrong way, you may want to demonstrate ways that the students have avoided their work (e.g., pretending to be sick, getting too silly, getting mad and complaining about the work). Discuss why someone might do it the wrong way (e.g., they are embarrassed to ask for help, they fear others will laugh at them). Counter such self-defeating thoughts by reminding them of Carol Dweck's Growth Mindset, which shows better outcomes for those who ask for help.

3. **Role-play and practice** the skill steps. First, warn students ahead of time that you will give them difficult work that they may not be able to do. Then consider the following activities to practice:

    a. Give the student a math problem that is just beyond their reach but that they can do with help.
    b. Ask them to spell a word that is likely to be something they have never seen, like the word *Bologna* (pronounced *Baloney*).
    c. Use their actual schoolwork to practice this skill, reminding them that they are not supposed to know how to do it yet.
    d. Try practicing this with non-academic tasks as well, like repairing something at home, cooking a new recipe, or practicing a sport, musical instrument, dance routine, or singing.

4. Remember to **review** how initial difficulty does not mean one is incapable or not smart but instead indicates they are about to learn something new.

5. This is an excellent skill to target on a **school behavior chart**, where students are rewarded for their effort to try, ask for help, take a break, and try again. **It is crucial that rewards are provided for effort, not outcome.** The focus should be on the process of trying, not on whether you get your work done right or wrong. Teachers may want to create an entire classroom reward system where the whole class earns points when anyone tries, asks to watch first, or asks for help. Class rewards could be an extra free period the class earns.

#11. DEALING WITH MAKING A MISTAKE

Rationale: In order to learn anything new, we will need to make mistakes. Mistakes teach us what to work on to grow.

1. Sometimes we are told that we did something incorrectly or we realize we did not do something the right way.

2. Say to yourself, "It's okay to make a mistake. Mistakes help us to learn."

3. Think about what you can do to learn from your mistake.

    a. Try it again until you get it right.
    b. Ask for help.
    c. Apologize if your mistake upset someone else.

Practice

Who will I try this with? _____

When? _____

What happened? _____.

#11. DEALING WITH MAKING A MISTAKE Activity Page

1. Your students' ability to deal with a mistake depends on your ability to demonstrate that you value dealing with mistakes more than doing things perfectly.

   a. To reinforce this concept, ask students to purposely make mistakes this week so they can work on DEALING WITH MAKING A MISTAKE and learn something new.

   b. Show enthusiasm when the student makes a mistake rather than getting upset. Say, "Great, you made a mistake. This is an opportunity to learn. What can you say to yourself to deal with this mistake?" Then praise the appropriate DEALING WITH MAKING A MISTAKE steps.

2. Role-play the steps for DEALING WITH MAKING A MISTAKE. Suggested role-plays:

   a. Pretend the student makes a mistake when doing schoolwork (e.g., reading, math, writing). You review the work and say he or she did something wrong and prompt him or her to correct it.

   b. Pretend the student makes a mistake when doing artwork (e.g., cutting, drawing, molding clay). Review the work and say they did something wrong and prompt him to correct it.

   c. Pretend the student makes a mistake during an athletic game (e.g., not catching a ball, not hitting or kicking a ball, not running fast enough). Point out that they are "out" or that they dropped the ball, and prompt them to deal with the mistake.

   d. Pretend the student drops or breaks something that belongs to somebody else. Prompt them to apologize and deal with the mistake.

3. Bait the skill. This means doing something that requires your student to show how to deal with a mistake. Tell the child that you want to see if they know how to handle mistakes, then purposely give them some difficult tasks to do and tell them you are more interested in how they deal with mistakes than whether or not they do something right, so you actually hope they will make a mistake.

4. This is an excellent skill to add to a behavior chart where students can get rewarded for handling a mistake rather than getting their work done correctly. This is highly recommended for any perfectionistic students.

1. Sometimes parents and teachers say "No" when you ask them for something.

2. If you say, "Okay," and do not get mad, they will be pleased with you. You might be able to ask for something else instead.

3. If the other person is pleased, they may let you do something you want to do later.

Sometime later ...

Practice

Who will I try this with? _____

When? _____

What happened? _____.

1. Explain the rationale and what is in it for them if they can accept no or wait for what they want. Give examples of the values of waiting (e.g., the longer you go to school, the better the job you can get, or the more you save your money, the more you can let your money work for you and the more you can buy).

2. Model and role-play the skill steps.

   a. Pretend the student asks a parent to go to the movies or a friend's house, and the parent says not right now. If they accept no, then say "Okay, I will take you later.

   b. Pretend the student wants expensive toys, games, shoes, or clothing at the store and you say no, you cannot have that. If they accept no, then say "Okay, you can have something else that you want then."

   c. Pretend students have to stop one activity, like using the computer, to go to another less desired activity, like tedious writing work. Tell them they can return to the computer later for stopping on time.

3. For students with high levels of impulsivity, this is a skill that must be primed before situations where they may be disappointed. Try to remind students of the rewards that may await them if they can accept no or wait for what they want prior to going somewhere where they will ask for something (e.g., a store, a classroom that has desired activities). You might want to offer to give them double of what they want if they can wait longer for it (e.g., after a minute, an hour, a day, or a week depending on the student's ability to wait). Or offer to get them something else if they can accept no for an answer. As the student's ability to wait increases, gradually lengthen the time before you provide any reward for waiting. Eventually fade out the need for any external reward, providing praise only for accepting no.

4. You can bait the skill to create opportunities to practice. This means doing something that requires your student to show how to accept no or wait. For example, tell them you might test them and then show them a favorite item or access to an activity and wait for them to ask for it. Then say, "No, you can't have it right now." If they accept no, then say, "great job, you accepted no, so now you can have it."

5. Create a DISAPPOINTMENT POSTER where students get points every time they wait or accept no. When they get enough points, they can get a special reward. In this way every disappointment has a silver lining as it becomes an opportunity to earn points towards something they want.

#13. STOPPING A FAVORED ACTIVITY

1. Sometimes parents or teachers tell you to stop doing something you enjoy (e.g., playing a video game, using a device). This is especially hard when they need you to do something less fun, like homework.

2. If you do stop on time, others will be pleased enough to let you do the favored activity again later.

   a. You can ask, "When can I get it back?"

3. If you do not stop on time, others may not trust that they can let you do the favored activity again because you cannot stop when told.

Practice

Who will I try this with? _____

When? _____

What happened?

#13. STOPPING A FAVORED ACTIVITY Activity Page

1. Explain the rationale of what is in it for them if they can stop a favored activity on time. Others will trust them to do the activity again.

2. Negotiate a schedule of when they can do their favored activity. More generosity in giving times to do their favored activity will generally make it easier for them to stop the activity since they know soon after they may get to return.

3. Model and role-play the skill steps.

   a. Pretend the student is asked to stop playing video games and come to dinner.
   b. Pretend the student must end playtime at the park and come home. Consider offering a visit to get ice cream if they stop on time.
   c. Pretend the student is told to stop a game in order to do homework. Perhaps negotiate extra time to do the favorite activity after homework.

4. For students with high levels of impulsivity, this is a skill that must be primed before they are told to stop playing. Try to remind students of the rewards that may await them if they can stop on time, like extra time at the activity at the next scheduled period they are allowed to play.

5. You can bait the skill to create opportunities to practice. This means doing something that requires your student to show how to stop on time. For example, tell them you might test them and then ask them to stop doing an activity. Sometimes it's easier to practice first with activities that are not their favorite before trying activities that are harder for them to stop. If they stop, then say, "Great job, you stopped on time, so now you can do it again later."

6. Create a STOP ON TIME POSTER where students get points every time they stop on time. When they get enough points, they can get a special reward. In this way every disappointment has a silver lining as it becomes an opportunity to earn points towards something they want.

#14. DEALING WITH ANXIETY AND FEAR: UNDERSTANDING THE ALARM REACTION

Rationale: Knowing what a True or False alarm can help avoid unnecessary anxiety.

1. In Skill #4 we learned about our limbic system (the Incredible Hulk) and our forebrain (Dr. Banner). The limbic system is like an alarm system that responds quickly to danger by readying us for fight, flight, or freeze. The forebrain responds slowly and carefully to solve problems.

2. When we feel like something will hurt us, the limbic system (The Incredible Hulk) can take over the brain and shut down Dr. Banner so we cannot think logically anymore to solve problems and we just start to fight, flee, or freeze up.

3. We need the Incredible Hulk if there is a **TRUE ALARM** like a car coming to hit us and we need to run out of the way quickly. But mostly we have **FALSE ALARMS**. A **FALSE ALARM** is when there is no real life-or-death danger. False alarms might include:

   a. Fear of socializing with people who might in fact be nice to us.
   b. Fear of new places that are not dangerous.
   c. Fear of trying any new work (even when help is available).

Practice Labeling True and False Alarms

Who will I try this with? _____

When? _____

What happened? _____.

1. Practicing this skill involves trying to label alarms as True or False during or after surges of anxiety or panic attacks. Often in the moment the individual will feel it is a true alarm. If the situation is in fact safe, try to tell the individual the following during these anxiety attacks:

   a. "Even though it feels like the situation is dangerous because your body is having an alarm reaction, the situation is safe."
   b. "If you can wait out the anxiety, it will pass, and you will learn that nothing bad will happen."

2. After the anxiety passes, review how it felt like an emergency, but in fact nothing bad happened. Review other times when they had false alarms and they feared something bad happening but nothing bad happened.

Rationale: Gradually facing your fears can help you overcome your fears.

1. Don't let FALSE ALARMS control you. You may not be able to stop the anxiety that comes with false alarms, but you do not have to listen to the part of your brain that tells you to avoid something that is not a "real" danger.

   a. Every time you face your fear, your brain learns that the situation is not really dangerous!

2. Create a fear ladder to help you *gradually* face your fear. Whatever you are afraid to do, make a list from the least to most fear-inducing situations, and then try to face each situation. A blank Fear Ladder is provided on the next page. Below is a sample Fear Ladder for a student afraid to go to try a new activity:

Steps of the ladder from least to most difficult	Fear level 1-5	Points earned
Just watch others do the activity	2	2
Partner with someone else to do the activity while you sit next to them	3	3
Participate in the activity for 10 seconds	3	3
Participate in the activity for 1 minute	4	4
Participate in the activity for 5 minutes	4	4
Participate in the activity for 10 minutes	5	5
Participate in the activity for the whole time	5	5

3. Even though you will feel the alarm, try to wait it out for the set amount of time. That, way your brain will learn nothing bad happens and it's just a false alarm.

4. If you cannot get started, ask for points towards a reward for trying each step on the ladder.

Practice Setting up a Fear Ladder for Your Fear

When will I try this? _____

Which step of the ladder do I feel like trying? _____

#15. MANAGE FEARS BY CREATING A FEAR LADDER
Activity Page

1. Help create a fear ladder breaking down the feared situation into less threatening steps. Ask the individual, on a scale of 1–5 (1 being the lowest, 5 the highest), how scary a particular step is.

Fear Ladder

For each situation, indicate how anxious it makes you using the scale below:

1 Calm   2 Slightly Nervous   3 Anxious   4 Very Anxious   5 Extreme Anxiety

	Situations	Anxiety Rating (1-5)
1.		
2.		
3.		
4.		
5.		
6.		
7.		
8.		
9.		
10.		

SOCIAL SKILLS TRAINING

2. Ask the individual which step they feel ready to attempt. Let the individual choose to attempt this to battle their own anxiety rather than feeling forced into it. Help prepare them by:

    a. Reminding them they will feel the fear reaction, but if they can wait out the anxiety, it will pass, and they will learn that nothing bad will happen.
    b. Using self-talk, saying, "I only need to do this for _____ seconds or minutes."

3. For those less motivated to face any step, consider using a point/token system towards desired rewards for attempting a particular step on the ladder.

#16. MANAGE FEARS BY THINKING LIKE A SCIENTIST

Rationale: Thinking like a scientist can help you overcome your false alarm fears.

1. Use your Dr. Banner forebrain to combat your fears. This means to think like a scientist. Some people call this Cognitive-Behavioral Therapy, which means using scientific thinking to overcome fears. When your worries stop you from doing things, ask yourself two questions and then find the evidence as a scientist would:
   a. Am I overestimating the probability of something bad happening?
   b. Am I overestimating how bad it would be if it did happen?

2. Have a trusted person help you gather the evidence about how likely the feared situation is and how bad it would be even if it did happen, then summarize the information in a Think Like a Scientist Evidence Card. See the example below of someone who was afraid of being stung by a bee or wasp and afraid they would die from it. See how the evidence shows that they are unlikely to be stung and will not die from it.

Example Think Like a Scientist Evidence Card		
Feared Situation	**Worry Thought**	**Scientific Evidence**
Getting stung by a bee or wasp	Being outdoors in the summer makes it likely for me to get stung	Bees and wasps are not aggressive away from nests and not likely to sting unless disturbed. If I avoid nests and wear shoes when walking, I am not likely to be stung.
Getting stung by a bee or wasp	Getting stung really hurts, and I could even die	It is not possible to die for me because I am not allergic. I can reduce the pain by immediately flicking out the stinger to limit the venom and applying ice.

Practice Setting Creating a Think Like a Scientist Evidence Card for your Fears

What will I try? _____

When will I do this? _____

SOCIAL SKILLS TRAINING

#16. MANAGE FEARS BY THINKING LIKE A SCIENTIST
Activity Page

1. Help the individual identify the situations they fear. Then ask them to consider the two questions about each fear, considering the probability and severity of their fear coming true:

   a. Am I overestimating the probability of something bad happening?
   b. Am I overestimating how bad it would be if it did happen?

2. You may decide to look up the information using reputable websites or trusted individuals to help gather information to more accurately answer the questions above. Use the information to create a Think Like a Scientist Evidence Card. See template below:

Think Like a Scientist Evidence Card		
Feared Situation	**Worry Thought**	**Scientific Evidence**
Write in the feared situation	Write what you worry will happen	Write why it is unlikely to happen
Write in the feared situation	Write how bad you think it would be if it happened	Write why it would not be that bad if it did happen

3. Use the Think Like a Scientist Evidence Card to help individuals face fears on their fear ladder. As with all these anxiety-reducing strategies, the main point is to help the individual face fears on their fear ladder.

Rationale: To help you reduce your anxiety enough to face your fears, there are several physical things you can do that lower anxiety.

1. Try using **relaxation strategies** prior to facing a feared situation. These might include:

    a. Listening to calming music. "Weightless" by Marconi Union is a spa-like track that has been shown to reduce anxiety (see the YouTube video of their song with calming scenes).
    b. Mindfulness meditation. Go to www.fragrantheart.com for free meditation guides.
    c. Slow deep breaths, especially breathing out slowly, have been shown to reduce anxiety. See handouts on breathing techniques on activity pages.

2. **Vigorous exercise** (for as little as 10 minutes or more each day) is a powerful anxiety and depression reducer. Try exercising the morning of the day you will face a feared situation. Some studies demonstrate that such vigorous exercise can be as effective or better in relieving depression and anxiety than antidepressant medications.

3. Various medications can greatly reduce anxiety and fear responses. Check with your doctor or a psychiatrist about these possibilities, and remember that taking a medication does not have to be forever, just long enough to help you start facing fears. as some of these can be habit-forming while others are not. Medications may be especially helpful when the anxious beliefs are "overvalued" (i.e., you are certain that the beliefs are true) and delusional (i.e., the beliefs are about things that are not really possible). This is different from the situation in which the individual believes that their beliefs are probably not true but continues to be bothered by them.

Practice Physical Ways to Lower Anxiety

What will I try? _____

When will I do this? _____

#17. MANAGE FEARS THROUGH PHYSICAL WAYS
Activity Page

1. Explore with the individual ways that help them to feel calm. There is no one right way to get calm, but rather, individuals should use what works for them. The point is to use calming techniques to help you face fears on the fear ladder.

2. Some of these techniques can be implemented while facing a fear, such as deep breathing, listening to music, and mindfulness meditation. Others are better to use before a feared situation, such as exercise or medication.

3. If the individual is willing to use deep breathing, practice with them so they do not hyperventilate but instead take slow, deliberate breaths, paying special attention to breathing out slowly. Pursing your lips like you are blowing up a balloon can help you release air more slowly. This kind of breathing has been shown to stimulate a relaxation response. See handouts on next page.

4. If the individual is thinking about using medication, consider the following:

    a. Check with their doctor or a psychiatrist about medications.
    b. Some of these can be habit-forming (like the benzodiazepines, which work immediately) while others are less likely to be habit-forming (like Selective Serotonin Reuptake Inhibitors, which can take several weeks to be effective).
    c. Medications may be especially helpful when the anxious beliefs are "overvalued" (i.e., the person is certain that the beliefs are true) and delusional (i.e., the beliefs are about things that are not really possible). This is different from the situation in which the individual believes that their beliefs are probably not true but continues to be bothered by them.
    d. Lastly, remind the individual that medications can sometimes be used briefly to begin the process of facing fears and then faded out when the individual has successfully confronted feared situations.

EXERCISE #1: The Relaxation Response (Benson, 1976).

Developed to: Help you cope better with stress and anxieties, sleep better and relieve fatigue, conserve the body's store of energy, and make you alert and focused.

Steps to follow:

1. Find a quiet calm environment with few distractions.

2. Sit quietly in a comfortable position.

3. Close your eyes.

4. Deeply relax all of your muscles, beginning with your feet and progressing up to your face (you can do this by squeezing each muscle tightly and then relaxing it).

5. Breathe through your nose. Become aware of your breathing. As you breathe out, say the word "one" silently to yourself.

6. Breathe in ... out ... "one" in ... out ... "one." Breathe easily and naturally.

7. Continue this for ten to fifteen minutes or as long as is comfortable.

8. Don't worry if you are not successful in achieving a deep level of relaxation. Let relaxation occur at its own pace. If you get distracted by your thoughts, try to ignore them by not dwelling on them and returning to breathing and repeating "one."

9. The more you practice this, the easier it will become.

EXERCISE #2: The Relaxing Breath

Dr. Andrew Weil's yoga-derived "Relaxing Breath" (aka "4-7-8 Breath") is a simple technique people can use to address various health problems, from stopping panic attacks to improving digestion.

1. Sit comfortably and place the tip of your tongue against the bony ridge near your upper front teeth. You will keep your tongue in this position throughout the exercise.

2. Exhale with a whoosh sound through your mouth.

3. Now close your mouth and breathe in quietly through your nose to the count of four.

4. Hold your breath easily to the count of seven. Then exhale through your mouth with a *whoosh* to the count of eight.

5. You have now completed one breath. Repeat the cycle three more times for a total of four breaths.

You can try to practice this twice a day. Do not do more than four breaths at one time for the first month of practice. Over time, you can work up to eight breaths. While you may notice only a subtle effect at first, breath work gains power through repetition and practice.

Rationale: Learning that obsessive worries are false alarms can help you not be overcome with anxiety.

1. What are anxious obsessions? These are different from positive obsessions associated with a particular interest. For example, a student might enjoy talking about his favorite movies over and over again. That's a calming obsession that does not cause anxiety. When we have frequent obsessive thoughts that are unpleasant and cause anxiety, they may be part of an anxiety disorder called Obsessive-Compulsive Disorder (OCD). Examples of unpleasant obsessions associated with OCD might include:

    *   Thoughts of being contaminated by germs leading to possible illness.

    *   Worries that one has forgot to do something (e.g., lock a door, turn off an oven) and that could lead to something terrible happening.

    *   Thoughts that we have caused harm to someone (e.g., one student feared that she might have accidentally hurt someone whenever she heard an ambulance go by even though she could not have possibly hurt anyone).

    *   Disturbing thoughts of harming people despite having no intent to do so. Unlike someone who is angry and wants to harm someone, here the person is upset by having such thoughts.

    *   Some students have had obsessive thoughts that they are defective, ugly, or perceived as bad or dangerous. When the focus is on a particular feature of one's face or body, this is often referred to as body dysmorphic disorder.

2. What are compulsions in OCD? Compulsions are repetitive, superstitious behaviors that an individual thinks will stop something bad from happening. With OCD, worry returns, and the person thinks they must keep doing the compulsion to stop the bad

event from happening. In this way the compulsion becomes an unnecessary and time-consuming addiction. Examples might include:

- Being obsessed with fears of germs. Compulsions might include frequent washing of hands and body. When washing becomes excessive, it can lead to health risks (e.g., dry, cracking, bleeding hands from being over-washed).

- Fears of forgetting something (like locking a door, turning off the oven). Compulsions might include frequent checking behavior. Checking behavior can become so time-consuming that the individual cannot get to school or work or socialize.

- Fears of "bad thoughts" like accidentally harming someone. In these situations, individual have what is called **thought/action fusion**, where they believe their bad thought can magically make bad things happen. In these instances the compulsion often involves redoing what they were doing when they had the bad thought to somehow have a different thought, or avoiding situations where they have such thoughts.

- Obsessing over an imagined defect or fear of being perceived as bad or dangerous. The compulsion may involve constant efforts to alter their appearance or behavior.

3. Treating obsessive-compulsive behaviors involves **gradual exposure to feared thoughts/situations** (what I call a Fear Ladder) and **response prevention** (not engaging in the compulsion). The goal is to learn nothing bad will happen if you have an obsessive thought and do not try to undo it with a compulsion. Thoughts cannot make bad things happen by themselves. The following are steps you can take to manage OCD:

   a. Create a **Think like a Scientist Evidence Card** for obsessive worries. Ask yourself if you are overestimating the probability or severity of something bad happening. Is there more evidence that your anxious thought is false than true?

b. Create a **Fear Ladder** to gradually face feared situations. With OCD this usually means facing a situation without doing the unnecessary compulsive or superstitious behavior. For example:

    i. For those obsessed with fear of germs, create a ladder where one touches possibly germy surfaces and waits longer and longer before washing.

    ii. For those whose fears focus on forgetting something (like locking a door, turning off the oven), try creating a ladder where you check fewer and fewer times.

    iii. For those who fear "bad thoughts" (like harming someone), create a fear ladder where one engages in fewer and fewer rituals. For example, try not to redo activities over and over to magically undo the bad thought. Remember, your thoughts do not make bad things happen, nor can they prevent them from happening. Thoughts and actions are separate.

    iv. For those who obsess over an imagined physical defect the fear ladder would focus on going out with less and less effort to alter your appearance.

c. Consider using some of the **physical ways to decrease your anxiety** like listening to music, meditation, special interests, deep breathing techniques, vigorous exercise, and possible medications.

Practice Gradual Exposure and Response Prevention

When will I make a Think Like a Scientist Card? _____

When will I create a Fear Ladder? _____

What step of the ladder am I willing to try? _____

SOCIAL SKILLS TRAINING

1. **Explain** the difference between pleasurable and unpleasant obsessions. Then give examples of compulsive behaviors used to neutralize unpleasant obsessions. Highlight that the compulsive behaviors may relieve anxiety for a moment but make things worse in the end by taking time away from life and sometimes causing harm.

2. Help create the **Think Like Scientist Evidence Card** using the format below:

Think Like a Scientist Evidence Card		
Obsessive Thoughts	Compulsive actions	Scientific Evidence
Write what you fear will happen	Write what compulsive behavior you do when this happens	Write why the negative event is unlikely to happen. Write why the compulsion does not work in the long run.
Write how bad you think it would be if it did happen	Write what compulsive behavior you do when this happens	Write why it might not be that bad if the negative event did happen.

3. Then create a Fear Ladder identifying situations/thoughts to face without engaging in compulsive behaviors for increasing amounts of time. Here is an example Fear Ladder for a young man with fear of germs and compulsive hand washing. Notice that he rated how scary each step was and received promise of points towards rewards for completing each step.

Steps of the ladder from least to most difficult	Fear level 1-5	Points earned
Not washing hands until touching any door handles, community property, or others' belongings	2	2
Touching door handles, community property, others' belongings, or something that fell to the floor and not washing for 5 minutes	3	3
Washing just once with warm water for about 20 seconds and rinsing for 10 seconds and then not washing again until the next time touching community property	3	3
Touching a door handle, community property, others' belongings, or something that fell to the floor and not washing for 10 minutes	4	4
Touching a door handle, community property, others' belongings, or something that fell to the floor and not washing for 20 minutes	4	4
Not washing more than once before eating	5	5
Not washing more than once after using public restroom	5	5
Not washing hands for at least 4 hours if not eating or using restroom.	5	25

4. Consider using a reward system with points towards desired activities or objects for facing each step on the ladder.

5. Select other strategies that may help **lower their anxiety** enough to confront their feared situations on the ladder. Consider deep breathing or pleasurable distractions. Often medication can be useful in more severe OCD.

6. When facing a step on the ladder, predict for the student that they will be anxious, but if they can wait it out for the time indicated on the ladder without engaging in a compulsion, their brain will learn that nothing bad happens.

SOCIAL SKILLS TRAINING

#19. DEALING WITH SOCIAL FEARS

Rationale: Social fears are often false alarms that stop us from doing what we want with others.

1. **What are social fears?** Social fears involve excessive anxiety about being judged or evaluated badly by others. These anxieties cause us to avoid social interactions, even in situations where we would like to interact. It can make us feel isolated and lonely. Fears might include not being able to talk or eat in front of others, or not being able to look at others.

2. Create a **Think Like a Scientist Evidence Card** to combat worries that others will judge you negatively. With social anxiety, we often think others do not like us because they do not talk to us, but often it is because we do not look at them, smile, or talk to them, so they assume we want to be left alone. Use the following as a format for creating your Think Like a Scientist Evidence Card.

Think Like a Scientist Evidence Card		
Obsessive Thoughts	**Socially Anxious Thoughts**	**Scientific Evidence**
Write a situation you fear will happen (for example, that others will ignore you)	Write what your anxious thought is. Maybe you think others do not like you?	Think about why the negative event is unlikely to happen or why your anxious thought might be wrong. For example, others may ignore you if you seem to be ignoring them. **Sometimes our anxiety makes it look like we are not interested in others!**
Write how bad it would be if the situation above happened.	Write why you think it is so bad.	Think about why it might not be that bad if the negative event did happen. For example, others may ignore you if you ignore them, but it does not mean they dislike you.

3. Consider what social situations may be desirable and manageable for you.

   a. It can be easier to interact with others doing and talking about an activity you are familiar with and enjoy.
   b. Sometimes structured activities that have a schedule and rules (like a class or sport) are easier than unstructured social times (like hanging out with friends with no plan).

c. Consider the noise level and crowd in certain social settings. Many find it easier to interact in smaller, quieter settings.

d. Most importantly, choose people who are positive, complimentary, and generally non-critical. You can observe people (in person or through online chats) to see how they act before deciding if you want to interact with them.

4. Create a **Fear Ladder** to gradually face desired social situations. Here is a sample from a student who feared talking to peers in school.

Steps of the ladder from least to most difficult	Fear level 1-5	Points earned
Look or smile at someone if they look at you	1	1
Greet someone back if they greet you	2	2
Initiate a smile and a greeting to someone you know	3	3
Initiate a conversation with someone you know (see conversation skills)	3	4
Join a conversation that people you know are already engaged in	4	4
Greet someone you have never spoken to but see in some regular way (e.g., because they are in your class or group)	4	4
Ask someone you know to get together to do an activity you both like	5	5

5. Consider using some of these physical strategies regularly to decrease your anxiety further so you can begin facing the fears on the ladder: listening to music, meditation, deep breathing techniques, vigorous exercise. If these strategies fail to help, you may want to consult with a doctor for anxiety/antidepressant medications.

Practice Gradual Exposure and Response Prevention

When will I make a Think Like a Scientist Card? _____

When will I create a Fear Ladder? _____

What step of the ladder am I willing to try? _____

#19. DEALING WITH SOCIAL FEARS Activity Page

1. **Explain** how social anxiety can contribute to us feeling lonely and isolated. The goal is not to socialize all the time but to do so enough to feel connected to others.

2. When creating the **Think Like Scientist Evidence Card**, keep in mind a common theme among those with social anxiety: students often think others do not like them, do not want to talk with them, or are simply disinterested in them. What they may not realize is that due to their shyness, they give off signals to others that they do not want to talk or engage, and then others leave them alone, leading them to falsely conclude they are disliked. So on the card, we can correct this thinking, explaining that it is not that others do not like them, but rather, they may be ignored because they do not talk or engage.

3. When choosing activities to socialize, we may want to create certain **modifications** to a school or other social settings like:

   a. Creating a quieter setting to eat lunch in school with peers.
   b. Creating social clubs centered on themes the student enjoys.
   c. Modifying recess to offer alternative activities that the student enjoys.
   d. Creating a peer buddy program (see Chapter 12).

4. When creating the **Fear Ladder**, include simple gestures like nodding, smiling, and saying an enthusiastic hello that communicates to others that we are friendly and open to engaging. Later steps can focus on initiating conversations and asking to get together. The student may need some scripts for starting and maintaining a conversation (see skill lessons on communication).

5. Getting points towards **rewards** may help to jumpstart facing fears on the ladder, but eventually, most students with social anxiety face their fears for the intrinsic payoff of no longer being trapped by their social fears.

#20. DEALING WITH BRIEF PERIODS OF DEPRESSION

1. This skill is not meant to replace ongoing talk therapy or medication for depression. This is simply a starting point to help get unstuck when depressed.

2. Create a Think Like a Scientist Evidence Card to combat overly negative thoughts about yourself. Use the format below to help you.

Think Like a Scientist Evidence Card		
Situation That Made You Feel Bad	**Negative View of the Situation**	**Scientific Evidence for a More Positive View**
Write a situation that made you feel bad about yourself.	Did you think it was all your fault and you cannot change?	Think about how the event might not be all your fault and that you can change or solve the problem.

3. Some of the main symptoms of depression are loss of energy and motivation to do anything, feeling worthless, and having no hope that things can get better. To combat these feelings, there are three simple things one can try:

   a. **Move your body every day.** This might be a walk, a brief workout, dance to music, or anything that can get your heart rate up. Ideally one would strive for at least thirty minutes, but even eight minutes a day of sustained exercise has been shown to relieve depression.
   b. **Interact with people you like.** Research has shown that being with people you like (whether just talking or playing a game) can relieve depression. Consider family members or peers who have been supportive and positive with you in the past.
   c. **Set small personal goals** every day that you can feel good about when you accomplish it. This might be as small and simple as cleaning your room, completing eight minutes of exercise, or doing some work on a school task or job. Remember: any amount of progress is better than none. This is not a time to be a perfectionist.

4. Do not feel bad if you are unable to accomplish these things, as that is part of being depressed. Any step towards these activities is progress. If symptoms persist beyond two weeks or you have thoughts to harm yourself, it is best to seek help from a professional therapist.

Practice

Which activities will I try? _____

When will I try these activities? _____

How did it make me feel? _____

#20. DEALING WITH BRIEF PERIODS OF DEPRESSION
Activity Page

1. **Explain** how everyone gets depressed sometimes. Usually, it's because something happened that made you feel bad about yourself and the future.

2. Help create the **Think Like Scientist Evidence Card** to combat negative thinking.

   a. People who are depressed tend to blame themselves entirely for negative events and believe that they are permanently defective and cannot change.
   b. Use scientific thinking to show how the negative event may not be the individual's fault and that whatever the problem is, it can be solved or improved. People can learn from mistakes and improve.

3. Help choose activities that the individual feels they can attempt. Consider:

   a. Manageable amounts of pleasurable exercise.
   b. Identifying people to interact with that generally make the individual feel better.
   c. Creating small goals, chores, tasks that are manageable.

4. If symptoms persist, help the individual overcome any embarrassment about reaching out for help. As Carol Dweck's growth mindset research shows, people who seek help have better outcomes in reaching goals.

5. Getting points towards **rewards** could help the individual to start being more active, but often folks with depression do not care about earning rewards until they feel slightly better. In that case, those around the individual may need to exercise with them or set up times to be with people they like rather than offering an incentive for the individual to do it themselves.

SOCIAL SKILLS TRAINING

#21. SHOWING AND READING WELCOME VERSUS UNWELCOME SOCIAL CUES

Rationale: Showing a welcoming impression increases the chances that others will like being with us. Sometimes when we are nervous or upset, we accidentally give off the impression that we do not welcome others when we might actually wish to connect with those people. Reading the cues that others welcome us helps us to continue to pursue interactions with those who want them and avoid interactions with those who do not want to interact. Pursuing people who do not welcome us can be frustrating and lead to trouble (e.g., if people accuse you of harassing them or following them).

1. The chart below shows what welcoming versus unwelcoming behaviors look like:

Behaviors	Welcoming	Unwelcoming
Body language	Turns body towards others, makes eye contact, smiles	Turns body away, avoids looking at them, frowns, makes angry or disgusted look
Tone of voice	Pleasant, friendly tone	Overly quiet, muttering to self, or overly loud and harsh
Choice of words	Friendly greetings: "Hi, how are you?" "Hello, nice to meet you."	Unfriendly greeting: "Whatever." Grunt
Reciprocity	Answers questions/texts, asks the same question back, accepts invitations, or explains why they cannot make it.	Does not respond to questions/ texts or ask questions. Repeatedly (three times in a row or more) turns down invitations to get together.

Practice

Where will I try this? _____

When will I try this? _____

How did do? _____

1. **Explain** the rationale for being able to show and read others' welcoming and unwelcoming behaviors. Link this ability to the student's goals for work, friendship, or dating. Read the chart on the previous page outlining the behaviors showing welcoming versus unwelcoming cues.

2. Model the expressions and ask for feedback.

   a. A charade-game format can be used here to review the material. The teacher models certain behaviors and the students decide whether it is welcoming or unwelcoming. Make sure you model all the categories of body language, tone of voice, and words.

   b. For the reciprocity category, one can ask the student questions about situations in which someone did or did not respond to one or several texts or invitations, and the students must try to assess the person's desire to get together.

3. Role-play with the students welcoming versus unwelcoming behaviors

   a. Student walks up to group at lunch or recess time: both the student and group can practice welcoming or unwelcoming behaviors.

   b. Student approaches another student at a class or group activity hoping to make a good first impression.

   c. Student sees classmates outside of school at a mall or an extracurricular activity.

4. This skill lends itself well to creating pictures where students can show welcoming versus unwelcoming behaviors. Such pictures are available in the *Social Skills Picture Book for High-School-Aged Students and Beyond* (Baker, 2005).

5. Prime and practice the skill: Using the chart on the previous page or a cue card, remind students of the skill before social situations in which they should consider how they express or read welcoming social cues. Situations might include:

   a. Before going to lunch where students sit near others.

   b. Before picking partners for group projects.

   c. Prior to going to a party, dance or potential dating situation.

   d. Prior to attending any new social situation (e.g., club, sports team, music, chorus, job).

#22. LISTENING POSITION

Rationale: Looking at someone makes them feel like you care about what they are saying.

1. Make eye contact.

2. Stay still. Quiet hands and feet.

3. Don't interrupt. Do not talk while others are talking.

4. If you are in class and you want to say something, raise your hand and wait to be called on.

Practice

Who will I try this with? _____

When? _____

What happened? _____.

#22. LISTENING POSITION Activity Page

1. Role-play the steps for LISTENING POSITION. Model the correct and the incorrect way to show a listening position and ask the student to tell what you did right or wrong. Suggested role-plays:

    a. Listening to a story time or lesson in class
    b. Listening to a parent give instructions
    c. Listening to another student during show and tell
    d. Raising your hand to ask a question about a lesson or to ask permission to go to the bathroom during class

2. Tell students you will test their ability to listen with their eyes rather than their ears. Tell them to pay attention to what you do with your hands and face rather than your words as you direct them in these activities:

    a. Gesture with your hands for them to draw a square while you say, "Draw a circle on piece of paper."
    b. Ask them to write down homework assignments. Then point to assignments written on the board as you tell them to "do this one, but not that one." See if they understood which ones to write down.
    c. Ask them to guess what you are looking at in the room.
    d. Without words, direct them to sit, stand, move to another seat, or attend to something special in the room.

3. Correct inappropriate listening. Have student demonstrate a good listening position.

4. Provide rewards for appropriate LISTENING POSITION.

    a. Give verbal praise for correct or partially correct LISTENING POSITION.
    b. Give tokens, pennies, or points for periods in which the students demonstrate a good listening position. When they get an agreed-upon number of tokens (e.g., five tokens), give a special reward (e.g., snack, stickers, privileges to play special game or watch a special show).

SOCIAL SKILLS TRAINING

#23. SHOWING INTEREST VERSUS BOREDOM

Rationale: Showing interest when others are talking increases the chances that others will like being with us. This is important when meeting new people or maintaining ongoing relationships.

1. The chart below shows what Interest versus Boredom looks like

Behaviors	Interest	Boredom
Face	🙂	😐
Body language	Show a **listening position**: Turn body towards others, lean in a bit, make some eye contact	Turn body away, avoid looking at them, look at your phone, watch, the exit doors, and yawn.
Tone of voice	Upward inflection: Oh, Ahh, I see.	Downward inflection that ends in a sigh.
Choice of words	Listener asks questions about what you just said.	The listener does not ask any questions, tries to change the topic, or does not say anything.

2. If you are bored and **do not want to listen**, it is polite to make an excuse so the other person does not feel bad. You can say: "I don't mean to be rude, but I cannot talk now as I have something I have to do right now—I'll talk to you later."

Practice

Where will I try this? _____

When will I try this? _____

How did I do? _____

1. Explain the rationale for being able to show and read signs of interest or boredom. Link the skill to the student's goals for work, friendship, or dating. Read the chart on the previous page outlining the behaviors showing interest versus boredom cues. Explain what to do if you or others are bored.

2. Model the expressions and ask for feedback.

   a. A charade-game format can be used here to review the material. The teacher models certain behaviors and the students decide whether they are interested or bored. Make sure you model all the categories of body language, tone of voice, and words.

3. Role-play situations in which others are interested or bored. Show how to make an excuse if you are bored and want to end the conversation.

   a. Student becomes bored when others in a group talk about something he or she has no interest in.
   b. In classroom setting, one may not be able to make an excuse to stop listening to a teacher. Instead, students might have to fake interest or quietly entertain themselves by drawing or doodling.

4. Make pictures or videos with the students to demonstrate what interest and boredom looks like. Also demonstrate how to make an excuse to end the conversation if bored.

5. Prime and practice the skill: Using the chart or a cue card, remind students of the skill before situations in which they should consider whether they are boring others or they might have to look interested even when they are bored. Here are some places to practice: lunch with peers, a classroom lesson, a job interview, club meeting, sports team, music lesson, party, or potential dating situation.

24. DON'T BE A SPACE INVADER

Rationale: People feel uncomfortable if you get too close to them.

1. Stand at least an arm's length away with most people.

2. Don't get too close unless the person is in your family.

3. Don't touch others' belongings unless they give your permission.

Practice

Who will I try this with? _____

When? _____

What happened? _____.

1. Role-play situations in which students must modify their personal space. For each situation, ask the student or observers to say when the actors get too close and when they are the right distance. Suggested role-plays:

    a. Greeting others the first time you see them and saying goodbye when you leave.
    b. Standing in line at school or in public (e.g., a movie, a store).
    c. Riding public transportation (e.g., not sitting or standing too close to others).
    d. Using a public restroom (e.g., not using the urinal right next to somebody else if there are others available).
    e. Requesting something from someone (e.g., asking for a snack or other food item that someone is holding, asking to play with someone's toy or game).
    f. Interrupting someone to ask a question about what was said or to ask permission to do something.
    g. Show what to do if you really liked someone else's laptop that they were not using and it was sitting on their desk. (Answer: ask to see it before touching it).

2. Some students have sensory needs that contribute to them touching others all the time. Give these students something else to touch, like a small stuffed animal, toy, doll, or other fidget object.

3. Prime them before crowded social spaces and correct inappropriate distance. Say, "Don't be a space invader, because it will make others uncomfortable and then they will not want to play with you. Keep an arm's length away." Explain that if a place is too crowded, it may not be possible to keep a full arm's length away, but we still should try to avoid contact if we can.

SOCIAL SKILLS TRAINING

#25. SARCASM VERSUS GENUINE EXPRESSIONS

Rationale: Looking at someone's body language can help us decide if they mean what they say.

1. Sarcasm is when someone's words do not match their body language and they really mean the opposite of what they say. Sarcastic body language may include rolling one's eyes and looking up or away, making a face of disbelief or confusion, and using a tone of voice that is mocking and draws out the vowel sounds.

2. What do people really mean?

Example	Not sarcastic	Sarcastic
Person says, "That was great!"	Person looks you in the eyes, nods, smiles. **They mean it was great.**	**Sarcastic body language:** looking away or rolling eyes, confused facial expression, mocking long vowel sounds tone of voice. **They mean it was NOT great.**

3. If you cannot tell if someone is being sarcastic, just ask, "Did you really mean that?"

Practice

Who will I try this with? _____

When? _____

What happened? _____.

#25. SARCASM VERSUS GENUINE EXPRESSION
Activity Page

1. Explain the rationale for being able to read sarcasm versus genuine expressions so that one can determine if the person means what they say.

2. Show genuine versus sarcastic expressions and ask students if they can guess your true message. There is no need for students to practice making sarcastic expressions, as it is more crucial for students to learn how to read such expressions. Sample expressions could include:

   a. "You are really good at math" expressed with sincerity. (True meaning: you are really good at math).
   b. "You are a really good writer" stated with sarcastic body language. (True meaning: they did not like your writing).
   c. "You are annoying, get away" spoken with eye contact and a firm, clear voice. (True meaning: The person is annoyed and wants you to go away).
   d. "Oh yeah, you are really the worst at computers" spoken with eyes rolling up, a look of disbelief, and a tone that draws out the vowel sounds. (True meaning: Person thinks you are really great with computers).

3. Consider creating pictures or videos with students demonstrating genuine versus sarcastic comments.

4. Practice this skill by having parents, peers, or teachers purposely make a sarcastic statement and then asking the student to guess the true intent of the statement.

Rationale: Keeping up your hygiene is important because good hygiene prevents disease and infection and it helps others to accept you.

1. Some typical hygiene routines are:

   a. Keeping your body clean by regularly showering or bathing. Some shower every day; others shower every other day. The frequency is based on personal choice and on how dirty or sweaty you become during the day.

   b. Using deodorant for underarms, which is common from puberty onwards to offset underarm odors.

   c. Washing your hair can be done daily or a couple times per week depending on how dirty or sweaty your hair gets. An anti-dandruff shampoo is often used if you have many visible dry flakes that may make others avoid you.

   d. Brushing your teeth twice a day with toothpaste. Using a mouthwash or mint if your breath is offensive to others (this can happen as a result of certain strong foods, mouth and stomach bacteria, acid reflux, or dehydration).

   e. Using tissues to wipe your nose rather than picking your nose. Using saline nasal sprays keep your nose moist so you won't want to pick.

   f. Sneezing, which should be done into a tissue or at least your elbow to prevent sneezing germs onto others.

   g. Wearing a mask around others if you have a contagious respiratory illness.

   h. Trying to go to a bathroom or private area if you need to pass gas rather than doing so near others.

   i. Burping or belching quietly by putting your hand over your mouth.

   j. Dressing in clean clothes that do not smell (undergarments and socks should not be worn for more than one day at a time without being cleaned).

2. To help with hygiene maintenance, you may want to keep a schedule with written reminders.

3. If you want people to stay away, consider better ways to do this, such as by asking others for space rather than making others repelled by you.

Practice

Who will I try this with? _____

What happened? _____.

#26. PERSONAL HYGIENE Activity Page

1. **Explain** the rationale for keeping up with hygiene, stressing both health-related and social concerns. Emphasize that others do not have to "conform" to social norms entirely (it is okay to be different), but by deviating too sharply from hygiene norms, they may incur rejection from peers. Even if they do not want friends, it is best not to have people feel negatively about them.

2. It may be necessary to **model and role-play** some hygiene routines that the student does not know how to do.

3. Students may also have sensory issues that prevent brushing teeth, bathing, or showering. You may have to experiment with alternative ways to keep up hygiene, like using small amounts of water, wipes, alternative toothpastes, etc.

4. Have students design a schedule of how often they should wash their bodies, hair, clothes, brush their teeth, shave, etc.

5. A game-show format can be used to answer questions about other hygiene matters. Sample questions include:

   a. If you are at a quiet dinner table with friends and family and you have to pass gas, what should you do?
   b. If you are in class and you have to burp, what should you do?
   c. What would you do if you feel something hard in your nose?
   d. What should you do when you have to sneeze?
   e. What could you do if you are in school and you just had gym and realized your armpits smell bad?
   f. What might you do after eating a pizza with triple garlic and before hanging out with your friends?

6. Use reminders and rewards if necessary. Parents may need to remind their children of hygiene expectations. Because these routines take effort and time, giving a reward for keeping to their hygiene schedule can be helpful at first to establish these routines.

SOCIAL SKILLS TRAINING

#27. DEALING WITH ODD MOTOR MANNERISMS

Rationale: Some of us may fidget or make certain motor movements when we are excited, nervous, or bored. These behaviors may help us to feel calm or expel energy. When they do not bother anyone else, it is fine to keep doing them. However, when the behaviors are very loud or distracting to others, we may want to find a way to do it more quietly or away from others, or try to explain it to others so they will accept it.

1. Some examples of fidgeting and motor mannerisms:

    a. Flapping or clapping hands.
    b. Licking or biting lips repeatedly.
    c. Picking pieces of skin.
    d. Pacing or walking in circles, sometimes walking around the periphery of spaces.
    e. Rocking your body in a chair.
    f. Bouncing legs or clapping knees together in your seat.
    g. Repeatedly scripting shows or singing songs from favorite movies.

2. If the fidget or mannerism bothers others, you can:

    a. Ask others to let you know if/when it bothers them.
    b. See if there is a way to do it more quietly. For example, if you tap pencils on a desk, try putting cotton balls on the ends to make it quieter. If you talk or sing out loud, try doing it in your head or at least a whisper.
    c. If your behavior is very loud or distracting, try to find a place away from others to do the activity.
    d. If it is not possible to alter the movements, you may want to explain it to others so they can be more understanding. For example, one student explained to his peers that when he gets restless, he likes to run around in circles to relieve excess energy.

Practice

Where will I try this? _____

When? _____

What happened? _____

1. **Explain** that fidgets and motor mannerism are fine to do unless they interfere with others because they are loud or highly distracting.

2. Sometimes, only with students' permission, it is helpful to videotape the motor mannerism they engage in so they can determine if it is something they are comfortable doing in front of others and to reflect on whether it is interfering with anyone else.

3. **When the student is unable to control their mannerisms** as is the case with Tourette's syndrome, it is better to conduct a peer sensitivity lesson to help others to be more understanding of the behavior (see Chapter 12).

#28. TONE OF VOICE

Rationale: If we are too loud or too soft when we speak,
others may not want to continue to speak with us.

1. Use **just enough volume** in your voice so others can hear you.

    a. Your voice should be softer when you are inside and there are few other noises
    around. We call this an "inside voice."
    b. Your voice may need to be louder when you are outside or there are many other
    noises around.

2. Try not to speak **too fast** or others will not understand you.

3. Use a **pleasant tone** of voice instead of an angry tone.

Practice

Who will I try this with? _____

When? _____

What happened? _____

How did I do? _____

#28. TONE OF VOICE Activity Page

1. Model and role-play different types of voice tone. You can make this into a game by giving tokens or prizes for correct responses. Prizes can be given to the student acting out the tone of voice or to observers who accurately indicate whether the voice tone was appropriate for the situation.

   a. Have the student communicate a message to another using the appropriate **volume** for each of these situations.
      i. Inside the class or home where no one else is talking (quiet voice).
      ii. Inside the class or home where many others are talking (louder voice).
      iii. Inside the class or home where you are right next to the listener (quiet voice).
      iv. Inside the class or home where you are far from the listener (louder voice).
      v. Outside on the playground (louder voice).
      vi. Outside watching a performance where the audience is quiet (quiet voice).

   b. Have the student communicate a message using an **angry or pleasant** tone of voice. A pleasant tone usually has softer articulations of consonant sounds, whereas an angry tone usually uses a more staccato, precise pronunciation. Try recording the student so they can review the tones in the following situations:
      i. The student asks permission to go somewhere or have something (pleasant tone).
      ii. The student tells someone to stop yelling or hitting her (angry tone).

   c. Have the student communicate a message in a faster rather than slower pace. Again, use a recording so the student can review it. Make up intricate messages to see if others can hear and remember what the student said. Give points or prizes when the communication is received clearly.

2. Bait the skill. This means doing something that requires the student to use an appropriate tone.

   a. For example, purposely stand far away or create background noise to see if the student adjusts his volume.

SOCIAL SKILLS TRAINING

3. Provide corrective feedback when the student's tone is inappropriate.

4. Please note: speech production issues may make it more challenging to adjust pace and volume of tone of voice for some students. In this case it is often better to help others be more understanding of those students rather than force the students to adjust their tone.

Rationale: Greeting others shows that you are friendly. Not greeting others may make others think you do not like them.

1. The first time you see someone during the day, you say, "Hi, how are you?"

2. When you pass someone in the hallway, you say, "Hi."

3. When someone is leaving for the day, you say, "Goodbye."

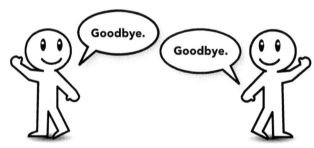

Practice

Who will I try this with? _____

When? _____

What happened? _____.

1. Model and role-play the skill using the following situations. Be sure to provide feedback on non-verbal cues such as smiling and use of a pleasant tone of voice when greeting others.

    a. Pretend it is the first time a student sees his teacher and classmates in the morning. Role-play the right way to say hello and good morning. Point out the wrong way, in which you either do not say hello or you say it over and over to the same person.
    b. Pretend to pass someone in the hallway. Practice saying "hello" or waving.
    c. Pretend it is the end of the school day or guests at your house are leaving. Role-play the right way to say "goodbye." Point out the wrong way, in which you either do not say goodbye or you say it over and over to the same person.

2. Bait the skill. Purposely walk close to the person first thing in the morning and do not say anything, waiting for them to say hello first. Do the same thing when they are leaving for the day and should say goodbye. If nothing is said, make the greeting and wait for them to respond. If nothing is said again, prompt them to make the greeting.

3. Provide corrective feedback when the student does not make a greeting.

4. Shyness can prevent individuals from greeting others. Help the individuals understand that some people may misinterpret their shyness as not being friendly. Help the individual find easier ways to say hello or goodbye, using nods and waves rather than verbal language if needed. Lastly, if they are unable to greet others, that is okay as long as they understand that others may ignore them. Sometimes students are upset when others do not talk to them and do not realize it is because they don't project a friendly appearance by greeting others.

Rationale: Sometimes we need to interrupt someone, but interrupting in the wrong way can make others annoyed.

1. Decide if you need to interrupt.

2. Walk up to the person or raise your hand if you are in a class and want to speak with a teacher.

3. If they are engaged in a conversation, WAIT for a pause in the conversation or WAIT for them to look at you. You may have to get closer and put your index finger up to get their attention. NOTE: YOU DO NOT HAVE TO WAIT IF YOU ARE REPORTING A DANGEROUS SITUATION.

4. Say, "Excuse me" or "Sorry to interrupt," then ask your question.

5. Do not interrupt if someone asks you to stop interrupting.

Practice

Who will I try this with? _____

When? _____

What happened? _____.

#30. INTERRUPTING Activities Page

1. Role-play the steps for INTERRUPTING. Suggested role-plays involve the following scenarios:

   a. Asking permission in class (e.g., to use bathroom, get a drink of water, borrow something).
   b. Needing help with something (e.g., schoolwork, getting a zipper up, tying a shoe, opening a jar).
   c. Being asked to be a messenger from one class to another or from one parent to another.
   d. Hearing people talking about something the student is interested in (e.g., a popular TV character, video game, weekend plans). After the student says, "Excuse me," they can say, "Were you talking about _____?" and then ask a question about it (see JOINING IN A CONVERSATION.)
   e. Coming to tell a parent or teacher about a dangerous situation (e.g., someone is hurt, something is on fire, a sibling ran away). Reinforce that the student should not wait but interrupt immediately in these situations.

2. Bait the skill. This means doing something that requires the student to interrupt.

   a. Take the student's pencil and then say, "Everyone, please take out a pencil."
   b. Purposely ignore when you see a child needing something so that the child must interrupt to ask for what he or she wants.

3. Correct inappropriate interrupting. Have student wait and then try interrupting again the right way.

4. Use visual supports for children who have great difficulty with this skill. Consider using:

   a. A red (stop) or green (go) card on your door or desk to indicate when it is safe for a child to interrupt you.

    b. Physical gestures, like holding your hand up or making a stop motion then a go motion, can help the child know when to approach you.

    c. Consider using a cue card that indicates how many times it's okay to interrupt a teacher or parent in a certain period of time. Or use a visual schedule to show when it's okay to interrupt (like right after class or when parents are off the phone).

5. Provide points/tokens towards rewards for following and rules shown on a behavior chart or cue card regarding INTERRUPTING. Example rules include "waits for a pause" or "waits to be called on" or "interrupts only three times per class period."

#31. TAKING TURNS TALKING (TWO-QUESTION RULE)

Rationale: If you do all the talking in a conversation, others may feel like you do not care about what they have to say. So it is important to take turns talking.

1. When others greet you, greet them back.
    If they say "Hello," then say "Hello" back to them.

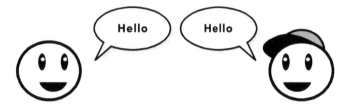

2. Two-question rule: When others ask you a
    question and you answer it, you can ask a
    similar question right back.

Practice

Who will I try this with? _____

When? _____

What happened? _____.

1. Role-play the steps for Taking Turns Talking. Suggested role-plays involve the following scenarios:

   a. Greet the students and prompt them to greet you back. Do the same for goodbyes.
   b. Ask them how they are and what they have been doing. After they respond, prompt them to ask back. Repeat with questions about future plans (e.g., what are you doing this weekend) and questions about the present (e.g., what are you playing, eating, doing?).
   c. Pick topics about which people have different preferences (e.g., movies, TV shows, food, school subjects). Prompt students to take turns sharing their preferences about each topic (e.g., "I like pizza, what food do you like?"). This activity can also be used to find out what students have in common as a basis for conversation and friendship.
   d. Use two colors of tokens, one for their questions and one for their answers. During conversations, dispense the tokens as students form questions and answers. The goal is for each student to have an equal number of tokens from each color.

2. Correct inappropriate turn taking by pointing out when one student dominates the conversation. Prompt them to ask others a question to maintain turn-taking.

3. Bait the use of the skill. Ask a student a question or share information about something you did and gesture for him or her to ask or share back. For example, say, "I went to the zoo this weekend." Instead of asking where the student went, simply wait for the student to share back what they did over the weekend.

#32. MAINTAINING A CONVERSATION

Rationale: Conversations involve taking turns talking back and forth. Asking the other person questions helps keep the conversation going.

1. Sometimes we answer others' questions and make comments. To keep the conversation going, we ask them "WH" questions to invite the others to speak.

ASK "WH" questions	Make comments
☺	☺
ASK	TELL
Who _____? Why _____? What _____? How _____? Where _____? What else ____? When _____?	I like _____. I am going _____. I also _____. My _____. I went _____.

2. Our comments and questions should be ON-TOPIC, meaning they are related to what the other person said. See example below where someone is responding to someone saying they **had fun going out to eat**.

On-Topic	Off-Topic
Where did you eat? What did you have? How was it? Who did you go with?	Where do you swim? How old is your brother?
I love going out to eat too.	I like flying kites.

Practice

Who will I try this with? _____

When? _____

What happened? _____.

1. To help with making comments and asking questions, use a visual support like the Maintaining a Conversation Chart in this section as a visual reminder of questions and comments. This chart is simply a prompt for starting sentences they can ask others. For students who cannot create their own sentences with these prompts alone, you may want to use flash cards with full sentences written on the cards for students to use.

    a. Only prompt students when they are stuck as you want them to learn how to generate questions. You might say, "Can you ask a 'wh' question?" then pause. If they need more help, then prompt, "Can you ask a 'who' question?" If they still need help, then prompt further, "Can you ask 'who' did you go with?"

2. For students who need help answering questions, you might use a conversation chart where you fill out answers to questions others may ask them, like "What did you do over the weekend?" and "Who did you go with?" and "What did you see there?" Fill out the answers to these questions, or use pictures for student who cannot read yet. Then when others ask them these questions, you can show them the conversation chart you filled out to help them answer. See example below:

Question	Answer
What did you do this weekend?	I went bowling
Who did you go with?	I went with my mom and sister.
How was it?	It was fun. I got two strikes.

3. Role-play MAINTAINING A CONVERSATION using the following scenarios:

    a. Do a show and tell where students can practice asking about some object you have shown them. Consider a musical instrument, special food, or a picture of a place you have visited or a past event. Have students take turns asking or telling about it.
    b. Try pairing students who have similar interests so they can discuss that motivating topic. Examples may include a show, video game, hobby, or place they both like to go.
    c. Have the student ask a parent, peer, or teacher about his or her day and try to keep the conversation on topic.
    d. Create a mystery bag with hidden items inside the bag (e.g., ball, food, other familiar items). Have the students ask questions or make comments until they can guess what is in the bag.
    e. Play a "guess who" game where someone pretends to be someone famous and the other person has to guess who they are by asking follow-up questions.
    f. Do a pretend interview of a famous person. One student will try to keep a conversation going with another student pretending to be a famous person. For example, if the famous person is a movie star, the other student can ask, "What's your new movie about?" or "Who is in your new movie with you?"

4. When practicing, consider using a point system where on-topic questions and comments earn points towards a rewards while off-topic questions and comments do not.

5. Correct off-topic comments by prompting an on-topic question or comment. See Shifting Topics for information on how and when to shift topics.

#33. STARTING CONVERSATIONS WITH PEOPLE YOU KNOW

Rationale: Starting conversations makes you look friendly.

1. Greet the person.
    Say "Hi" or "How are you?" the first time you see a person during the day.

2. Ask questions about what the person is doing in the PRESENT SITUATION.
    "What are you [doing] [talking about] [eating] [reading]?"
    "How do you like this [class, lunch, project, game]?"
    "Where did you get the cool [shirt, hat, sneakers, watch]?"

3. Ask questions about the PAST.
    "How was your [day, week, weekend, vacation, holiday]?"
    "Did you hear about [what happened in the news, the new TV show, a sports game]?"

4. Questions about the FUTURE.
    "What are you going to do [after school, this weekend, this week, for vacation]?"

5. Ask about one of **THE PERSON'S INTERESTS**. According to research, asking about something you already know the other person likes or does makes you more likeable to them. Examples:
    "How is soccer?" "How is your dog?" "Are you still playing the piano?" "What games are you playing lately?" "How is your job?"

6. Remember to ask follow-up questions and make on-topic comments.
    WHO, WHAT, WHERE, WHEN, WHY, HOW, WHAT ELSE ...?

Practice

Who will I try this with? _____

When? _____

What happened? _____.

#33. STARTING CONVERSATIONS WITH PEOPLE YOU KNOW Activity Page

1. Activities to review or generate CONVERSATION STARTERS include:

    a. Ask students what they would say to start a conversation in each of the situations listed at the bottom of this page. Use a quiz show format with points or play money for appropriate responses.

    b. When students are in their language arts classes, see if they can be assigned to write sentences and paragraphs that are conversation starters for various situations. In other words, when students are working on grammar or paragraph formation, they can also be working on CONVERSATION STARTERS.

    c. Make lists of people you know and things that they do. For example, write down what jobs they have, their hobbies or interests, and what classes they take. Use this as a basis for conversation starters. For example, if you know that a fellow group member likes basketball, then ask, "Have you seen any good basketball games lately?"

2. Role-play CONVERSTATION STARTERS. Suggested role-plays:

    a. Use the situations listed below or ask the students to tell you actual situations they have experienced. Let each conversation continue for several minutes so the students also work on maintaining a conversation.

    b. Play the conversation freeze game. Have students wander the room until the teacher/parent says freeze. Each student must then turn to the nearest student and ask one of the conversation starters. The teacher/parent can give them the question (e.g., "What are you going to do after school?"). Then they must exchange the information. The teacher/parent then asks each student what they learned from the other student. In this way the students must actually listen to each other. Points can be given out for remembering what their partner says. Then the teacher/parent can ask them to wander again until the next "freeze" where a new question will be posed to a new partner. The teacher/parent can do this daily with the same set of conversation starters until the students have memorized the questions.

c. A variant of the above game is to post conversation starters on posters in various places. Students are asked to go to an area with a partner and ask the conversation starter that is posted on the wall in that area. The teacher or parent then asks the students what they learned from their partner to test if they listened to each other (see Poster Summary Skill #39).

3. Bait the skill. This means doing something that requires your student to Start a Conversation.

a. For example, purposely stay quiet when you see the student for the first time during the day or when you have something in your hand you know might be interesting to the student (e.g., a picture of something, a new game, a book). Then prompt or wait for him to start the conversation.

4. Correct inappropriate ways to start a conversation, such as launching into a monologue about a subject of little interest to others. Prompt by saying, "First ask how the other person is doing or how she has been. Then ask if she wants to hear about what you want to talk about."

Situations for CONVERSATION STARTERS

Past:
1. You overhear someone talking about her vacation.
2. You see your friend on a Monday morning.
3. You see your classmates after a school break.
4. A friend just came back from taking a hard test.

Present:
5. You are eating lunch with your classmates.
6. You see someone playing on their phone.
7. You see someone wearing a T-shirt that has the name of a school on it.
8. You are in line at a movie theater and you see someone from school who is also in line.

Future:

9. It's Friday before school lets out for the weekend and you are with your classmates.

10. It's the end of the school day on Wednesday and you are saying goodbye to your friends.

11. You overhear your friends talking about their school break plans.

Others' Interests:

12. The other person has been talking recently about training their new dog.

13. The other person plays a sport regularly.

14. The other person has a job at a local library.

15. The other person likes to cook.

16. The other person loves playing video games.

17. The other person loves a particular television show.

18. The other person's mom was not feeling well last time you spoke to them.

#34. JOINING A CONVERSATION

Rationale: Joining in conversation makes others know you are friendly.

1. Listen to what the people are talking about to identify the topic of conversation.

2. Walk up to the people talking.

3. Wait for them to look at you or wait for a pause in their conversation.

4. Say, "Excuse me, were you talking about _____?"
    (Topic)

5. Ask a question about the topic:

    Who ... What ... When ... Where ... Why ... How ... What else?

Practice

Who will I try this with? _____

When? _____

What happened? _____.

How did I do? _____.

#34. JOINING A CONVERSATION Activity Page

1. Role-play the steps for JONING A CONVERSATION. Suggested role-plays involve the following scenarios:

   a. Have two students start a conversation about what they did over the weekend, or what they will do after school or group, or another topic you choose (e.g., favorite movies, sports teams, food, TV shows, something in the news, video game, vacation spot). Have a third student join the conversation by listening for the topic and asking or telling something relevant.

   b. Have a group conversation and prompt students to ask questions or make on-topic comments, thus participating in and joining the conversation. This can occur in a small group, where students review their week or discuss a specific topic such as those listed above.

2. Prompt those who withdraw from conversation to JOIN IN. Prompts can be simple (e.g., "Can you ask or tell something about what they are saying?") or more scripted (e.g., "They were talking about movies. Can you ask them what movie they liked best?").

3. Bait the use of the skill. Talk about their favorite topic or interest in front of them until they spontaneously join in with a question or comment.

4. To practice this in real life, have students first consider what groups of peers they might want to Join In with. Not all peers may be friendly so first identify peers that have proven themselves over time to be more accepting. Then choose a time, place, and loose script to try the skill.

#35. INTRODUCING TOPICS OF INTEREST TO OTHERS

Rationale: Introducing a topic can make you interesting to others.

1. When you want to tell someone something, wait for a good time to talk, like when there is a pause in the conversation or the person is not busy with something else.

2. Then ask if it is okay to talk. You could say:
   "Can I tell you something?"
   "Did you hear about...?"

3. Try to pick a topic that others might be interested in. Examples:

   a. Telling about something that **happened** to you or something you did recently.
   b. Telling about something that **happened in the news**, like a breaking story or a sporting event.
   c. Asking about something you might have in **common** with the other person. For example, discuss a TV show, game, place, or food you both like.
   d. Asking others for **advice or opinions** about something. For example, if you have a problem, ask others what they think you can do about it.

Practice

Who will I try this with? _____

When? _____

What happened? _____.

1. If you have a small group, have students first review different topic areas such as TV shows, foods, hobbies, books, games, sports, and school subjects. Find out which topics are common interests. Post a list of interests they have in common. This will serve as a basis for introducing interesting topics to each other.

2. For middle schoolers and older students, have them keep track of current news events in a journal. They can use this later as a basis for discussion.

3. Role-play the steps for INTRODUCING TOPICS OF INTEREST. Suggested role-plays involve the following scenarios:

   a. Have students introduce a common interest for discussion. Contrast this with students introducing a topic only of interest to them and lecturing others about it.
   b. Have students discuss an experience they had and then ask others if they ever had a similar experience. For example, "I went to the museum yesterday and saw _____ . Has anyone else ever gone to the museum?" Contrast this with talking about an experience without asking others anything and demonstrate how this could become one-sided.
   c. Have students introduce topics from the news. "Did you hear about…?"
   d. Have students ask other students for advice. They can ask advice on dealing with a school project, a conflict with a friend or parent, or even a potential dating situation.

4. Correct inappropriate introductions of topics when a student talks at others about their interest with little sensitivity to their audience. Redirect them to talk about a common interest, event, or experience or ask for advice.

#36. DON'T TALK TOO LONG

Rationale: When you talk for a long time or add too many details, listeners often become bored.

1. When you are talking about a topic, look at others' faces to see if they are interested or bored.

Bored   **Interested**

2. If they look bored, say, "Do you want to hear more?"

Do you want to hear more?

3. If they say no, stop talking or ask, "What do you want to talk about?"

What do you want to talk about?

4. If they say they don't mind hearing a little more, then give a brief one- to two-sentence summary of what you wanted to talk about without the details.

Practice

Who will I try this with? _____

When? _____

What happened? _____.

SOCIAL SKILLS TRAINING

#36. DON'T TALK TOO LONG Activity Page

1. It is equally important for both talkers and listeners to respond appropriately when practicing this skill. Talkers must read the signs of boredom and ask if others want to hear more, and listeners must politely indicate they do not want to hear more, shift the topic, or end the conversation (see skill on ENDING A CONVERSATION). If asked by the talker whether they want to hear more, listeners can be instructed to say, "Maybe another time," rather than saying, "No, I do not want to hear more."

2. The goal of this skill is not to inhibit students from talking about their interests, but rather to become more aware if they are going on too long OR they are talking to others who do not share those interests. Students should be encouraged to talk with others who share their interests when possible.

3. Role-play the steps for Talking Briefly. Suggested role-plays involve the following scenarios:

    a. Since some students with ASD have a tendency to talk obsessively about their interests, it may be useful to use their interest in the role-play. Pick an interest of one student's that is not shared by the other students and have them begin to talk. Have other students show interest and then show subtle signs of disinterest. Subtlety is important, as we do not want the listeners learning how to demonstrate extreme boredom. Have the student identify when the other listeners become bored and have them ask if they want to hear more. Prompt the listeners to say, "Maybe another time."

    b. Role-play the same situation above with the student starting a conversation as others indicate they have to leave. Often students may launch into a discussion when class or group is over. Help them to see that this is not the time to begin a lengthy discussion.

    c. If you have a small group discussion as a regular part of a group, you can do the following activity to demonstrate to certain members how much talking they actually do. Give out tokens for every comment or question made by each student.

At the end, review who has the most tokens. If one student has more than everyone else, then they may be doing too much talking. This exercise is often helpful for students who complain they do not get enough time to talk, not realizing that they dominate the conversation.

    d. Have students practice shortening their description of an experience into one to two sentences, leaving out details unless someone asks a follow-up question.

4. Correct lengthy talking by drawing the student's attention to their audience. Prompt them to ask others if they want to hear more and perhaps stop talking or ask the others a question to engage their interests.

5. Bait the use of the skill. As students are talking to you, begin to look slightly bored or fidgety until they ask you if you want to hear more.

#37. INTRODUCING YOURSELF AND OTHERS

Introducing Yourself

Rationale: When you are in the same location repeatedly with someone you do not know, it is polite to introduce yourself.

1. Decide if this is a person you want to meet. Will you be in the same class with them every week? Are you taking a long journey sitting next to them? Do you sit near them at lunch every day? Did they start a conversation with you?

2. Wait for a pause before talking.

3. Make eye contact and use a pleasant tone of voice.

4. Say, "My name is _____, what's your name?"

5. Then say, "It's a pleasure to meet you."

Introducing Others

Rationale: When you are with several people that you know, but they do not know each other, it is your job to introduce them to each other.

1. Say to Person #1, "_____, I would like you to meet _____."
   (Person #1)   *(Person #2)*

2. Say to Person #2, "_____, I would like you to meet _____."
   (Person #1)   *(Person #2)*

3. Then you can explain who each person is to you. For example, "_____ is my friend," or "_____ is my mother."

4. Sometimes we forget people's names. When that happens, you can tell the two people: "Do you already know each other?" If not, then say, "Oh, then you can introduce yourselves to each other."

Practice

Who will I try this with? _____

When? _____

What happened? _____.

1. Role-play the steps for INTRODUCTIONS. Suggested role-plays involve the following scenarios:

    a. Have students pretend to introduce themselves to new children in class, or to children they meet in the park, or in the cafeteria.
    b. Have students pretend to meet adult friends of their parents, teachers, or community leaders.
    c. Have students pretend to introduce their friends to their parents and vice versa.
    d. Have students pretend to introduce their old friends to some new friends.

2. Prompt students to introduce themselves to any new individual in class or at home. Also prompt students to refrain from introducing themselves to the same people more than once, or to strangers with whom they would have no basis to meet (e.g., they are not individuals who will be in the same location for an extended period).

3. Bait the use of the skill. Have new people purposely come to the classroom or to their home and then prompt the use of the skill.

#38. GETTING TO KNOW SOMEONE NEW

Rationale: Making new friends involves actively learning about new people.

1. Start the conversation by asking a question about something you see in the present moment or about something you might have in common with the person:

   a. Ask, "What are you [doing, reading, eating, playing]?"
   b. If you are in the same class or in the same place, ask, "So how do you like this [class, place]?"

2. Introduce yourself.

   a. Say, "By the way, my name is _____, what's your name?"

3. Ask questions to get to know the person.

Okay Topics	Okay Questions
SCHOOL	Where do you go to school? What grade are you in?
AGE (for kids only)	How old are you? (Do not ask an adult)
NEIGHBORHOOD	What town do you live in? Where do you live?
INTERESTS	What do you like to do for fun? What games do you like? What TV shows do you watch? What else do you like to do?
FAMILY	Do you have a big family? Do you have brothers and sisters? Do you have any pets?

4. Do not ask about "sensitive topics" unless the other person brings it up first. Sensitive topics are subjects that can make others upset. For example,

   a. Don't ask about someone's race or religion when you first meet them.
   b. Don't ask about something that makes the person look different or sound different.
   c. Don't ask the person about any problems she may have.

Practice

Who will I try this with? _____

When? _____

What happened? _____.

1. Expand on the rationale of this skill to build motivation. Some students are reluctant to take the initiative to meet new people. If they have friends, they may not need to. However, a recent Harvard study on what makes others happy found that social connection was one of the best predictors of happiness. Tracking folks for over eighty-five years, researchers found that those who actively sought out connection with others to maintain social connections were happiest.

2. Role-play the steps for GETTING TO KNOW SOMEONE NEW. Suggested role-plays involve the following scenarios:

    a. Have students pretend to meet a new child in class. They can start by asking how the new student likes the new class or school.
    b. Students can pretend to meet someone at the park, asking if they like the park or playground equipment they are using to begin (e.g., "Do you like the swings? Me too. My name is …").
    c. Students can pretend to meet someone in the cafeteria. They can begin with "What are you eating?" or "The lunchroom is pretty loud, right?"
    d. Students can pretend to meet someone at a party. They can begin with "So how do you know … ?" referring to the host of the party.

3. Prompt students to GET TO KNOW any new individual in class or at home. Correct the use of any sensitive topics during this first encounter.

4. Bait the use of the skill. Have new people purposely come to the classroom or to their home and then prompt the use of the skill.

#39. POSTER: SUMMARY OF STARTING AND MAINTAINING CONVERSATIONS

Getting to Know New People

Name: What's your name? Mine is _____.

Town: Where are you from? Where are you living now?

School: Where do you go to school? What are you studying?

Work: What kind of work do you do or want to do?

Fun: What do you like to do for fun? Hobbies, TV, movies, books, places they like to go, games, sports, food.

Family: Do you have a big family? Parents, siblings, or pets?

Talking with People You Know

Tell: Guess what (something you did)?
Did you hear (some news you heard about)?

Past: How was your _____ (week, weekend, day, vacation)?

Present: What are you _____ (doing, reading, working on, eating)?

Future: What are you going to do _____ (after group, this weekend, over vacation)?

Interests: How is _____ (something they are interested in or they do like work, hobbies, sports, or a common interest)?

Keep Conversations Going

ASK		TELL	
Who _____?	Why _____?	Ah huh.	I also _____
What _____?	How _____?	I see.	I never _____
Where _____?	What else ____?	I like _____	My _____
When _____?			

#40. CONVERSATION REPAIR: SAYING I DON'T KNOW, I DON'T UNDERSTAND, AND GIVING BACKGROUND INFORMATION

Rationale: Sometimes there is a breakdown of communication where one person does not understand what the other person said. In order to be friendly, it is best not to blame anyone for the communication problem but rather to do something to fix the problem. These are several repair strategies.

1. **SAYING I DON'T KNOW:** When others ask you questions that you do understand, but you do not know what the answer is, say, "I don't know" or "Let me think about it" if you need more time to think about the answer. Do not just keep silent; let the other person know that you are thinking about it or do not know the answer.

2. **ASKING A QUESTION WHEN YOU DON'T UNDERSTAND:** When you do not understand what someone is saying, you should say, "I do not understand." If the person repeats what he or she said and you still do not understand, then you can say, "I still do not understand. Can you explain it in a different way?" or ask someone else to explain it to you.

3. **GIVING ENOUGH BACKGROUND INFORMATION:** Since other people do not know all that you know, you may have to give background information about what you are saying. The background information you give depends on how much information the other person may have. For example, your grandmother may not know about a new online game you play, but a peer who has played the game will know what it is if you begin discussing the game by its name. As a general guideline:

    a. If you are talking about people, explain who they are. Is it a FRIEND, FAMILY MEMBER, TEACHER, OR A FAMOUS PERSON?
    b. If you are talking about a thing, explain what it is. Is it a GAME, TV SHOW, PLACE, OR TOY?

4. **WHEN YOUR PARTNER DOES NOT UNDERSTAND:** If you express an idea and the other person does not seem to understand, then try to restate what you said using other words.

Practice

Who will I try this with? _____

When? _____

What happened? _____.

#40. CONVERSATION REPAIR: SAYING I DON'T KNOW, I DON'T UNDERSTAND, AND GIVING BACKGROUND INFORMATION Activity Page

These are four skills that all share a common theme: repairing communication breakdowns. The most important part to teach is that each of us should try to fix the problem without getting mad or blaming the other person.

1. **Ideas for modeling and role-plays:**
   a. **Saying I don't know.** These are questions that perhaps one understands but does not know the answer to:
      i. Where is your mother right now?
      ii. Who do you think will win the World Series this year?
      iii. Who was the first person to fly across the Atlantic Ocean?
   b. **Saying I don't understand.** These are questions where one may not understand what is being asked, such as:
      i. Someone asking you to do something in a foreign language.
      ii. A vague question like "Can you grab that?" in which the person gives no indication of what to grab.
      iii. A question in a field that you do not know much about, so the question is hard to understand, like "If the Heisenberg Principle is correct, then can we really know the activity of sub-atomic particles?"
   c. **Giving background information:** Students can play a game where they talk about something without saying what it is and others have to figure out what they are talking about. These are sample situations in which one should provide more background information:
      i. Saying that Phil and Eileen are coming over to the house (without explaining who they are to those who do not know them). In real life, these are my in-laws.
      ii. Telling someone who does not know about camera technology that you bought a 7.2-megapixel digital one with a docking station.
      iii. Saying you like it with mushrooms and peppers (without saying you are talking about pizza).

        iv. Indicating you are going to get a hybrid (without indicating you are talking about a car).

    d. **When your partner does not understand.** These are situations in which the student can say, "Let me say that differently."

        i. Any of the situations from the "giving background information" can be used to practice.

        ii. Explaining something using overly complicated vocabulary such as "I believe my epidermis is blemished with crimson blotches due to the beta ray exposure." (Translation: I think my skin is freckled from the sun).

2. **Prime** the student before the following situations in which the students may need to use these skills:

    a. Attending challenging classes where they may not understand or know the answer to many questions

    b. Expressing complicated concepts to others (e.g., teaching, presenting in front of a class, participating in a group project, speaking with other individuals who do not share the same knowledge base)

3. Daily life offers many opportunities for communication breakdowns. However, to create more opportunities, parents or teachers can **bait** the students to use these skills by:

    a. Asking questions that the student does not know the answer to

    b. Asking questions or giving directions that are overly complicated so that the student will need to ask for clarification

    c. Pretending not to know about someone or something the student is talking about so they have to fill in the background information

    d. Pretending not to understand what the student is saying so they have to explain it again

#41. SHIFTING TOPICS

Rationale: Shifting topics too quickly can make others
think you do not care about what they are saying.

1. Wait for the right time to change the topic. This includes:

   a. When the other person stops talking or says they are done.
   b. After the other person had a chance to talk about a topic and you showed interest by asking **at least one follow-up question**.

2. Prepare the other person for a change in topic by asking if it is okay to change the topic or by using a transition phrase.

   a. Examples of ways to **ask if it is okay** to change the topic.
      "Can I change the topic?"
      "Can I talk about something else?"

   b. Examples of transition phrases:
      "By the way, did you hear about ...?"
      "Speaking of ..." (Here you are referring to something the other person said and using it to start a new topic.)

3. Begin discussing the new topic.

Practice

Who will I try this with? _____

When? _____

What happened? _____.

#41. SHIFTING TOPICS Activity Page

1. Practice creating transition statements to get from one topic to another. Give students a list of two topics and have them compose the transition statement. This requires finding a category that both topics can belong to. For example:

    a. Going to the zoo to going to a museum (say, "Speaking of trips …")
    b. Watching a baseball game to playing soccer (say, "Speaking of sports …")
    c. Being teased to having a test (say, "Speaking of stressful experiences …")

2. Model and role-play the steps for SHIFTING TOPICS. Suggested role-plays involve the following scenarios:

    a. You were not listening to your friends, so you have no idea what they were saying, but you desperately wanted to tell them about a new computer you got. (Hint: try to listen and ask a question about what they said first or at least wait for a pause, then ask to switch the topic.)
    b. Someone is talking about a movie you are not really interested in, and you would rather talk about a movie you liked. (Hint: remember to ask or comment positively about their movie before transitioning to yours.)
    c. Pretend others are talking about a topic like their favorite TV shows and you want to talk about what you are going to do over the weekend.
    d. Role-play it again asking permission to change the topic, but do not wait for the topic to end. In other words, keep shifting the topic without asking any questions about the former topic as if you are not interested. Discuss the importance of waiting before shifting the topic.

3. Correct abrupt shifts in conversations. Prompt students to wait until a pause, then make a transition statement or ask to talk about something else.

4. Prime students ahead of time to use the skill when entering a room where people have already been talking.

SOCIAL SKILLS TRAINING

#42. ENDING A CONVERSATION

Rationale: Ending a conversation too quickly can
make others think you do not care about them.

1. Decide if you need to end the conversation.

    a. Is it because you have to do something else or because you are late in getting
       somewhere?
    b. Is it because you are bored?

2. Ask one more follow-up question or make one more on-topic comment to show you
    care about what the person is saying. For example, say, "I hear what you are saying."

3. Decide what to say to end the conversation.

    a. If you are late, say, "I am sorry but I have to go because I am late."
    b. If you have to do something else, say, "Well, I have to go because I have other
       things I am supposed to do."
    c. If you are bored, do not tell the other person you feel bored. Make an excuse that
       you have other things to do. Say, "I am sorry but I have to go because I have other
       things to do now."

4. Say, "See you later," and then leave or walk away.

Practice

Who will I try this with? _____

When? _____

What happened? _____.

#42. ENDING A CONVERSATION Activity Page

1. Model and role-play the steps for ENDING A CONVERSATION. Suggested role-plays involve the following scenarios:

   a. A student is talking with another student about their favorite video game, food, movie, TV show, sport, or other activity. One student realizes he is late for class.
   b. Two students discuss one of the topics above. One of the students begins to go on and on about his interests while the other student gets bored. The bored student must end the conversation appropriately.
   c. This time, one of the students has homework that he will not be able to finish unless he stops talking. He must end the conversation appropriately.

2. Correct inappropriate or abrupt endings. Have the student show interest with a question and then make an appropriate excuse to end the conversation.

3. Bait the use of the skill. Purposely talk on and on in a boring way or start talking when the student wants to play or leave, then prompt the appropriate ending.

#43. ANSWERING THE TELEPHONE

Say "Hello."

↓

Get their name. "Who is calling, please?"

↓

Find out why they are calling. "Who are you trying to reach?"

You	Someone who is home	Someone who is out	They are a salesperson
(Use this format for receiving a text as well as a call)			
Say, "Hi, how are you? So what's going on?"	Say, "Hold on, I will go get them." Put the phone down.	Say, "They cannot come to the phone right now, can I take a message?"	Say, "Sorry, I am not interested."
Ask follow-up questions and make on-topic comments.	Go tell the person at home that they have a telephone call from _____. Don't yell this information from another room.	Say, "Hold on, I need to get a pen and paper." Ask for their name, telephone number, and any **message** that they want to leave.	Don't give them any information about you or your family.
When you want to get off the phone, wait for a pause and explain, "Sorry, but I have to go do some other things right now. It was good to talk with you. Talk to you later." Then wait for them to say goodbye before you hang up.	Give the phone to the person at home.	Repeat the message to them to check if it is right. Say, "Let me make sure I got this right." If they say it's right then say, "Okay, goodbye." Wait for them to say "goodbye" before you hang up.	Say, "Goodbye." Then hang up the phone.

Practice

Who will I try this with? _____

When? _____

What happened? _____.

#44. CALLING A FRIEND ON THE TELEPHONE

Say hello and give your name. "Hello, this is _____ calling."

↓

Ask for your friend. "Is _____ there?"

If you friend is home
(Use this script for texting as well as calling)

Say, "Hi, how are you?

Say why you called.
"I wanted to ask you something."
"I wanted to know if you wanted to get together."
"I was bored and just wanted to talk with you."

Keep the conversation going with a new topic:
"So what have you been doing lately?"
"So what are you doing now?"
"So what are you going to be doing _____?"
"Did you hear about _____?"
Ask and tell to keep it going.

When you want to get off the phone, wait for a pause and then say, "I have to go do some other things right now. It was good to talk with you. Talk to you later."
Then wait for them to say goodbye before you hang up.

If your friend is not there

Say, "Can I leave a message?"

If they say yes, give them your name and telephone number and any message you want to leave.

"This is _____ and my telephone number is _____. Please tell _____ that I called."

Wait for them to say okay or that they got the message. Then say, "Thank you. Goodbye now."

Practice

Who will I try this with? _____

When? _____

What happened? _____.

#43 and 44. PHONE CALLS Activity Page

1. **Explain** the importance of talking on the phone to reach career and personal goals. Making phone calls is typically an important part of maintaining friendships and conducting business in the job world. Validate for students that most people are somewhat anxious calling people they do not know, but the more they practice using the phone, the more comfortable they will get. This same skill can be modified slightly to text friends. Sometimes it is more polite to text friends on their personal cell phones rather than call them as it is less intrusive. One can text first to see if it is an okay time to call them.

2. **Model and role-play the skill steps.** Have conversation pairs practice in the same room but with their backs to each other so they cannot see each other (as is the case with typical phone calls). Remember to demonstrate appropriate beginnings and endings to conversations. The following are situations that can be used:

   a. You call up a friend to ask about a work assignment and your friend is not home (practice leaving a message).
   b. You call up a friend to ask about a work assignment and your friend is home (practice getting the requested information and having a brief conversation).
   c. You call a friend just to talk.
   d. You answer the phone at home and take a message from someone trying to reach your parent.
   e. You answer the phone, and it is your friend calling to ask to get together.

3. **Priming and practicing in real life:** When students set out to practice making or receiving a phone call, they can have with them a copy of these skills at hand since the other person on the phone will not notice. They should use this visual before making or when expecting a phone call or text.

#45. Use Your H.E.A.D. When You Are Involved in a Conversation

Rationale: Sometimes it is useful to have an acronym to remember what to do in a conversation.

 APPY VOICE: Use a happy, medium volume voice when having a conversation. Don't scream or whisper.

 YE CONTACT: Look at people's eyes at least occasionally when talking or listening to them.

 LTERNATE: Alternate between talking and listening. Take turns talking.

 ISTANCE: Keep about an arm's length away from people when talking. Don't be a "Space Invader" by getting too close.

Practice

Who will I try this with? _____

When? _____

What happened? _____.

1. For many students with good verbal rote memories, the acronym H.E.A.D. can remind them of several important skills related to having a conversation. All of the skills embedded in this acronym appear as separate skills elsewhere in the book. For example, "happy voice" is the skill entitled TONE OF VOICE, "eye contact" is part of the LISTENING POSITION skill, "distance" is part of the DON'T BE A SPACE INVADER skill, and "alternate" is part of the TWO-QUESTION RULE. The decision on whether to teach these skills separately or all together using the acronym H.E.A.D. should be based on the student's verbal rote memory and subsequent desire to use acronyms to guide behavior.

2. Role-play each part of this skill:

   a. **Happy Voice** (see TONE OF VOICE)
      Consider using a tape recorder so students can hear themselves trying each of the following types of voice.
      i. Use an "outside" (high volume) rather than an "inside" (regular volume) voice.
      ii. Use an angry rather than a pleasant tone of voice.
      iii. Use a fast or slow rather than an appropriate pace of speech.

   b. **Eye Contact** (see LISTENING POSITION)
      i. Make eye contact in class to the teacher.
      ii. Make eye contact to a peer in conversation.
      iii. Make eye contact when greeting others and saying goodbye.

   c. **Alternate** (see TWO-QUESTION RULE)
      i. Role-play exchanging greetings (e.g., say, "Hi" and ask the student to say "Hi" back).
      ii. Role-play conversation starters (e.g., ask the student what she did over the weekend and prompt her to ask back).

iii. Tell a story about what you are going to do after school and prompt students to tell you what they will do after school.

d. **Distance** (See DON'T BE A SPACE INVADER)
   i. Role-play getting too close and too far. Have students give you a thumbs-up sign when you are an "okay" distance apart and a thumbs-down sign when you are too far.
   ii. Show the right and wrong distances when using a greeting.
   iii. Show the right and wrong distances when discussing the past weekend.
   iv. Show the right and wrong distances when discussing after-school plans.

3. Use a game-show format to quiz students about what each letter stands for and examples of each. For example, ask what the "H" stands for in H.E.A.D. and ask for an example. Give tokens or fake money for right answers. Make sure everyone gets to respond and earns a prize.

4. Consider videotaping students practicing using the acronym H.E.A.D. while conversing with a partner. Then have them review if they did each step of H.E.A.D.

#46. T.G.I.F.
(Means more than "Thank Goodness It's Friday." It's about Having a Conversation)

Rationale: Sometimes an acronym can remind us of the steps to start and maintain a conversation.

T

IMING: The time to start a conversation is when the other person is not talking or there is a pause in their conversation.

G

REETING: A greeting is the first thing you say to someone when beginning a conversation.

Hi.   Hello.   What's up?   How are you?

I

NITIAL QUESTION: An initial question is something you ask to start a conversation about a particular topic.

How was your __?   What are you __?   What will you be __?   Did you __?

F

OLLOW-UP QUESTIONS: These are the questions you ask to get more information about a topic and to keep the conversation going.

Who?   What?   What else?   Where?   When?   How?   Why?

Practice

Who will I try this with? _____

When? _____

What happened? _____.

1. For many students with good verbal rote memories, the acronym T.G.I.F. can remind them of several important skills related to having a conversation. All the skills embedded in this acronym appear as separate skills and are covered in more detail elsewhere in the book. For example, "Timing" is like the skill INTERRUPTING, "Greeting" is covered separately in the skill by the same name, "Initial Question" is dealt with in more detail in the skill called STARTING A CONVERSATION, and "Follow-Up Question" is covered more fully in the skill MAINTAINING A CONVERSATION. The decision on whether to teach these skills separately or all together using the acronym T.G.I.F. should be based on the student's verbal rote memory and subsequent ability to use acronyms to guide behavior.

2. Role-play each part of this skill:

   a. **Timing**
      - Demonstrate by waiting versus interrupting an ongoing conversation to ask how others are doing.
      - Demonstrate by saying hello to someone who has just taken a break from work versus when they are busy working.

   b. **Greeting**
      - Role-play starting a conversation with someone you see for the first time during the day with and without saying hello.

   c. **Initial Question**
      - Role-play starting conversations about the past, present, future, or their interests (see skill STARTING CONVERSATIONS for greater detail on role-plays).

   d. **Follow-Up Questions**
      - Role-play keeping the conversation going with questions and comments that are on-topic (see MAINTAINING A CONVERSATION for more role-play ideas).

3. Use a game-show format to quiz students about what each letter stands for and examples of each. For example, ask what the "T" stands for in T.G.I.F. and ask for an example. Give tokens or fake money for right answers. Make sure everyone gets to respond and earns a prize.

4. Consider videotaping students practicing using T.G.I.F. to start a conversation with a partner. Then have them review if they did each step of T.G.I.F.

#47. ASKING SOMEONE TO PLAY

Rationale: Playing with others helps you make friends, and there are some games you cannot play alone.

1. Decide if you want to play with someone.

2. Find something to play that you both may like.

3. Walk up to the person.

4. Wait for a pause or for them to look at you.

5. Ask, "Do you want to play with me?"

6. If they say, "No," then ask someone else, try a different game, or ask an adult to help you.

Practice

Who will I try this with? _____

When? _____

What happened? _____.

#47. ASKING SOMEONE TO PLAY Activity Page

1. Model and role-play the steps for ASKING SOMEONE TO PLAY. Suggested role-plays:
   a. Pretend it is snack, free-play, or recess time at school and no one has started playing yet. Have the child initiate play with someone. Have the recipient say yes and also no sometimes so that student must remember to ask someone else or get another game.
   b. Extend the role-play above to the point where no child will play any game and the child must seek the teacher's help rather than express anger at the other children, thereby risking loss of friendship.
   c. Pretend it's a playdate at someone's house. Role-play selecting games that the other child really likes and games that the other child does not like to highlight the importance of choosing games that both enjoy.
   d. Pretend that children are busy reading or finishing their work in school. Role-play waiting until they are done with their work versus asking them to play in the middle of their work.

2. Bait the skill. This means doing something that requires the student to initiate play. For example, purposely display an interactive game that the child really likes in front of him without asking to play. If he does not ask to play, prompt him to ask. For example, say, "If you want to play, ask me to play the game with you."

3. Correct inappropriate ways of asking others to play, such as demanding that others play or insisting on playing games that others do not like. Also prompt students who sit on the periphery, fearful of asking others to play.
   IMPORTANT NOTE: If you are going to encourage shy students to ask others to play, direct them to students whom you have previously coached to accept such offers (see Chapter 12 for details on peer sensitivity training).

4. Social anxiety can prevent a child from initiating play. It may be helpful to break down initiating play into smaller goals on a fear ladder (see skill on managing social anxiety). Perhaps at first just target playing with peers after the teacher or parent facilitates the play. Then try having the other students initiate, and then finally have the targeted student try initiating. We can provide rewards for each step towards ASKING SOMEONE TO PLAY.

48. JOINING OTHERS IN PLAY

Rationale: Joining in the right way can help you to play the game you want and to feel like part of things.

1. Walk up to the people playing a game you like.

2. Wait for a pause or for them to look at you. You may need to get closer and raise your finger up to get them to look at you.

3. Say something nice about what they are doing.

That looks fun!

That's cool!

4. Ask if you can play too.

Can I play too?

5. If they say, "No," then ask someone else.

Practice

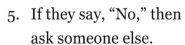

Who will I try this with? _____

When? _____

What happened? _____.

#48. JOINING IN PLAY Activity Page

1. Model and role-play the steps for JOINING IN PLAY. Suggested role-plays:

   a. Have two children play a recess game (e.g., two-square) and a third student wanting to join in. Have students say yes to join in and sometime also no, so the student has to remember to go ask someone else.
   b. Have siblings invite friends over to play a game. Have the student ask to join in.
   c. Have peers play a game with a teacher, and have the student ask to join in.

2. Bait the skill. This means doing something that requires the student to join in. For example, purposely play something that they really like in front of them without asking them to join in. Prompt or wait for them to ask to join in.

3. Correct inappropriate ways to join in, such as barging in on a game and taking over. Also prompt students who sit on the periphery, fearful of joining in.
   IMPORTANT NOTE: If you are going to encourage shy students to join in, direct them to students whom you have already coached to allow the student to join in to ensure success.

4. Social anxiety can prevent a child from joining in play. In this case it is helpful to break down joining in play into smaller goals on a fear ladder (see skill on managing social anxiety). Perhaps at first just target playing with peers after the teacher or parent facilitates the play. Then try having the other students ask the child to join in, and then finally have the targeted child try to join in. We can provide rewards for each step towards JOINING IN PLAY.

#49. COMPROMISE

Rationale: Compromising allows people to get along well.
Demanding people do things all your way can push others away.

1. Find out what the other person wants to do.

   What do you want to do? Soccer?

2. Tell the other person what you want to do.

   I want to play baseball.

3. COMPROMISE: Offer to do some of what the other person wants and some of what you want to do.

   Let's play soccer and then a little baseball.

4. When you are alone, you can do things all your way, but when you are with others, it is best to compromise.

Practice

Who will I try this with? _____

When? _____

What happened? _____.

#49. COMPROMISING Activity Page

1. Model and role-play the steps for COMPROMISING. Suggested role-plays:

   a. Two children both want to play with the same toy. (Hint: take turns.)
   b. Two children are going to play together but they both want to play different games. (Hint: play a little of both.)
   c. Siblings are arguing over who will get to watch what they want on TV. (Hint: take turns or see if there are two TVs.)
   d. Two children want the last piece of cake. (Hint: Split it.)

2. Bait the skill. This means doing something that requires the student to compromise. For example, purposely say you want to do something other than what the student wants to do and say, "I wonder if we could compromise."

3. Correct demands by the student to have it all their way. Have the student suggest a compromise.

4. Because this is a difficult skill where individuals must accept not getting all that they want, it may be helpful to provide points towards rewards for appropriate COMPROMISING.

SOCIAL SKILLS TRAINING

Rationale: To get along with others, it is important to find a fair way to decide what to play or work on when in a group. If your goal is to make friends, it is more important to get along than to get your way all the time.

How to make decisions when working on a group project

1. Allow each person to say their idea for the game or work project

    a. Say what you want to do.
    b. Don't insult others' ideas. If you do not like someone's idea, say, "That's an interesting idea, but I think this is better because ..."

2. Discuss which ideas you like and be willing to compromise. Remember, it is more important to get along than to make everyone select your idea. In order to get along, you might:

    a. Combine everyone's ideas.
    b. You can try to convince others of your idea in a respectful way. "I like your idea, but I think this is even better because ..."
    c. Offer to do someone else's idea.

3. Take a vote on what idea(s) to select and go with the group.

    a. If the majority wants one idea, but you want something else, then go with the majority unless their idea is dangerous.

Roles you might select as you make decisions together

In a group, each person can play a particular role for the group to function. The following lists some of the roles you might play when participating in a group. There can be more than one person for each role, but all roles must be filled for the group to function.

- **Leaders:** The leaders *do not* decide what ideas to do; the leaders only keeps everyone focused on the task of deciding what to do.

- **Idea contributors:** Everyone should be an idea contributor, telling others their thoughts and ideas.

- **Record keepers:** They keep notes of ideas so the group can come back to the play or work at a later time and remember what they were doing.

1. **Explain** the rationale for focusing on the goals individuals have. Do they want to get along and be accepted by others or simply impose their will on others? Explain how they can get all that they want when they're alone, but to stay part of a group, they must also get along.

2. **Model** the process of making decisions in group. As an example, pretend that a group is deciding on a pretend role-play game at recess where animals escape from the zoo and scare people in their homes, while a zookeeper must catch them. Decisions about who plays the animals, zookeeper, and homeowners must be made. They can take turns playing these roles as a way of compromising. Also, they can vote on what kind of animals will escape and how to catch them.

3. Break up students into groups of two or three. **Role-play** the process of making group decisions by using the following activities. In each activity, make sure students identify who will be a record keeper and keep track of everyone's ideas, as well as combined ideas and the final selected idea. Each activity can take several sessions to complete, so it is advised that students do only a portion of each activity in each session.

    a. Decide what a group of friends will do when they hang out together.
        i. Start by coming up with ideas for activities: restaurant, movies, sports, gaming.
        ii. Discuss what most people like to do and if anyone objects to certain activities. Consider ones that all may be able to tolerate.
        iii. Then vote on which activities to do.

    b. Come up with a commercial for a new imaginary invention. (Three-session project).
        i. Come up with the name.
        ii. Decide what it does.
        iii. Create a story board for the commercial. For example, first an announcer introduces the product and explains what it does, then customers demonstrate how it works, then another announcer tells how and where to get the product.

      iv. Decide on who will act out which parts.

      v. Perform the commercial.

   c. Create a short film or movie.

      i. Come up with the idea for the movie.

      ii. Come up with a story board.

      iii. Decide who will play what part.

      iv. Rehearse and then perform for the camera.

4. **Prime and practice in real life:** Students should be primed to use these steps before arranging group get-togethers and before doing group projects. In schools, this means teachers should be informed of these skill steps to describe to their students before assigning group projects. It is especially important to stress "getting along" more than "getting your way." Teachers may want to consider giving extra credit to groups that show cooperation instead of extra credit for the content of the work.

5. **Review:** Students should be redirected to the skill steps whenever they begin to argue, insult other students, or refuse to work with others.

Rationale: Sharing with others makes you look friendly and makes it more likely that others will share with you.

1. Remember, others might share their things with you if you share with them.

2. Offer to share something you have.

3. Ask to share something they have. Don't just take it.

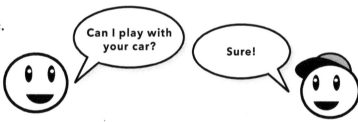

Practice

Who will I try this with? _____

When? _____

What happened? _____.

1. Model and role-play the steps for SHARING. Suggested role-plays:

   a. Two children (peers or siblings) both want to play with the same set of building blocks or some other toy in the classroom or at home. (Hint: this involves sharing and taking turns.)
   b. One child wants to play with a game that the other child owns at home or in school. He must ask before taking, and the other child should share or indicate a time when he will share it.
   c. Students (or siblings) do an art project without having separate materials so that they must share.
   d. During snack time, one student has nothing to eat. He must ask rather than take while others practice sharing.

2. Bait the skill.

   a. Have students (or siblings) do an art project without giving separate materials to each. Have only one set of markers, one glues, etc., so that they must share.
   b. Give out snacks and pretend to run out, forcing people to share with each other. In case they do not share, have enough snacks on hand.

3. Correct unwillingness to share. Some children will more readily share materials or toys when they are told that it is temporary and that they will get the materials right back again.

4. **Note:** Some children may be able to share better if they are given a set of their own materials labelled with their name on it and then told that there are other materials labelled as "group materials" that are for sharing.

5. Because it is difficult to share, some children will do well to receive points towards a reward for SHARING. This will offset the sense of loss they experience from sharing.

#52. TAKING TURNS

Rationale: Giving others a turn helps you to make friends with others.

1. Taking turns means you let other people play with something while you wait. Then you play while they wait.

First she has a turn on the computer while he waits.

Then he has a turn on the computer while she waits.

2. You may have to wait, but you will win a friend if you take turns.

Practice

Who will I try this with? _____

When? _____

What happened? _____.

#53. DECIDING WHO GOES FIRST

Rationale: Coming up with a fair way to decide who goes first can help you stay friends with others.

1. Try letting others go first as it will make you seem friendly.

2. If you do not want to let others go first, then pick a way to decide who will go first:
   a. **Play "Rock, Scissors, Paper, Shoot."** This is appropriate for two people. In this game, each person forms a rock, scissors, or paper with their right hand behind their back. After saying "rock, scissors, paper, shoot," they simultaneously show their hand to the other. Rock beats scissors, scissors beats paper, paper beats rock.
   b. **Play "The odd finger is it."** This is appropriate for more than two people. In this game, everyone forms one or two fingers behind their back. After they say, "the odd finger is it," all show their hands. The person who has a different number of fingers out than everyone else gets to go first. Keep playing until only one person has a different number of fingers than everyone else.
   c. **Toss a coin.** This works for two people. One person calls heads or tails while the coin is in the air.
   d. **Play "Eeny, meany, miny, moe, catch a tiger by the toe, if he hollers, let him go, eeny meany, miny, moe."** Here someone points to each player in turn while saying each word. The person who is being pointed to at the last word (moe) gets to go first.

3. Next time you play a game, someone else gets to go first. If you wait your turn, the other person will be happy and want to play with you.

Practice

Who will I try this with? _____

When? _____

What happened? _____.

#52 and 53. TAKING TURNS and DECIDING WHO GOES FIRST Activity Page

1. Model and role-play the steps for TAKING TURNS and DECIDING WHO GOES FIRST. These skills go together because part of taking turns involves deciding who gets to go first. Children can decide whether to just let others go first or to use a fair way to decide. Suggested role-plays:

    a. Two or more children want to use the one computer available at home or in school.
    b. Two or more children want to use some playground equipment that only one person can go on at a time.
    c. Children need to decide who will go first in a board game. They then need to decide what color or game piece they will be using.
    d. Role-play the same items above, but pretend it is another day, and the person who went first the previous day should now go second or last.

2. Bait the skill. Pretend you want something that the student is about to ask for so that you must take turns. Pretend you want to go first or you want the special game piece that the student wants so you must use a fair means to decide.

3. Correct those who don't give others a turn. Remind them that giving others a turn is temporary; they will get to play again or go first the next time.

4. Because this skill involves "giving up" something desirable, some children will benefit from getting points towards rewards for appropriate TURN-TAKING.

#54. PLAYING A GAME

Rationale: In order to avoid arguments, it is helpful
to play games by a common set of rules.

1. Find out the rules of the game.
    a. "What is the object of the game?"
    b. "How do you play?" Agree on the rules before playing to avoid arguments.

2. Decide who goes first.
    a. Let others go first to make friends.
    b. Decide through a game of chance, like flipping a coin, rolling dice, or playing "Rocks, Paper, Scissors, Shoot."

3. Wait your turn during the game.

Practice

Who will I try this with? _____

When? _____

What happened? _____

#54. PLAYING A GAME Activity Page

1. Model and role-play the steps for PLAYING A GAME. Suggested role-plays:
   a. You can use any standard board game to work through the skill steps.
   b. You can have students take turns making up a new rule for a standard game until you have a new game. This requires that they pay close attention to the rules and allows them to become more flexible in their willingness to play new games. You may want to give examples of new rules so that they have a template to make their own rules. For example, one can play tag where multiple persons are "it" and you have any number of "safe" zones where you cannot get tagged. Or one can play checkers where you can jump others backwards and forwards even before getting a King.

2. Bait the skill.
   a. Start playing a standard game and do not tell students the rules unless they ask. Keep changing the rules until they protest, then remind them to get the rules prior to the game.
   b. As you play, insist on going first and occasionally go when it is not your turn unless anyone protests. Then prompt others to take turns fairly.

3. Correct lack of turn-taking or forgetting to get the rules.

4. Some children will have difficulty accepting new rules to a game. It may be helpful to initially provide points towards a reward in those cases.

#55. DEALING WITH LOSING

Rationale: Being a good sport helps you to make and stay friends.

1. Say to yourself: "It's only a game, there will be other games."

2. Remember, although you lost the game, you can win a friendship (which is more important) if you show good sportsmanship.

3. To show good sportsmanship, you should tell the other person:

    "Congratulations"   "Good game"   "You played a good game"

4. Shake the other person's hand and help him put away the game or materials.

Practice

Who will I try this with? _____

When? _____

What happened? _____.

#55. DEALING WITH LOSING Activity Page

1. To teach this skill, parents and teachers may need to temporarily exaggerate the idea that losing calmly is better than winning a game. Adults should remind students just before they play a game that they are more interested in how the students deal with losing than whether they win the game. As the game is played, the adult can anticipate which child is losing and remind them that if they do not get mad, they will win a friend and can receive a reward for staying calm. The adult should show little enthusiasm when someone wins, and show great enthusiasm when someone deals well with losing.

2. Model and role-play the steps for DEALING WITH LOSING. Suggested role-plays involve short games so that the skill can be practiced without waiting for a long game to end:

   a. Use a coin toss (heads or tails) or "odds or evens" (each student puts out one or two fingers after one child calls "odds" or "evens") to decide who will go first. Whoever loses should be coached through the steps of DEALING WITH LOSING. The one who lost is applauded for staying calm.

   b. Tic-Tac-Toe is another quick game that is good for practicing this skill. As a two-person game, it can be used for students to role-play in front of a larger group. It is imperative to applaud the student who loses and stays calm before they have a chance to get upset.

   c. "Musical chairs" and "Simon Says" are ideal quick group games. As students lose and are reminded to go through each step of DEALING WITH LOSING, they may be applauded as they sit out to await the next game. For the child who gets very upset, try to distract them rather than use reason. Repetition of the experience will eventually reduce the outbursts. If all else fails, let them win and say, "We will let you win today and then maybe next time you will be able to DEAL WITH LOSING A GAME."

   d. For older children (fourth grade and up), use board games or sports. The skills involved in DEALING WITH LOSING can be used not only when you lose the game, but also for any perceived loss in the game (e.g., striking out, a low roll of the dice, missing a shot).

3. Prime the skill before any game. This is key to short-circuiting an Incredible Hulk meltdown. Say, "We are going to play a game, and let's see if you can deal with losing. Since it's much harder to deal with losing than to win this game, we can give you extra snack or points towards a reward if you can handle it."

4. This skill can often benefit from a good reward program with points for handling losing that add up towards a desired reward.

Rationale: Showing good sportsmanship when winning a game can help you make and keep friends.

1. If you win a game, you can also win a friend if you show good sportsmanship.

2. Sportsmanship means:
   a. Do not brag or show off that you won. This makes others feel bad.
   b. Say, "Good game."
   c. If the others are upset because they lost, remind them that it is only a game and they might win next time.

Practice

Who will I try this with? _____

When? _____

What happened? _____.

#56. DEALING WITH WINNING Activity Page

1. Just as in Dealing with Losing, we need to remind students that the goal is not to win a game, but to win a friend. Highlight that we are interested in their ability to win friends as they play.

2. Model and role-play the steps for DEALING WITH WINNING. These suggested role-plays are the same as for DEALING WITH LOSING, and both skills should be role-played simultaneously. We use short games so that the skill can be practiced without waiting for a long game to end:

   a. Use a coin toss (heads or tails) or "odds or evens" (each student puts out one or two fingers after one child calls "odds" or "evens") to decide who will go first. Whoever loses should be coached through the steps of DEALING WITH LOSING while the other is coached through the steps of DEALING WITH WINNING. Both are applauded and praised for staying friends by not getting mad or bragging. No one is applauded for their skill in the game, as the gameplay itself is secondary to their friendship skills.

   b. Tic-Tac-Toe is another quick game that is good for practicing this skill. As a two-person game, it can be used for students to role-play in front of a larger group. Again, both are applauded and praised for staying friends by not getting mad or bragging.

   c. "Musical chairs" and "Simon Says" are also ideal quick group games.

   d. For older children (fourth grade and up), use board games or sports. The skills involved in DEALING WITH LOSING and DEALING WITH WINNING can be used not only when you win or lose the game, but also for any perceived win or loss during the game (e.g., striking out or hitting a home run).

3. Bait the skill by doing something that requires your student to deal with winning in a gracious way. For example, as you lose a game, say, "You are so much better than I am. You are the greatest ever. I am terrible." See if the student can try to cheer you up rather than gloat over the victory.

SOCIAL SKILLS TRAINING

Rationale: Ending a play activity in a positive way helps you to stay friends.

1. Decide if you do not want to play anymore.

    a. Is it because you want to do something else?
    b. Is it because the person you were playing with did something you did not like?
    c. Is it because you do not like the other person?

2. Do not just walk away. Try to finish the game if the other person wants to finish.

3. Tell the person in a nice tone of voice why you do not want to play anymore.

    a. If you want to do something else, say, "I want to stop because I want to play something else."
    b. If you do not like what the other person did, say, "I do not want to play anymore because _____ [what the other did]."
    c. If you do not like the other person, make an excuse that you have other things you want to do. Say, "I have to stop because I have other things I need to do now."

Practice

Who will I try this with? _____

When? _____

What happened? _____.

#57. ENDING A PLAY ACTIVITY Activity Page

1. Model and role-play the steps for ENDING A PLAY ACTIVITY. Suggested role-plays involve the following scenarios:

   a. You are playing a game and it is getting boring. Practice telling the other person you want to play something else versus just walking away.

   b. After playing a game with someone, you do not feel like playing anymore. Practice finishing the game and telling the person you want to take a break versus walking out in the middle of the game.

   c. Pretend you are playing a game and one person keeps cheating. Practice telling the person why you do not want to play with them anymore in a calm way rather than getting mad.

   d. Pretend you were playing a game with someone you do not really like. Practice making an excuse that you do not feel like playing rather than telling the person you do not like him or her.

2. Correct inappropriate or abrupt endings. Have the student wait to finish the game and/or make an appropriate excuse.

3. Bait the use of the skill. Tell the student you are going to test their ability to end games appropriately. Purposely play games that are tedious or begin to cheat and make the game frustrating until the student appropriately ends the game.

Rationale: Friends do not always just come to you. You may need to do some work to find friends. The first part of that work is to put yourself in situations where you can meet potential friends.

1. **WHAT IS A FRIEND?** A friend is someone you like and who likes you. There is a difference between being "friendly" and "being friends." Friendly means being nice and polite to others. "Being friends" means you seek each other out to communicate, get together, and share life's experiences. Common interests, similar ways of thinking, and common experiences are some of the things that bring friends together.

2. **WHERE CAN YOU FIND POTENTIAL FRIENDS WHO MAY SHARE SOME OF YOUR INTERESTS?**

    a. Schools and community centers often have **clubs** based on interests (e.g., radio, music, television/video, photography, journalism, science fiction, sports, gaming, theatre). If no club matches your interests or experience, you may want to consider starting **your own club** in your school or community.
    b. Schools and community centers often have **teams** to join like athletics, debate, chess, math, and chorus or musical bands.
    c. **Support groups** that help students with a variety of issues (e.g., grief, social isolation, substance abuse) may be places to meet friends with common experiences.
    d. **Proximity and friendliness** are other reasons to consider being friends. If you see peers frequently who are very nice, you may want to make the effort to be friends.
    e. **The online world** can be an easier way to find people with common interests through websites that allow you to converse about particular topics or play online games. One can initiate a conversation by simply commenting positively about someone else's work (e.g., art, writing or gaming ability).
        - Consider places where folks post their **artwork or story writing**.
        - Consider **online gaming** and the platforms where people discuss games.
        - **Caution** is advised on the web, as there are predators on the internet who try to steal from or potentially abuse unknowing victims. If you plan to

meet someone in person that you met online, it would be wise to do that with a parent or another adult in a public place to ensure your safety. In addition, do not divulge any financial information (e.g., credit card or bank account numbers) to individuals you meet online, as they may be trying to steal form you. Also, never send unclothed pictures of yourself as this is illegal if under 18 years old.

Practice

Who will I try this with? _____

When? _____

What happened? _____.

SOCIAL SKILLS TRAINING

#58. WHERE TO FIND FRIENDS Activity Page

1. **Explain** the importance of making an effort to find friends. Then discuss the importance of some commonality in interests or experience that form the basis for people coming together to be friends. Outline the different places that students may find suitable friends.

2. This skill cannot be easily modeled or role-played. Instead, students can **create an action plan** that details their interests and where they might search for potential friends as described in the following steps:

   a. Have students list their interests among possible school, community, or online resources using the clubs and activities described in the skill sheet.

   b. Ask students to indicate which activities they already participate in and which they might be willing to explore.

   c. Ask them to identify any peers they have seen in those settings who might share their interests or experiences or simply seem friendly.

   d. Ask them to write what they might say to begin a conversation with those individuals. Consider starting simply with a compliment about something the other person did. (More rules for talking with potential friends are provided in the next skill lesson, as well as in the skill Getting to Know Someone New.)

   e. Students with a great deal of anxiety about initiating conversation with someone new may need to review Dealing with Social Fears (Skill #19).

#59. MAKING A GOOD FIRST IMPRESSION WITH A POTENTIAL FRIEND

Rationale: Once we have identified possible friends, we want to communicate with them in ways that increase the likelihood they will like us.

1. We can be seen as friendly if we smile and greet the potential friend when we see them in person.

2. Complimenting others is a good way to help others see us positively and want to spend time with us. Whether online or in person, you can:

   a. Say something nice about **something they did** like artwork, writing, general classwork, gaming ability, or anything else they did or posted.
      • "I really liked your (artwork, story, performance, game strategy)!"

   b. Say something positive about **how they look**, what they are wearing, or a new haircut.
      • "You look great," "That's a great (dress, tie, shirt, pair of shoes, new haircut)." Avoid any comments about their body, as this may be perceived as a threat and make them uncomfortable.

   c. Say something positive about **some ability** they have.
      • "You are really good at (math, English, this game, sports, dancing, singing)."

3. Get to know them more by asking about potential common interests.

   a. If you both like gaming, ask, "Did you ever play ...?"
   b. If you both like music, ask, "Did you ever listen to ...?"
   c. If you both like artwork related to certain shows, ask, "Did you ever see ...?"

4. Use the **Getting to Know New People** skill (Skill #38) to find more common interests between the two of you.

5. **Avoid giving uninvited criticism** or advice about how to do something better unless they ask for critical feedback. Even if you think they could do something better, KEEP IT TO YOURSELF unless they specifically ask for your feedback on what they could do better.

Practice

Who will I try this with? _____

When? _____

What happened? _____.

#59. MAKING A GOOD FIRST IMPRESSION WITH A POTENTIAL FRIEND Activity Page

1. **Explain** the importance of making a good first impression to interest a prospective friend. Appearing friendly and complimenting others is like making a deposit in the friendship bank. Insulting or criticizing is like making a withdrawal.

2. **Create a script** for complimenting prospective friends and asking about a potentially shared interest:

    a. For online artwork related to anime or other shows, consider saying, "Loved your art! Have you ever seen [fill in with potentially related show]?"
    b. For online gaming, say, "Liked the way you play! Have you ever played [fill in with a game you both may like]?"
    c. For people you are in a group/club with, write a potential compliment like "I like what you said" or "You are really good at _____!" or "How did you do _____ so well?"

3. Create a script for possible shared interests to ask about. Questions like, "Did you ever see _____?" or "Do you play _____?" or "Do you like _____?" can be used, filling in the blanks with possible shared interests.

4. Before participating in an in-person or online group, review your script of what to say (and what NOT to say—that is, no criticisms).

5. For students whose social anxiety interferes with executing this skill, create a **fear ladder** as shown in Skill #19 and use the **Think Like a Scientist** strategy to minimize fears.

#60. GUIDELINES FOR CONTACTING OTHERS AND ARRANGING GET-TOGETHERS

Rationale: Friendship is based on mutual interest where both people freely choose to connect with each other either in person or online. We must connect sometimes to be friends.

1. WHEN YOU MEET SOMEONE THE FIRST TIME and discover you have common interests, you may want to follow these steps to pursue the friendship.

   a. You can suggest getting together with them **"sometime"** around a common interest **(do not specify a time or date yet)**. This loose suggestion of getting together can help you "test out" if the other person is interested in you.
   b. If they say they want to get together with you (and their facial expression and tone of voice indicates excitement too), then make a firmer plan with a specific date and time.
   c. If they say maybe or make an excuse that they would not be able to get together, then don't ask again during this first encounter.

2. AFTER A SECOND MEETING WITH SOMEONE, you can try to get to know them further using Skill #38, Getting to Know Someone New:

   a. If you continue to have things in common with them, suggest, "Maybe we should get together sometime?" If they respond positively with words, tone and facial expression, then set up a time and date.
   b. If they make an excuse or say no, then do not pursue them again. Let them make the next move. If they are interested in you, then it is their turn to ask you.

3. DO THEY INITIATE CONTACT WITH YOU AS MUCH AS YOU DO WITH THEM?

   a. If you are doing all the initiating or messaging, then it may be that you like them but they are less interested in you. However, it is possible the other person is just very shy. In that case, consider contacting about once per week as long as they occasionally respond.

b. Use the **three strikes** rule. If you have asked to get together or made at least three attempts over several weeks to contact them and they said no or did not respond, then they may not be interested, and you should not pursue them unless they later ask you to get together. The exception to this rule is if they have another compelling reason for saying no or not responding (e.g., they were out of town, sick, very anxious about getting together, their phone was broken).

4. IF SOMEONE CLEARLY SAYS NO and that they are not interested in pursuing a friendship with you, then do not pursue them. To do otherwise at this point would be considered harassment. Look to other possible friendship opportunities.

Practice

Who will I try this with? _____

When? _____

What happened? _____.

#60. GUIDELINES FOR CONTACTING OTHERS AND ARRANGING GET-TOGETHERS Activity Page

1. **Explain** the importance of balancing making an effort to find friends and giving friends enough space to discover for themselves that they like you. Some students need much more encouragement to make any effort to connect while others err on the side of asking others too much. Know your customer before stressing one side or another of this equation.

2. **Model and role-play** the skill, highlighting the non-verbal and verbal signals that others may give to indicate interest or disinterest in pursuing a friendship. Try using the following situations to model and role-play:

   a. You meet someone in a school activity (e.g., band, chorus, after school club, school play, sports team). Use the Getting To Know Someone New skill to get to know them (Skill #38). Suggest getting together and have the person respond in the following ways: with an emphatic yes, with an ambivalent-sounding yes, with an uninterested maybe, or with a no. Review what these different responses may mean.

   b. Pretend you just had a get-together at the mall with a friend that lasted most of the day and you want to extend it to dinner that night. Role-play with another student showing varying levels of interest in this plan.

3. Use a game-show format to help students think about whether they should pursue another student. Use the following questions to provoke discussion:

   a. You met someone from a school club and had two conversations over two different times with them. You asked them to get together and they said "Yes, call me." You called them twice during the week and they did not return your call. What would you do? (Hint: consider the three strikes rule, so try one more time, but also ask if they are "okay" since you have not heard from them to see if something happened that kept them from returning your calls.)

   b. You just had your first get-together with a new friend and it seems to have gone well. Should you suggest getting together again tomorrow? Should you suggest getting together again next week? Should you not suggest another get-together but just say you will call them soon?

    c. You overhear a new friend of yours saying that they are going to go somewhere you really want to go (e.g., a movie you want to see, a store you want to visit). Should you ask to come along? Should you say you wanted to go to that place sometime? Should you say nothing and see if they invite you?

4. In order to read other people's interests, it can be helpful to review with a student an email or messaging stream they had with the other person to look for clues to how the other feels. Sometimes it is impossible to read the signals and thus students need very concrete instructions such as "Try three times to connect, and if they do not respond, look elsewhere for friends."

#61. SHARING FRIENDS

Rationale: Letting your friends hang out with other people shows
you are not controlling and makes others like you more, not less.

1. When friends hang out with other people without you, it may make you jealous.
Remember:

   a. If you do not get mad and you let your friends be with other people, they will feel
   relaxed with you and enjoy your friendship more.

   b. If, on the other hand, you get annoyed when they want to be with others, they
   may feel uncomfortable with your friendship. Instead of wanting to be with you,
   they may feel like they are forced to be with you.

2. Let them be with others, and they may want to return to you to get together.

   a. If your friend is going somewhere, having a party, or getting together with others
   to do something you would also like to do, you can say that you like that kind of
   activity too, but do not invite yourself along. Let them invite you if they want to.

Practice

Who will I try this with? _____

When? _____

What happened? _____.

SOCIAL SKILLS TRAINING

#61. SHARING FRIENDS Activity Page

1. **Explain** the importance of sharing friends. Tell the ancient story of the bird in the cage whose master let him fly free each day. The bird returned to the master each day because the bird liked him. Contrast this to the master who never let his bird fly free. Once he opened the cage, the bird flew away, never to return. Explain that although you cannot guarantee that your friend will always return to be with you, it is still better to have a friend who wants to be with you than to have one who simply feels coerced into being with you.

2. **Model and role-play** the skill highlighting the non-verbal and verbal signals that indicate being okay with or annoyed at your friend for being with others. Try using the following situations to model and role-play:

   a. You are sitting in the cafeteria, and your friend passes by you to sit with someone else. Show how you would act.
   b. Pretend you are talking with your friend about a movie you want to see, and he says he is going to see that movie with another friend. Show how you would avoid inviting yourself along.

3. Students who get jealous with certain friends need **priming** ahead of time to prepare them for seeing or hearing about instances when their friend may be with others. Remind them of the positive outcome of sharing friends (i.e., the friend may feel more comfortable with them and return later).

4. If students have difficulty sharing certain friends, they can be given an assignment to purposely give that friend more space (e.g., by not calling or initiating conversations for a while).

SOCIAL SKILLS TRAINING

Rationale: We should avoid accidentally saying things that upset others. Doing this too often may make others dislike us. In addition, we may want to be careful about sharing private information about ourselves with people we cannot trust. Revealing too much to the wrong person can make us victims of teasing.

1. **Sensitive topics** are words and ideas that others may regard as personal or insulting and may make people feel uncomfortable.

2. Insults are negative comments about others. One should **try not to ever make insults** about:

   a. how others **look**
   b. their **personality**
   c. where they **live** (e.g., their home)
   d. something they **made** (e.g., food, artwork, writing)
   e. something they **performed** (e.g., sports, speech, singing, dancing)

3. Sensitive topics are not necessarily insulting but may make others uncomfortable. These are topics that **you should not discuss unless the other person brings it up first:**

   a. **Sex, violence, race, religion, and sexual orientation** are usually sensitive topics when you first meet someone. It may be okay to discuss these topics if they bring it up first.
   b. Someone's **age** (okay to ask children but not adults).
   c. A **physical difference** (uses wheelchair, missing limb, blind, or deaf).
   d. A **learning difference** (difficulty reading or understanding class work).
   e. A **behavioral difference** (difficulty paying attention or sitting still, saying odd things). If their behavior bothers you (e.g., if they interrupt you), you can ask them to stop the behavior without insulting their character. Say, "Can you stop interrupting?" instead of "You have a problem interrupting."
   f. **A loss of a job or death** of a family member or friend.

4. Sensitive information about yourself are things you do not want everyone to know about you.

   a. Do not tell all your private information to people you do not yet trust to keep the information private.
   b. Decide whether the person you are talking to is a friend and someone you can trust not to tell others. Then ask them to keep the information confidential (i.e., do not tell others).

Practice

Who will I try this with? _____

When? _____

What happened? _____.

#62. AVOIDING SENSITIVE TOPICS Activity Page

One way to begin teaching this skill is to walk into the room with something odd-looking, like a bag for a hat or a fake huge pimple on your nose. Do not say anything about it unless a student asks. Pretend that you do not know what they are talking about until other students also point it out. Then begin a discussion about "sensitive topics," pointing out that you may see something different about someone, but you may not want to say anything to protect the person's feelings.

1. **Explain** the rationale and the definition of "sensitive topics" with the skill written up on the blackboard or a poster. This skill is difficult to role-play because the right response is usually to do nothing. As such, it is helpful to discuss numerous situations rather than act them out. You may decide to adopt a "game-show" format to review these situations.

2. **Use the game-show format.** For each situation, students can indicate whether they think it is a sensitive topic and if they would say anything. In some situations, students should say nothing, while in others, the student should wait for the other person to bring it up, and in other situations the student can say how they feel. Example situations:

    a. You say someone has nice sunglasses (not sensitive).
    b. You say someone has really thick glasses (sensitive).
    c. You say you are annoyed because a student keeps interrupting you when you try to say something (not sensitive, you can tell them to stop without insulting their personality).
    d. Someone says it's a nice day (not sensitive).
    e. A student asks how old his teacher is (sensitive).
    f. A teacher asks how old her student's little brother is (not sensitive).
    g. You ask your friend if he gets any special help in school (sensitive).
    h. You ask why the student in your class is so strong in gym (not sensitive).
    i. You ask why the student in your class is so overweight (sensitive).
    j. You ask why the girl in your class is so good at gymnastics (not sensitive).

k. Sometimes you wish that you were the opposite sex (possibly sensitive, only tell those friends who will not spread rumors about you).

l. You ask why the girl in your class can't understand her assignment (sensitive).

m. Your friend's grandfather died (sensitive, but you can say "Sorry to hear that").

n. Your teacher has a large belly, and you want to ask if she is pregnant (sensitive).

o. You heard that your friend's dog died and want to ask about it (sensitive).

p. You heard that your friend won a spelling bee and want to say congrats (not sensitive)

3. Students who do not regularly edit themselves will need to be primed (prompted) before entering situations in which they will see individuals who are different from them.

4. Anytime the student makes an insensitive remark, label it a "sensitive topic" or insult and explain how the remark can hurt others' feelings.

63. RESPECTING OTHERS' OPINIONS AND SUGGESTIONS
(When Others Do Things Differently)

Rationale: Respecting others' rights to share their ideas, even when you disagree, is crucial to maintaining friendships.

1. Definitions: Facts are ideas that are agreed upon by most everyone because they can be confirmed by trusted sources or observation with our own eyes. If there is significant disagreement about what the facts are, then at least some people view this information as opinion rather than fact. Opinions are ideas that are not agreed upon by everyone. People have different opinions.

2. Respecting others' opinions: There will be times that you know you are right and others are wrong. You may even think that others are silly or unintelligent to believe what they believe. If you want to get along with them, then here is how you might handle this situation:

   a. Don't insult them by referring to their idea as silly, unintelligent, or just wrong. Respect others' right to have their own opinion. Say, "Well, that's your opinion. I have a different opinion."

   b. State your ideas as strong opinions, not facts. Use words like, "From my point of view ..." or "I believe ..."

3. When you disagree about what to do and you have to **work together**, be willing to compromise. That means doing a little of what you want and what they want (see skill for Compromising).

4. Teachers and parents may change the rules about how a game or task is to be completed. You may not like these new rules, but you must respect others. You can:

   a. Accept the new rules. You may have to if the person is an authority figure, like a teacher or parent.

   b. Respectfully express your disagreement: "In my opinion, the older rules were better." Do not use insulting remarks like "These rules are stupid, silly, or wrong."

Practice

Who will I try this with? _____

When? _____

What happened? _____.

SOCIAL SKILLS TRAINING

1. **Explain** the importance of talking to others in a respectful way even when you disagree with them. With the phrases written up on a poster or blackboard, explain how to talk with someone when you disagree.

2. **Model and role-play** the skill steps. Suggested role-plays:

   a. Initially, discuss students' preferences for less emotional topics like food, TV shows, sports teams, and video games. As they discover differing preferences, instruct them to show respect for others' preferences by saying that they respect the others' preferences. In contrast, role-play insulting others' preferences (only the instructor should do this to keep it from provoking a fight). For example, show how it is not okay to say things like, "Your favorite team stinks" or "You like that video game, that's for babies."

   b. Instructors can also change the rules for how some tasks should be completed and coach the student to respect the new rules even if they prefer the old rules. One can do this with classic games or any routine.

   c. The next activity requires the permission of the students; you will be asking if it is okay to really challenge them to remain calm and respectful. As the instructor, share an opinion that you know will be in deep contrast with the opinions or values of each student and require them to say that they respect your right to your opinion even though they disagree with it. More challenging to tolerate may be comments on religion and politics. You can say to a member of one political party that the other political party is correct about a particular subject. Prompt them to calmly show respect for your right to your opinion, and then state how they disagree with it.

3. Certain situations can be anticipated in which the student will be confronted with others with markedly different opinions. The following are some of the situations before which to **prime** students to be ready to respect others' opinions:

a. When they will be working on group projects and have to select ideas together.

b. When they will be talking to someone who has very different opinions about valued topics (e.g., sports teams, politics, religion).

c. When a task will be done differently than they expect.

4. Students may initially need incentives to be willing to accept new rules, compromise, and stay respectful. Hopefully one can fade that out and the reward of getting along with others can become part of their valued identity.

5. Provide feedback if students begin to get angry and disrespectful in the way they handle their disagreements with others. Redirect them to respectfully handle their disagreement.

SOCIAL SKILLS TRAINING

#64. DON'T BE THE "RULE POLICE"

Rationale: Generally, people do not like it when you tell them what
to do or tell on them for violating a rule. In fact, if you act like the boss
or tell on them, some students will begin to tease or harass you.

1. **Don't be the rule police:** It is not your job to make others follow the rules. Generally, you should not tell others what to do or tell on them.

2. Here are some **exceptions** when it is okay for you to tell people what rules to follow or tell on them if they violate a rule. Here is a list of those situations:

    a. When you are the teacher, the boss, or put in charge of others.
    b. When people ask you what the rules are.
    c. When people break a rule that could cause great danger to themselves or others. You may have to tell on them.
    d. If people do something to hurt you. Here you can use an "I message" or tell on them. For example, "I feel _____ when you _____ because _____. I want you to _____."

Practice

Who will I try this with? _____

When? _____

What happened? _____.

#64. DON'T BE THE RULE POLICE Activity Page

1. To introduce the skill to those who often tell others what rules to follow, start by overly criticizing each thing they do, saying that is not allowed or against the rule. Discuss how it made them feel about you. Then **explain** the rationale for not telling others what to do and outline the exceptions to that rule.

2. Use a **game-show format** to review the information. Students take turns answering questions that require them to discriminate between situations where they must tell others what to do or say nothing. Suggested questions are detailed below, but you may want to add questions that are especially relevant to your students (e.g., describing situations in which they were the rule police). Offer points towards rewards for answering questions:

   a. Why should you not tell other people what to do?

   b. If someone is chewing gum in school, which is breaking a school rule, what should you do? (Probably nothing; this situation is not dangerous despite being a rule violation).

   c. If someone is drawing when the teacher tells everyone to read a book, what should you do? (Probably nothing, because it is not your job to tell on the other person).

   d. If someone is lighting toilet paper on fire in the bathroom, what should you do? (Tell an adult what is happening because it is dangerous. You might want to avoid using the student's name or avoid direct confrontations in this dangerous situation).

   e. If everyone in the cafeteria lunch line is supposed to take just one milk but someone takes two milks, what would you do? (If there will still be enough milk for everybody, then maybe do nothing).

   f. If a classmate is annoying you by whispering to you when the teacher is talking, what can you do? (Probably tell the classmate to stop because he is directly annoying you).

   g. If a classmate is annoying another classmate by tapping him on the shoulder, what should you do? (Probably nothing, because this is not dangerous and does not directly impact you.)

SOCIAL SKILLS TRAINING

3. Some students go out of their way to be the Rule Police because they themselves get in trouble frequently and they do not want to be the only ones in trouble. In this case it would be helpful for the student to understand better ways to feel good about themselves rather than getting others in trouble. They can also learn how they begin to get "friendship credit" with others for not telling them what to do or not telling on them when they do something wrong.

4. Students may not realize when they are acting like the Rule Police and may need feedback. Redirect instances of being the "Rule Police" by asking the student, "Was is dangerous? Was the person hurting you? Are you in charge? If not, then do not tell them what to do."

#65. MODESTY

Rationale: When you are modest, people have more respect for you. They will feel you treat them as equals, so they will feel good being around you.

1. **Modest** means that you do not brag about your talents or accomplishments in front of others. It is okay to be aware that you are better than someone at something, but it is unfriendly to say that out loud. It is also unfriendly to insult someone else's abilities (see skill on Avoiding Sensitive Topics).

2. Modesty looks and sounds like:

   a. Thinking, but not saying, what your talents and accomplishments are unless someone asks you.
   b. Refraining from comments about you being better at something than the person you are talking with.
   c. Presenting your strengths as good but not better than all those around you. For example, "I am pretty good at ..." rather than "I am better than all of you at ..."
   d. In the classroom, do not brag about doing all the homework or say that it was really easy. Also, answer some but not every one of the questions the teacher asks the class.

3. The exception to this rule is in a job interview, when you can tell people about your talents and accomplishments.

Practice

Who will I try this with? _____

When? _____

What happened? _____.

1. **Explain** the rationale and steps for being modest. In teaching this skill, make sure students do not become self-deprecating. They can present themselves in a positive light without bragging and without putting themselves down.

2. **Model** describing a talent modestly without acting better than others.

3. **Role-play** the skill using the following situations or situations that actually occurred in the student's daily lives:

   a. Have each student write down some of their strengths and talents (e.g., school-work, sports, musical, artistic talents). Have each one practice describing their abilities to the other students in a modest fashion versus bragging about them. Correct any negative self-statements as well.

   b. Role-play a student answering all the questions in a classroom lesson. Discuss how the other students feel about that student.

   c. Pretend one student is having trouble with their work. Practice offering help in a bragging versus modest way (e.g., saying "That's easy let me show you how" versus "That's a tough one, let me see if I can help.")

   d. Pretend a student is talking about a time that they had trouble playing a sport or musical instrument or completing some school or work task. Show how another student could respond in a bragging way (e.g., "I am much better than you at that" or "I can help you because I am much better than you") versus a supportive way (e.g., "Yeah, that happened to me once too" or "Do you want any help with that?").

4. Students who are particularly good at a subject should be primed (reminded) not to brag or flaunt their abilities. Students who tend to brag may also need to be primed before any competitive situation.

5. Correct arrogant behaviors by reminding them how others will feel if they say such things.

#66. EMPATHIC LISTENING

Rationale: One of the most important parts of being a good friend is the ability to listen to your friend in a way that shows you understand them. People sometimes do not want you to "fix" their problem but prefer you just show that you understand how they feel. Good listening is really a gift you give to your friends that make them like being with you.

Steps to empathic listening

1. Empathic listening means listening in a way that shows you understand how the other person feels. Use this skill when someone says they have something important to talk about or they are upset. Try to do at least the first four steps below; the fifth is optional.

    a. **Show a good listening position:** Face them with some eye contact that indicates you are listening (don't look at your phone).

    b. **Reflect back what you heard:** After the person has spoken, check to see if you heard what they said. Say, "Let me see if I got that. You said that ..." (Repeat back in your own words what you heard them say. Then say, "Is that right?")

    c. **Ask, "Is there more?"** You want to let them have the time to say what is really on their mind and not rush to interrupt or try to tell them what to do.

    d. **Validate their feelings:** This means indicating that you understand how they might feel given what they described, even if you yourself might not feel the same way. You can say, "It makes sense that you feel that way given what happened." This may be particularly hard if the other person is upset with you. But remember, you do not have to agree, you just have to show that you understand.

    e. **Empathize.** This last step involves communicating to the other person that you feel what they feel. First, your face and tone must communicate a similar feeling to how they feel (e.g., looking sad if they are sad, or excited and happy if that is how they feel). You can say, "I feel _____ too given what happened to you."

Avoid invalidating their feelings

1. Try not to offer a solution to the problem before you have shown that you understand the other person's feelings.

2. Don't say things that will make the other person feel like it is not okay to feel the way they do, such as "That's no big deal, get over it."

3. If the other person is upset with you, do not say they are wrong to feel that way. Validate their feelings (e.g., say you understand how they feel) and then ask if you can tell them how you feel. You can explain how you think and feel differently even though you understand how they feel. You can use an "I message" here: "I feel _____ when you _____ because _____. I want _____."

Practice

Who will I try this with? _____

When? _____

What happened? _____.

1. **Explain** the rationale and steps for empathic listening using the example phrases provided. Emphasize that listening is a gift and can be more important than solving the other's problems.

2. **Model** each skill step the right way and perhaps the wrong way to show how one can accidentally be unsupportive or invalidating. Have someone else pretend that they had an argument with their parents about buying a video game, and you listen to their story, demonstrating the right and wrong way for each step.

   a. Show the right and wrong listening positions.
   b. Show accurate versus inaccurate reflective listening.
   c. Show how to ask if there is more to the story versus interrupting the person with ideas about what to do to get the video game.
   d. Show how to validate someone's feelings, demonstrating an understanding of how upset they may be versus invalidating their feelings by saying it is not big deal.
   e. Show how to communicate that you feel upset with them versus saying that you would never feel upset over something minor.

3. **Role-play** the steps by having students talk with each other. Each student can come up with one thing that made them very happy or very upset, or they can use the following situations to practice.

   a. A student describes winning an academic award and is very happy.
   b. A student describes how their older brother won a scholarship and they feel they never win anything so they are feeling upset.
   c. A student tells his friend that he is upset because the friend never sits with him at lunch. Show how to validate the student's feelings.
   d. Have a student talk about something another student may not care much about so that the listener has to work hard to show their understanding. For example, have a student say he is very upset because someone walked in front of him on his way to an elevator and slowed him down slightly. See if the student can validate the other's feelings even if he does not understand why this is so upsetting.

SOCIAL SKILLS TRAINING

4. Students may need to be reminded to be empathic listeners whenever their friends are upset. Sometimes this can be anticipated when one has heard news that a friend has experienced an event that probably caused strong emotions.

5. Provide immediate feedback to students if they say something invalidating to others. Try to stop it before the student says too much to upset the other person. Redirect them to the skill steps, particularly how to show their understanding even if they would not feel that way if it happened to them.

#67. SHOWING CARING FOR OTHERS' FEELINGS
(Preschool-Elementary)

Rationale: Showing you care about others' feelings makes them like you more.

1. Look for signs others are upset.

2. Ask, "Are you okay?"

3. Ask if you can help.

4. Help them if they want help.

Practice

Who will I try this with? _____

When? _____

What happened? _____.

SOCIAL SKILLS TRAINING

#68. SHOWING CARING FOR OTHERS' FEELINGS
(Middle School and Up)

Rationale: Showing that you care for others may be the most important skill for maintaining close relationships. In addition to listening empathically (see previous skill), there are a variety of responses you can make to show you care for the other person.

1. Look for signs that the other person is upset. The specific emotion someone is feeling can be identified later by asking the person. But initially, it is important to know whether someone is basically happy or upset in order to know how to approach them (see Skill #1, Recognizing Emotions).

2. If someone is happy, say, "You look happy. Did something good happen?" Tell them you are very happy for them.

3. If someone looks upset, ask calmly so as not to bother them, "Are you okay?" or "What's wrong?"

4. Use the empathic listening skills to hear what upset them.

5. Then, depending on what they say, you can make a **supportive comment**.

   a. Share a time you had a similar experience. Say, "I know how you feel because it happened to me ..."
   b. Validate the other person's feelings. Say, "It makes sense that you feel that way given what happened to you."
   c. Refute any negative information. For example, if the other person says everyone hates them, say, "I like you, and I know others who do too."
   d. Ask the person if it would help to do something fun to get their mind off the problem.
   e. Ask if you can help.

6. Do not laugh or tease them, and do not invalidate their feeling by saying that they should not feel the way they do.

Practice

Who will I try this with? _____

When? _____

What happened? _____.

1. **Explain** why it is important to show caring for others' feelings. Review Skill #1, Recognizing Emotions, if needed, but stress that it is less important to read the exact emotion and more important to know if someone is happy or upset.

    a. Model the facial expressions and tone that accompany positive versus negative feelings and see if the students can guess if you are happy or upset.

2. **Model and role-play** the steps for showing care for others. Suggested role-plays:

    a. Pretend someone fell down and hurt themself and needs help getting up.
    b. Pretend someone lost something, got upset, and needs help finding it.
    c. Pretend a student is having a hard time with schoolwork and looks upset. Offer to help the student with their work.
    d. Pretend someone is sad because they did not get to play with others. Offer to play with them.

3. For middle school ages and up, a good way to practice this skill is a game I call **"Make Me Happy."** Students take turns acting out situations that make them upset (see below or use an actual situation that happened to them). This part of the game is like charades but can be played allowing the acting student to speak. Once the other students have guessed what the situation is, all the other students take turns making supportive statements. The statements can be pulled from the skill sheet. Sample situations and supportive responses include the following:

    a. Someone fails a test. ("I know how you feel; it happened to me lots of times." "You will probably do great next time." "That test wasn't even fair." "Want me to help you study next time?")
    b. No one will dance with someone at a school dance. ("I can never find anyone to dance with either." "They do not know what they are missing; you are a good dancer." "Let's play a game instead of trying to dance with them.")

c. Someone is teased by being called ugly. ("You are not ugly." "I get teased too sometimes. Don't believe what they say.")

d. Someone's parent is very ill. ("Sorry to hear that. Is there anything I can do to help?" "I know someone who was sick with the same thing and was fully cured." "Want to do something fun to get your mind off it for a while?")

4. Correct inappropriate ways to show understanding, such as when the student does not see that someone is obviously upset or tries too hard to help when the other person does not want help.

#69. DEEPENING RELATIONSHIPS; SHARING PERSONAL INFORMATION

Rationale: When friends decide to share personal information with each other, it is a sign that they are becoming closer friends who know that the other will keep their personal information confidential.

1. **What kinds of personal information do close friends share?** Usually this is information about your emotional world, your worries and insecurities, and things about you that you think some people might judge negatively. General information about your name and interests is not considered personal unless your interest is something that others have been known to see negatively (e.g., if your interest is not considered age-appropriate by some people).

   a. Something about yourself that you believe not everyone accepts, like your political or religious beliefs, your diagnosis if you have one, your sexual orientation, or a hobby that is not typical of your age.
   b. Worries and wishes you have about the future or others.
   c. Past traumatic events or other experiences that you fear others would judge harshly.

2. **Who should you choose to tell personal information to?** You need to be able to trust that the person will accept you and not insult you and will keep the information confidential if that's what you want.

   a. People you have observed to be accepting towards others may be people you can trust. Maybe they indicated that they have ASD or perhaps they said that their good friend has ASD, so you assume they are accepting of ASD. Perhaps in listening to them, you hear that they respect and appreciate all religious and political orientations, so they will likely accept yours.
   b. After you have had a conversation with a person about less personal topics (e.g., name, school, work, interests, other topics listed in the skill "Getting to Know

SOCIAL SKILLS TRAINING

Someone New"), you may be able to tell if they seem supportive or unkind. If they are complimentary and did not say anything insulting, then you may take the risk to share something more personal. If, on the other hand, they seemed insulting to you, you may decide to avoid taking the risk of sharing more personal information.

3. **When others share their personal information with you,** it is crucial that you respond in a caring way if you want to maintain a good friendship. You can:

    a. Be an empathic listener (see skill on Empathic Listening).
    b. Show caring through supportive statements (see skill on Showing Caring for Others' Feelings). Share a similar experience or validate their feeling.
    c. Keep the information confidential (i.e., do not tell others) unless they say you can tell others.

Practice

Who will I try this with? _____

When? _____

What happened? _____.

1. **Explain** the rationale for sharing personal information to create a special, closer relationship with someone. Discuss who is and is not an appropriate recipient of your personal information.

2. **Use a game-show format to review what might be considered personal information.** For each situation below, students can indicate whether they think it involves personal information and whether they would tell anyone or just close friends:

   a. Telling others what school you go to. (Probably not too personal and might be shared with most people.)

   b. A student shares that he was abused or molested as a child. (This is probably private information you may only want to share with those who you trust to be supportive and keep the information confidential.)

   c. Telling others what shows or movies you like to watch. (This may or may not be personal. If the shows are common for your peer group, then it may not be personal. However, if the shows are for students much younger than you, then some people may tease you for watching them and it would be best to only share this with those students you trust to be kind.)

   d. Telling others where you work. (This is probably not personal, unless the job is something that some students would tease you about.)

   e. Telling others about your attraction to others. (This is personal information to share only with those you trust to keep the information confidential.)

   f. A student tells others that sometimes he wishes he was the opposite sex. (This is personal information to share only with those you trust to be kind and keep the information confidential.)

   g. You tell others that you did not understand an assignment. (This is personal because some students may be unkind while others will be kind and help you.)

SOCIAL SKILLS TRAINING

3. Students may want to consider making a list of people they would trust with their personal information and with whom they would like to further develop their friendship. They can make a plan to share information with those people.

4. Some students will need to be **primed** or prompted before entering situations in which they will be around individuals who cannot be trusted to hear about the student's private matters.

5. Small group-therapy situations can be ideal for sharing personal information after confidentiality rules are presented.

6. **Provide corrective feedback.** Anytime the student shares personal information too soon or with those who cannot be trusted, discreetly provide feedback about people with whom they might want and not want to share this information. Similarly, if the student does not respond supportively when hearing about their friend's personal information, then direct them to be more empathic and supportive.

#70. GETTING ATTENTION IN POSITIVE WAYS

Rationale: Getting attention is not the same as being liked. Getting attention in positive ways helps people to like you, but getting attention in a negative way can push others away.

1. Attention is when people look and listen to you.

    a. **Positive attention** is when people look and listen to you and like what you are doing.

    b. **Negative attention** is when people look and listen to you but do not like what you are doing.

Positive Ways	Negative Ways
1. It is okay to try to tell a joke if you are not insulting others or using sensitive topics.	Make others laugh at the wrong time (e.g., during a class), after someone says to stop or by using sensitive topics.
2. Listen to others and ask questions about what they are discussing.	Do all the talking without listening to others.
3. Start a conversation about shared interests.	Talk only about your interests.
4. Compliment others.	Insult others.
5. Compromise about what to do.	Demand to do everything your way.
6. Ask to play or get together. If the person you ask says no, ask someone else.	Get mad or jealous if they do not want to talk or get together with you.
7. Tell the truth.	Make up stories to try to impress others or gain their sympathy by pretending to be hurt.

Practice

Who will I try this with? _____

When? _____

What happened? _____.

1. **Explain** the rationale, definitions, and examples of positive and negative attention. The amount of information in this skill may be overwhelming for some students. Sometimes it is wise to focus on only one example of positive and negative attention. If a student has a problem with getting attention in negative ways, focus on what that student does (e.g., being too silly all the time) and one thing he or she could do instead (e.g., making sure it is the right time to be silly and assessing his audience's response).

2. After teaching the skill through explanation, you can use a **game-show approach** to review the situations described in the skill. Students take turns answering questions that require them to describe ways to get attention and maintain friendships. Suggested questions:

   a. Does getting attention mean that others will like you? (No, getting attention in negative ways will push people away.)
   b. Will being silly all the time make people like you more? (No. If people tell you to stop being silly, you should so that they will not be annoyed with you.)
   c. Name and show one positive way to get attention.
   d. Show another positive way to get attention and tell what you did.
   e. Show another positive way to get attention and tell what you did.
   f. Can you think of a joke that is not insulting and that does not mention sensitive topics? (Hint: There are joke apps that may provide endless jokes from which to choose.)

3. **Role-play** positive and negative ways to get attention. Students can take turns acting out the different positive and negative ways while other students guess what they are doing. This can be facilitated by writing negative and positive ways to get attention on separate slips of paper. Each student can select a slip of paper and then enact what it says to do while others guess what they are doing. NOTE: If you have students who have trouble stopping negative attention-seeking behavior, then do not role-play the negative ways at all, as doing so may inadvertently encourage them.

4. A key to the effectiveness of this skill is teaching peers who surround a student not to encourage or laugh at negative ways to get attention. Some teachers use a point system where students get points by refraining from inappropriate comments as well as by ignoring inappropriate comments from other students.

5. Though I am not a fan of any punishment system, if students are not angry (i.e., not the INCREDIBLE HULK) and they continue to choose negative versus positive ways to get attention, it may be okay to try a **response cost system** (see below). The student here is provided with the promise of rewards (snack and game time), but if they make inappropriate comments, they get a warning. After the second warning, they lose the snack, then increments of game time if the comments continue. The goal is to inhibit inappropriate remarks. Be warned: with anger-prone students, this can backfire and should be avoided.

Warning	Warning	Lose snack
Lose 5 min game time	Lose another 5 min game time	Lose another 5 min game time

Rationale: Even with close friends, one must respect their wishes for how physically and emotionally close they want to be.

1. People have the right to be alone or to keep things to themselves.

   a. If you respect others' space and belongings, they will respect you.

2. Respecting others' space means:

   a. Keeping some physical distance from them. For example, stay about **an arm's length away** unless you are invited to come closer.
   b. Allowing others to have time by themselves.
   c. Letting friends talk and do things with other people. That is, don't push them to talk and do things only with you.
   d. Not asking them to talk about private information when they say they do not want to discuss it.

3. Respecting others' belongings means:

   a. Not touching others' belongings unless given permission or invited to do so.
   b. Not taking or borrowing others' belongings without permission.
   c. Keeping others' property clean and in good condition if you borrow it.

Practice

Who will I try this with? _____

When? _____

What happened? _____.

1. After teaching the skill through explanation, you can use group discussion with students or a game-show approach to review the situations described in the skill. Students take turns answering questions that require them to describe different ways to respect others' boundaries. Suggested questions:

   a. How far should people be from each other when talking or playing together?

   b. If your friends want to do something by themselves when you want to get together with them, what should you do and why?

   c. If you ask your friend to get together and they say they can't meet with you because they are going somewhere with some other friends, what should you do or say? Why?

   d. You ask your friend why they never discuss certain things (e.g., their parents, where they used to go to school, why they do not change in the locker room, why they are never available on Saturdays) and they say they do not want to discuss it, what should you do or say? Why?

   e. If you see one of your friends' belongings that you really want to pick up and look at, what should you do? Why?

   f. Is it okay to borrow something from your friend without asking them? Is it ever all right to do that (e.g., to borrow a pencil)?

   g. If you borrow your friend's CD player and it breaks, what should you do? Why?

2. Review any inappropriate violations of others' boundaries and help the student come up with a plan to correct the problem.

#72. OFFERING HELP

Rationale: Offering help to others makes others see you as friendly, can help you feel good about yourself, and may lead to others helping you when you need it.

1. Look for signs that others may need help:

    a. They are having trouble with their work.
    b. They are having trouble carrying something heavy.
    c. They are missing a pencil or piece of paper that you could lend them.
    d. They are being ignored and need someone to invite them to play or talk.
    e. Their hands are full, so they cannot open a door.

2. Say, "May I help you?" and then help them.

3. If they say they do not want help, then leave them alone.

4. Be careful not to help people in ways that hurt others. For example, reminding teachers that they forgot to assign homework may make the other kids in class annoyed with you.

Practice

Who will I try this with? _____

When? _____

What happened? _____.

1. Model and role-play the skill steps using the following situations or situations that actually occurred in the student's daily lives:

    a. A classmate is having trouble with their work.
    b. A parent or teacher is having trouble carrying something heavy.
    c. A classmate is missing a pencil or piece of paper.
    d. A friend is being ignored and needs someone to invite them to play or talk.
    e. A student, teacher, or parent has their hands full, so they cannot open a door.
    f. Role-play any of the above situations again in which the other person does not want the help.
    g. A student ignores someone on crutches struggling to open a door while opening the door for the teacher. Review with the students how other classmates might feel about this behavior.

2. Prompt others to help when they are ignoring those who may need it.

3. You can bait the skill by acting like you need help without directly asking for it. For example, struggle to open a door with your hands full, or complain that you cannot figure out how to put something together.

#73. DO'S AND DON'TS ON SOCIAL MEDIA

Rationale: Everything we post on social media becomes a permanent record for everyone to see. Therefore we must be careful about what we say in order to maintain friends and acceptance from online communities.

1. Things to **DO** that help make you look friendly online:

   a. Compliment others' posts.

   b. Ask about possible shared interests. For example, "Do you like _____ [particular game, show, artwork]?"

   c. Offer emotional support if someone is upset by saying things like "Hope you feel better" or "That has happened to me too" or "Is there anything I can do to help?"

   d. Respond to messages from friendly people in a timely way, or make an excuse if you could not respond for many days.

2. **DON'T** do the following, as it can push others away:

   a. Express anger, rage, or complain about others online; doing so may scare others away. It is better to talk to a trusted friend privately or a counselor.

   b. Offer criticism of others' work when no one asked for critical feedback.

   c. Seek revenge when someone criticizes you. If you disagree with their comment, you can say why you disagree, but do not attack back.

   d. Yell or insult someone else's gaming skills. You can make a suggestion about strategy, but if they are not able to take your advice, find another person to play with.

   e. Discuss sensitive topics like race, religion, politics, sex, or violence, unless they bring it up first and you are in a private conversation with them.

   f. Seek revenge when others "ghost" you. Instead, find someone else to talk with.

3. Safety from cyberbullies and sexual or financial predators

   a. If you are being teased online, report it to the website administrator. Keep a record of all insulting comments. If they make physical threats, you can report it to the police. Block the person from messaging you or commenting on your page.

   b. Do not agree to meet anyone in person unless your parents or a trusted guardian is with you.

   c. Do not give out any financial information, including banking or credit card info, to someone who asks for it unless you contacted the official website or telephoned the institution so you know it is legitimate.

Practice

Who will I try this with? _____

When? _____

What happened? _____.

#73. DO'S AND DON'TS ON SOCIAL MEDIA Activity Page

1. Online communities can be great places to meet like-minded people and allow shy students to think about what they want to say before responding to others. Self-control is one of the most important skills in communicating online so that we do not say things that offend or push others away. **Students should be encouraged to seek out advice from trusted helpers (e.g., parents, counselors) before sending online messages to others.** For more information on how to be safe online, my book *No More Victims* outlines ways to be safe from cyber bullies and predators.

2. Discuss the following situations to review the skill:

   a. How would you start a conversation with someone you have been observing online and whose artwork or writing you admire? (Hint: Compliment their work, or ask about possible shared interests.)
   b. How soon should you respond to someone's message to you?
   c. What might you say if someone online says that they have low self-esteem because they have been teased a lot in the past?
   d. What should you do if someone criticizes something you posted online?
   e. What should you do if you are very angry at someone for ghosting you?
   f. What would you do if you're teaming up with someone for an online game and they do not follow your advice to win and you both begin to lose the game?

3. Students who are extremely shy may need help with creating a fear ladder (see Managing Social Fears) to gradually attempt to interact with others online.

4. Students who frequently get angry with or overly critical of others and who get rejected from online communities would benefit from individual counseling to help them edit remarks online and learn to discuss their upsets with their counselor.

#74. WHEN TO TELL ON SOMEONE

Rationale: Telling on others when they do something wrong can make people angry with you. Yet sometimes it is important to tell on someone.

1. Try not to tell on others most of the time, because it may make them feel mad and sad.

2. Tell on others if:

   a. They keep bothering you after you told them to stop and tried to ignore them.

   b. They do something dangerous that could hurt themselves or others.

Practice

Who will I try this with? _____

When? _____

What happened? _____.

#74. WHEN TO TELL Activity Page

1. This is very similar to the skill "Don't Be the Rule Police," but it is often more appropriate to teach preschoolers through second-graders. After teaching the skill through explanation, you can role-play actual situations that occurred in the classroom or at home in which the students tell on each other, or you can use the situations described below. For children who can imagine hypothetical situations, you can use a game-show approach to review the situations described in the skill. Students take turns answering questions that require them to discriminate between situations where they must tell on others or say nothing. Suggested questions:

   a. If someone keeps tapping you with a pencil, what should you do? (Tell them to stop first; if they do not, only then can you tell on them.)

   b. If someone is chewing gum in school, which is breaking a school rule, what should you do? (Probably nothing; this situation is not dangerous despite being a rule violation).

   c. If someone is drawing when the teacher tells everyone to read a book, what should you do? (Probably nothing, because it is not your job to tell on the other person).

   d. If someone is throwing toilet paper at you in the bathroom, what should you do? (Tell them to stop; if they do not, then tell an adult.)

   e. If everyone in the cafeteria lunch line is supposed to take just one milk, but someone takes two milks, what would you do? (If there will still be enough milk for everybody, then maybe do nothing).

   f. If a classmate is annoying you by whispering to you when the teacher is talking, what can you do? (Probably tell the classmate to stop because they are directly annoying you; only tell if they do not stop).

   g. If a classmate is annoying other classmates by tapping them on the shoulder, what should you do? (Probably nothing, because this is not dangerous and does not directly impact you.)

2. Redirect or correct instances of tattle telling by asking, "Is it dangerous? Was the person hurting you? Did you tell them to stop first?"

3. You can bait the skill by breaking non-dangerous rules in front of them (e.g., chewing gum in a school, having eleven items when checking out at the ten-items-or-less lane at the supermarket).

SOCIAL SKILLS TRAINING

Rationale: "Assertive" means trying to get what you want without hurting others. It is a positive way of communicating.

1. With friends and family, it is usually better to be assertive than passive or aggressive.

    a. **Aggressive** means communicating in a way that hurts others. Insulting others or yelling quickly ends communication and the possibility of resolving a conflict.

    b. **Passive** means doing nothing, such as letting people do things that bother you without saying how you feel. (Note: Sometimes being passive can actually seem aggressive. For example, if someone asks you to help them and you do not respond, that may be perceived as hostile. The "silent treatment," in which you do not respond to someone, is often considered a "passive-aggressive" action and perceived as a hostile response.

    c. **Assertive** means to communicate what you want in a respectful way *without* hurting others. This is a positive method for trying to resolve conflicts.

2. Decide if you need to be assertive.

    a. Someone is asking you to do something that is dangerous or makes you feel bad.

    b. You want or need someone to do something.

3. Use an "I" statement to be assertive (avoid insults):

    I FEEL _____ (feeling word)
    WHEN YOU _____ (what they did or said)
    BECAUSE _____ (the reason it upset you)
    WHAT I WANT OR NEED IS _____ (what you want from them)

Practice

Who will I try this with? _____

When? _____

What happened? _____.

1. **Explain** the rationale for being able to express what you want without offending others. Contrast that with being passive (not saying what you want) and aggressive (communicating in a threatening way where others will not listen or will get mad).

2. **Model** the correct way to use an "I" statement without using insults.

	Right way	Wrong way
I FEEL	upset	you are mean
WHEN YOU	yell at me	are a horrible person
BECAUSE	it scares me	you are the worst person
WHAT I WANT	is for you to say it without yelling	is for you to disappear forever

3. **Role-play** using an "I" statement with the following situations:
   a. Someone keeps bumping into you.
   b. Someone borrows some money and does not pay you back when they said they would.
   c. Someone demands to play a game that you do not want to play.
   d. You are doing a group project in school and no one is listening to your ideas.
   e. Someone borrows your pencil and you need it back.
   f. The teacher or parent gives everyone a snack except you.

4. Bait the skill. This means doing something that requires the student to assert themselves. Tell them you are about to do something to help them practice asserting themselves, then:
   a. Take their book-bag when they need it.
   b. Give everyone a snack or a chance to do a favored activity except a couple of students until they make an assertive statement. Best to tell them ahead of time that you will be testing them.

5. Correct inappropriate ways to express frustration, like aggressive or passive responses.

#76. CONFLICT RESOLUTION

Rationale: Eventually we will all have some conflicts or disagreements with others. Handling conflicts in a positive way can help you get along better with others.

1. Ask the person if you can **schedule a time** to talk; say, "When would be a good time to talk with you about something?" Sometimes people need time to prepare for a difficult discussion, so it is best to schedule a time rather than just start telling them how you feel.

2. **Prepare yourself** for the discussion; think about what they did or said that upset you. Do you want them to stop doing something, apologize, or help you in some way?

3. Tell the other person what you want in an **assertive** way with an "I" statement in a **calm** tone of voice:

   I FEEL _____ (feeling word)
   WHEN YOU _____ (what they did or said)
   BECAUSE _____ (the reason it upset you)
   WHAT I WANT OR NEED IS _____ (what you want from them)

4. Then give them a chance to talk while you listen.

   a. **Reflect what you heard:** Say, "Let me see if I got that. You said that ..." (Repeat back in your own words what you heard them say). Then say, "Is that right?" APOLOGIZE if you hurt the other person's feelings.
   b. **Ask, "Is there more?"** Let them have the time to say what is really on their mind and not rush to interrupt.
   c. **Validate their feelings:** Show you understand how they might feel given what they described, even if you do not feel the same way.
   d. When they are done, **ask if it is okay for you to say more.**

5. As you take turns talking, you can **offer solutions that work for both of you,** taking into account your feelings and theirs.

Practice

Who will I try this with? _____

When? _____

What happened? _____.

1. **Explain** the rationale, stressing the importance of understanding the other person's perspective in order to resolve a conflict and reach an agreement with others. Then explain the steps for effective communication, including scheduling time to talk, taking turns talking, and listening empathically.

2. **Model** these steps with another person. Pretend you are mad at them because they did not respond to your text messages and invitations to hang out. Pretend the other person wanted to get together but their parents took their phone and grounded them. Allow this information to come out as you take turns asserting yourselves and listening empathically so that they can resolve the problem. Model apologizing if we hurt the other person's feelings.

3. **Role-play** using actual situations that your students have experienced or use these role-play scenarios:

   a. A friend keeps criticizing the way you dress.
   b. Someone borrows some money and does not pay you back when they said they would.
   c. A friend demands to go somewhere with you, but you want to go somewhere else.
   d. You are doing a group project in school and no one is listening to your ideas.
   e. A teacher accuses you of cheating when you did not.
   f. A parent gives everyone in the family a gift except for you.

4. Help students to use the skill when they complain of a conflict with peers, family, or authority figures. Have them role-play what they might say to that person.

#77. DEALING WITH TEASING (Pre-K to 2nd Grade)

Rationale: This skill is about ways to react to teasing.
The goal is to stop it, without making it worse or getting in trouble.

1. Tell the person to stop.

2. Show the person that you do not care what they say.

3. Ignore the person or walk away.

4. Tell an adult if it continues.

Practice

Who will I try this with? _____

When? _____

What happened? _____.

Rationale: This skill is about how to think about and react to teasing. The goal is to stop the teasing and to stop it from hurting your feelings.

1. **Stay calm.** If they want to hurt you or get your attention, getting upset will only make them want to do it more.

2. **Check it out** before getting upset.

   a. Ask, "Did you mean that?" Sometimes they are just kidding. You can still ask them to stop if you do not like this kind of kidding around.

3. **Don't take it personally.** The other person's teasing may have more to do with them than you. They may have problems that make them put others down. Think to yourself, "It does not matter what the other person says. What's important is what I think and what my friends think." You may not be able to stop others from teasing, but you can learn to not let it hurt your feelings.

4. Use the following **four-step strategy** to try to get them to stop. If they stop with an early step, then you do not have to go to the next step.

   a. Tell the person to **stop** calmly.
   b. Tell them you **do not care** what they say.
   c. Walk away or **ignore** the person.
   d. If they continue despite your walking away or if they threaten to harm you, **tell an authority** (school personnel, supervisor, or your parent). Some teasers will not stop until authorities are informed. It is best for authorities not to tell the teaser you were the one who told on them, but rather to say they heard from many people that the person was teasing others.

5. Don't insult them back, as this often makes things worse. On the next page are more words you can use to respond to teasing without teasing them back.

More Words to Respond to Teasing

There are many words one can use to respond to teasing. It is best to avoid using insulting words, which usually provoke more teasing or a fight. If you tease back, it's best to do it in a non-insulting way (see below).

(Circle the items you might use or write your own)

Telling Them to Stop

"Stop!"

"I'm serious, cut it out!"

"Quit it!"

Ignoring

Ignore (do not look or listen)

"Is someone talking? I don't hear anything."

"Talk to the hand because the ears don't hear."

Win them over to your side

"You are too nice to want to tease me."

"It's too easy to pick on me; pick on someone who is a challenge."

Tease back in a joking way that does not provoke a fight

"Are you a comedian? That's almost funny."

"I do not really care what you say."

"I've got better things to do than listen to this."

"Very mature."

"Takes one to know one."

"It's sad you have to tease others to feel good about yourself."

Tell on them

Do not be afraid to tell on them when they threaten or hurt you.

When a group teases you

"Why does it take all of you to try to hurt one person's feelings?"

Practice

Who will I try this with? _____

When? _____

What happened? _____.

1. **Protect** others from teasing rather than simply teaching victims how to respond. Our job as adult authorities, teachers, or supervisors is to try to improve the peer environment so that our students do not get teased. We may need to:

   a. Increase monitoring of teasing hotspots (students hanging outside of school before class, on the bus, lunchroom, locker room, and other unsupervised areas).

   b. Report students who do the teasing to an authority (e.g., vice principal in a school, supervisor in an employment setting.). We may need to report this frequently until the students are warned of the consequences of their actions. I often talk to students doing the bullying in the following way: "I do not know if it is true, but there have been reports that you are *teasing other students*. I want others to respect you, and I need you to respect others. If anyone bothers you, you can tell me and I will take care of it, but if we get reports that you are continuing to tease others, you will have to talk with the administration, who will discuss with you the consequences." I do not use the "victim's" name here because I do not want the teaser to retaliate against them. If students continue to tease after this warning, there needs to be a consequence. At this time they may discover who reported them. That person must then be protected and the teaser warned about consequences that would ensue if they retaliated.

   c. Because adults will not always see teasing among peers, it is crucial to train positive peers to help protect potential victims. See Chapter 12 on ways to provide sensitivity training to create peer support for potential victims of teasing.

2. **Model and role-play** the skill steps for Dealing with Teasing. Never actually tease the students without first getting their permission. Always ask students what they want to be teased about as a way of practicing the skill. Do not allow other students to choose what the student should be teased about, as this will damage self-esteem. When you role-play, practice with the teaser stopping after the victim responds, and practice with the teaser not stopping, requiring the victim to tell an adult. Also, discuss what the victim can think so as not to take it personally.

a. The best role-play is one that mirrors what the student actually gets teased about. Ask students if there is anything they have been teased about so they can practice dealing with it.

b. If the student is reluctant to discuss what he gets teased about, use less threatening words to practice (e.g., "I do not like your sneakers, hat, or shirt" instead of saying something about the student's personality, body type, or behavior).

3. Have the student create their own responses to teasing by choosing words from the "More Words to Respond to Teasing" sheet.

4. Review any aggressive reactions to teasing by highlighting that in certain places like school, they only make things worse. Redirect the student to respond more assertively by using the skill steps described. More importantly, instances of teasing should be a call to action for better monitoring by adults and addressing the teaser's behavior.

#78. GIVING CONSTRUCTIVE CRITICISM

Rationale: When you criticize someone in an aggressive way, it my make others annoyed. If you must criticize, it should be done in a "constructive" way.

1. When to offer criticism:

    a. If someone asks for your critical feedback about something they did.

    b. If someone does something that directly hurts or bothers you.

    c. Otherwise: IF YOU HAVE NOTHING POSITIVE TO SAY, DON'T SAY ANYTHING AT ALL.

2. Constructive criticism focuses on what the person can do to improve rather than focusing on what they are doing wrong or insulting them.

    a. If someone asks for feedback about something they did, use the Sandwich Method to provide feedback:

      • Say something positive about what they did. For example, "I really liked how you ..."

      • Offer advice on how to improve. For example, "This part could be even better if you ..."

      • End with something positive again.

    b. If someone does something that directly hurts or upsets you, use an "I" statement (see skill on Assertiveness).

      I FEEL _____ (feeling word)

      WHEN YOU _____ (what they did or said)

      BECAUSE _____ (the reason it upset you)

      WHAT I WANT OR NEED IS _____ (what you want from them)

Practice

Who will I try this with? _____

When? _____

What happened? _____.

1. **Explain** the reason to avoid giving criticism unless it's requested or the person is bothering you. Explain the Sandwich Method for giving constructive criticism.

2. **Model, role-play, or discuss** when to say nothing and when to offer constructive criticism. Consider modeling aggressive criticism as well so students can understand what not to do. Use situations that have actually happened if possible or the following situations:

   a. A teacher asks a student to read aloud in class. The student reads very slowly, which begins to annoy another student. Role-play what that other student should do (e.g., do not say anything because the student may have a reading problem, but quietly read ahead if he cannot wait).

   b. A peer is in a wheelchair on a trip to the museum. Another student is annoyed that the child in the wheelchair is slowing them down. Role-play what this student can do and should not do (e.g., do not criticize, but ask if he can go ahead with another adult and meet the rest of the group later).

   c. A friend is playing a video game online with the student and making lots of mistakes. They have not asked for advice. Role-play what the student should do (e.g., say nothing and consider playing with someone else next time if their friend is slowing them down).

   d. A peer keeps interrupting a student when they are talking. Role-play what the student could do (e.g., use an "I" statement to express his annoyance at the interruptions).

   e. A peer throws a pencil at another student. What can the student say or do? Here, it is okay to criticize in a positive way using an "I" statement.

3. Students can be primed just before meeting with others who are known to do or say things that might be unconventional or irritating. Thus, students can be prepared to refrain from criticizing different but harmless behavior and to constructively criticize irritating behavior.

4. Provide feedback to students when they criticize others, directing them to be constructive and assertive rather than aggressive or insulting. Explain that your feedback to them is an example of constructive criticism as you tell them what they could do better.

#79. ACCEPTING CONSTRUCTIVE CRITICISM

Rationale: The ability to accept others' constructive criticism will both help you get along and allow you to learn new things. If you cannot accept any criticism, it is hard to correct anything and learn.

1. Decide if the criticism is **constructive** or **hurtful**. **Constructive** criticism may point out what you did wrong but also focuses on what you can do to improve. **Hurtful** criticism only points out what you did wrong and may contain insulting remarks.

2. If it is **constructive criticism**, then this is an opportunity to grow. It's not only okay to make mistakes, but it is the process of trying to correct them that helps us learn more.

   a. Say, "Okay, I'll think about that" or "I'll try to work on that."
   b. If you are asked to correct work, it is often best to just do it rather than argue over it because then you will be able to finish sooner.

3. If it is **hurtful criticism**, use an "I" message to tell them it was hurtful. If they continue, just treat it like teasing and tell them to stop, ignore it, or consider avoiding them if possible.

Practice

Who will I try this with? _____

When? _____

What happened? _____.

1. **Explain** the rationale that accepting constructive criticism helps one learn and get along with others. One might use stories of famous inventors, athletes, or performers who received a great deal of criticism to help mold their successes. Contrast constructive versus hurtful criticism and how to respond to both.

2. **Model and role-play** situations in which the student should accept criticism or correction. Use actual situations that have occurred or the following situations:

    a. A student is asked to stop interrupting so that he and his classmates can continue to learn.
    b. A student is asked to stop biting his fingernails to prevent getting an infection.
    c. A student is told to correct their work before going to the movies with friends. If he argues, it will further delay going out with his friends.
    d. A student is told that they are not good at drawing or art-making with no suggestions for how to improve. This might be treated as an insult and they can use an "I" message to express their hurt, or treat it like teasing (see DEALING WITH TEASING).

3. **Prior to giving feedback to a student** on a test or other performance, prime the student with the rationale for accepting criticism. Help them to anticipate and welcome imperfection as an opportunity to learn and grow. Then ask if they are ready for constructive feedback so they have time to prepare themselves. If they say they cannot handle criticism at the moment, then consider delaying the feedback.

#80. DEALING WITH PEER PRESSURE AND AVOIDING SETUPS

Rationale: Sometimes following your peers' suggestions can be very helpful; other times, it can lead you to serious trouble. It is important to understand when pressure from peers is helpful and when it is not.

1. Understand the difference between good and bad peer pressure.
   a. **Good peer pressure** is when friends ask you to do something that might help you or others, like encouraging you to be kind, do your schoolwork, practice a sport or hobby, or help a friend.
   b. **Bad peer pressure** is when friends ask you to do something that will get you in trouble or hurt others, or when they insist they will only be your friend if you do it. This can include:
      • Playing a trick on someone
      • Doing something dangerous to yourself or others, including harmful drugs

2. What can you do when you **do not know if it is good or bad** peer pressure? Sometimes peers may pretend to help you while actually pressuring you to do something bad. We call this a **SETUP**. If you are not sure whether it is good or bad, ask a person you trust for advice. This might be a parent, coach, mentor, or friend with a proven record of helping you.

3. Use the following steps to **handle bad peer pressure**:
   a. Ignore them.
   b. If they continue to pressure you, say no and refuse to do it.
   c. Explain why.
   d. Walk away if they continue to pressure you.

4. **What if you are so desperate for friends** that you do things that peers suggest even when you know doing so may not be good? People who try to make you do bad things are not really your friends; they are just using you. Instead, seek out people who will really care about you (see skill on "Where to Find Friends").

Practice

Who will I try this with? _____

When? _____

What happened? _____.

#80. DEALING WITH PEER PRESSURE AND AVOIDING SETUPS Activity Page

1. **Explain** the rationale for handling peer pressure and the definitions of good and bad peer pressure. Discuss the pull to conform to such pressure when one is desperate to make friends.

2. Help them see other options for finding positive friendships with people who do not have them do dangerous or hurtful things just to feel accepted. Have students make a list of people who care about and do not ask them to do dangerous or hurtful things. Use the skill WHERE TO FIND FRIENDS to help them see options for other friendships.

3. Have students also make a list of students, parents, and others that they can trust to give helpful advice when peers ask them to do things.

4. One can use a game-show format to model and role-play how to react to different peer-pressure situations. For each situation below, students can be asked to decide if it is good, bad, or unclear peer pressure and how they would respond.

   a. Peer asks the student to join him in stealing candy from a store and explains that everyone else does it. (Bad)
   b. Peer encourages the student to finish schoolwork so he can go out to the mall. (Good)
   c. Peer encourages the student to cut school so he can go out to the mall. (Bad)
   d. Peer asks for money in exchange for friendship. (Bad)
   e. A group of peers say the student has to be tough and defy the teacher to be cool and accepted into their group. (Bad)
   f. Peer encourages the student to keep practicing a sport or musical instrument. (Good)
   g. Peer tells the student that a friend wants to go out with her and that she should ask him out. (Unclear; go ask someone you trust, as this could be a SETUP)
   h. Peer tells the student that another student is mean and to avoid being friends with him. (Unclear; go ask someone you trust)

5. Students should be primed before interacting with peers known to engage in risky behaviors. Help them anticipate pressure to do bad things and know how to respond.

6. Provide feedback to students if they have succumbed to negative peer pressure, exploring with them why it may have happened. Did they know it was negative peer pressure? Did they want to do it anyway just to belong? Remind them of other friendship opportunities and the need to ask for advice if they are unsure of the consequences of certain behaviors.

SOCIAL SKILLS TRAINING

Rationale: A rumor is information being passed from person to person that may or may not be true. It is important to check out the truth about something before reacting to it.

1. If you hear someone may have said something bad about you, find out if they actually did before getting upset with them.

    a. Ask to talk directly with the person who reportedly said something bad about you. Say, "I need to speak to you for a moment. When is a good time to talk?"
    b. When they are ready, tell them what you heard they said about you.
    c. If they deny saying anything, let them know that you hope that is true.
    d. Warn them that if the rumors do not stop, you will have to report it to an authority (teacher, parent, or boss).

2. If you hear rumors about others, do not automatically believe they are true.

    a. Do not spread a rumor by telling others. That will upset others, and the rumor may well be false.
    b. If you are not sure whether it is true, you can ask someone you trust, like a teacher, or parent who will not spread the rumor further.

Practice

Who will I try this with? _____

When? _____

What happened? _____.

1. **Explain** the rationale for not automatically believing and spreading rumors. Students often do not know whether to believe a rumor. They will often need advice from a trusted friend or adult, so they should make a list of students, parents, and staff that they can trust to give helpful advice. These should be the people the student will seek out when a peer says something that may or may not be true.

2. **Model and role-play** or simply discuss how to handle situations that represent different types of rumors. If possible, use situations that actually occurred in the students' lives where they were uncertain of the truth about a rumor. For each situation, discuss how they would respond if they heard that rumor about themselves or others. Suggested situations:

   a. Peer tells the student that one of their female classmates is pregnant.
   b. Peer tells a student that their teacher is really an alien from Mars.
   c. Peer tells a student that there will not be any school for a week because of a special teacher convention.
   d. Peer tells a student that the teacher was just kidding about the test she said they would have tomorrow.
   e. Peer tells a student that a terrorist attack is going to occur in the school tomorrow. What might happen if they spread such a rumor?

3. Students should be primed not to automatically believe rumors especially when they are around students known to make up information and gossip a lot. They should instead ask a trusted friend, parent, or teacher.

4. Provide feedback to students if they spread a rumor about others, redirecting them to question the truth of such a rumor and telling them not to spread information that hurts others. Also provide redirection to students who become angry when they hear false rumors about themselves. Direct them to calmly check out whether the person really did say something about them before getting angry at the person.

#82. DEALING WITH BEING LEFT OUT

Rationale: Any of us may get left out of a social event sometimes. Dealing with this positively can help us be included or at least not make it worse.

1. Think about possible reasons why you were left out.

2. Was it because no one knew you wanted to be included? If so, tell others that you also want to join in.

3. Did you tell people but they said you cannot join in? Then ask why you can't join. Maybe they have no more room or you did something that upset them.

4. If others offer no reason for why they left you out, try not to take it personally. Some people reject us without ever getting to know us. You can:

   a. Find others who are more willing to have you join in. Look at the skill WHERE TO FIND FRIENDS.
   b. Ask an adult for help joining in.

Practice

Who will I try this with? _____

When? _____

What happened? _____.

#82. DEALING WITH BEING LEFT OUT Activity Page

1. Most of the responsibility for not being left out is on the part of the adults that surround the student (e.g., teachers and parents). We must create social opportunities for our students, and this may involve sensitizing peers to the needs of the student and encouraging them to engage the student (see Chapter 12 on Sensitivity Training). However, we can also help the student deal on a personal level to avoid being left out as described in this skill.

2. Discuss, model, and role-play the steps for Dealing with Being Left Out. Suggested role-plays:

   a. A bunch of students are playing a game at recess and one student is sitting by themselves. Role-play where the student says nothing to join in and then review that this is why they were left out. Role-play again where the student tries to join in and this time it works. Roleplay a third time where the student asks to play and is turned away. Have the student practice asking why they cannot play and/ or asking an adult for help finding someone else to play with.
   b. Do the same as above, but this time pretend you are looking for a partner or group to do a school group project.
   c. Lastly consider in these role-plays if there was anything the student may have done that led them to be left out (like interrupting or being bossy or too loud). Talk about ways to correct or apologize for these behaviors and then ask again to join in.

3. Have students make a list of students who may be more likely to let them join in. Also make a list of the adults they can ask for help if they are left out of an activity they want or need to join.

4. Correct inappropriate ways to deal with being left out like passively doing nothing (e.g., never asking to join) or aggressively responding to others (e.g., yelling at them) which would ensure they would be left out.

SOCIAL SKILLS TRAINING

#83. ASKING RESPECTFULLY FOR WHAT YOU WANT

Rationale: In general, we will get more from others when we use respectful words and a calm tone of voice.

Dos	Don'ts
Respect personal distance: Keep an arm's length away.	**Do not touch** anybody. Do not get closer than an arm's length away.
Use "request" words. "May I …?" "Can I …?" "Would you mind …?" "Would it be okay if …?"	Do not use "demand" words. "Do this now!" "I will not …" "You should …"
Use a calm "request" tone of voice.	Do not use an angry or "demand" tone of voice.
If others will not give you all you want, ask if you can compromise (get some of what you want but not all).	Do not demand to have it all your way.
If others refuse to compromise about a particular item or activity you requested, then **accept no** and ask if there is something else you can have/do instead.	Do not raise your voice or become aggressive if you don't get what you want.

Practice

Who will I try this with? _____

When? _____

What happened? _____.

#83. ASKING RESPECTFULLY FOR WHAT YOU WANT
Activity Page

1. Some children understand how to be respectful but choose not to because of chronic anger or depression. These children need more than this skill. They should be referred to a competent mental health professional for an evaluation to determine all the factors that contribute to their condition. For those with occasional disrespectful attitudes and who may not fully understand how they are impacting others, this skill lesson can be quite helpful.

2. This skill is really a composite of several previous skills like DON'T BE A SPACE INVADER, TONE OF VOICE, COMPROMISING, and ACCEPTING NO. One can use role-plays from each of these skills to review this composite skill. The one new step in this skill is understanding the difference between requests and demands. Some sample role-plays:

   a. Review appropriate distance when requesting something from others.
   b. Role-play the difference between requesting and demanding something like a snack, a trip to the playground, a special game, or to stop working.
   c. Review compromising versus demanding to play what you want to play. Use different games to practice.
   d. Pretend a parent refuses to compromise about getting a violent video game. Have the student practice ACCEPTING NO and asking if there is something else they can have instead.

3. Correct disrespectful actions and redirect to the appropriate behavior (e.g., watch the tone, make a request rather than demand, keep your distance). Consider using a video recorder so students can hear how they sound.

4. Using a reward program here can be especially helpful. Points towards rewards can offset disappointment when students do not get all that they want.

SOCIAL SKILLS TRAINING

#84. WHERE TO FIND POTENTIAL DATES

Rationale: Although it would be wonderful if you did not need to do anything to find a date and potential romantic partners would just come to you, this rarely happens. Most of us have to work to find a date.

1. **What is a date:** Going out with someone in a setting such as a restaurant, cinema, or cultural event with the intent of getting to know them better to see if you both would be interested in developing a romantic relationship.

2. **Where to find a date (see also the skill on Where to Find A Friend):**

   a. **Dating sites.** The advantage of these platforms is that the people here are interested in dating, so they will not be upset if you ask them out. The same is not true when you meet people in other settings. The downfall of these platforms is people you meet on the web may not actually be who they say they are, and many predators use the internet to find potential victims. If you plan to meet someone in person that you met online, it would be wise to do that with a trusted adult (parent or mentor) in a public place to ensure your safety. In addition, do not divulge any financial information (e.g., credit card or bank account numbers) to individuals you meet online, as they may be trying to steal from you. A common scam is for someone to profess their love to you and then later ask for money. The following lists some common dating sites available at the time of this book's printing. This is not an endorsement of any particular site, and clients should be cautious and ask a trusted mentor for help in navigating these sites. Lastly most sites are for eighteen-year-olds and up with the exception of the TEEN sites listed last:

ASD-specific:

https://www.hikiapp.com/

https://uneepi.com/

https://autisticdating.net/

https://www.autismdate.com/

http://www.aspie-singles.com/

https://www.aspergersdatingsite.com/

http://www.spectrumsingles.com/

https://www.facebook.com/autisticdating/

General Mental Health Issues:

http://www.nolongerlonely.com/

All disabilities including physical:

http://www.dating4disabled.com/
http://www.datedisabled.com/
http://www.datingdisabled.net/
http://www.whispers4u.com/

**Some Neurotypical sites/APPS
(many are geo-located to reveal people in your area)**

General: Hinge, Bumble
Serious relationships: Match, Plenty of Fish, OKcupid
Casual Dating: Tinder

Specifically for teens (ages 13-17)

Yubo, Spotafriend, Skout, Mylol, Tinder for Teens

b. **Singles events.** Many organizations sponsor singles events to meet people. One program called "Speed Dating" may be especially helpful in that you talk with many new people as they break up the members into dyads for a series of brief conversations so that each person gets a chance to talk to many others.

c. Schools and community centers often have **clubs** based on interests (e.g., radio, music, television/video, photography, journalism, science fiction, sports, gaming, theatre, religious youth clubs.). Though not specifically a location to find a date, having shared interests can lead to friendships which could eventually lead to dating.

d. **Family and friends.** One of the best sources for meeting others is through mutual friends or family. Polls show that most married couples met each other through mutual friends. Letting your friends know you are looking to date someone can help. Ask if they know anyone that they could set you up on a date with.

e. **Bars** (for those twenty-one and older), dance clubs, and parties are also other possibilities.

Practice

Who will I try this with? _____

When? _____

What happened? _____.

1. Explain the rationale that one has to work to find possible dating opportunities. Describe the places where students can meet potential dates.

2. Students should create an action plan that lists places that they frequent and the type of person that they want to ask on a date. Go through the list of places and help the student identify favorable scenarios.

3. Students should then list people they trust to ask for advice in communicating with possible dating interests. This is especially important when using online options to avoid possible scams and predators.

   a. If parents are involved, they should try to avoid threatening to remove a teen's phone if they are communicating with questionable people as then teens may not say when they get suspicious texts. If parents can help their teens keep the line of communication open, then they can better guide their teenager.

   b. If teens continue to engage in risky online communications, parents can install any one of several software programs to track communications, signal when risky texts come in, and track their teen's whereabouts. Here is a list of safety programs parents can utilize: 1. FamiSafe Android Parental Control App. 2. Kaspersky Safe Kids. 3. mSpy Parental Control. 4. Net Nanny. 5. Norton Family Parental Control. 6. Screen Time Parental Control App. 7. ScreenLimit. 8. Family Time. 9. ESET Parental Control Android

4. Students can be primed prior to entering social situations that these are places that they might meet someone. Even before trying to talk with someone in these settings, it is important to consider many of the non-verbal skills related to dress and hygiene to maximize the student's chances.

5. Speed-dating is an activity that helps singles structure their socializing to meet many people in one outing. In this format, individuals have scheduled conversations with one other person before rotating to another person. Usually there are a series of five-minute conversations with up to ten or more people. It would be helpful for high schools, colleges, or other organizations to use this format to help people meet each other rather than leaving it up to individuals to initiate conversations on their own.

#85. ASKING SOMEONE OUT ON A DATE

Rationale: As much as we wish others would ask us out, sometimes we have to do the work to arrange a date. The most successful people in the dating game are those who are willing to take the risk and ask someone out.

1. Use the skill Getting to Know Someone New (Skill #38) to find out what you may have in common. **DO NOT BRING UP SEXUAL ACTIVTY** unless they bring it up as this can scare people away! **Focus on their interests** more than your own unless they specifically ask you about your interests.

2. If the person seems interested in talking with you (e.g., they ask about your interests and they do not make an excuse to stop talking with you), then you might **ask if it would be okay** to exchange phone numbers or email addresses so that you can talk again sometime.

3. If they provide you with their phone number or email, contact them no more than twice in a week unless they tell you to call more often.

4. If they respond to your emails or phone calls or they initiate the call, then they might be interested in at least being your friend. At this point you can suggest getting together with them in a place/activity that you will both enjoy (based on your common interests). You could say, **"Speaking of _____, would you like to get together to go to _____ sometime?"** Restaurants, concerts, sports activities, and other special events are good choices.

5. If they say yes, offer to meet at a convenient time for them.

6. If they say no, you can ask if they might want to go out another time. If they say no, then do not ask them again, but rather say, "If you change your mind, let me know." Asking too many times may upset and annoy the other person, so if you have asked twice, then let them ask you next time.

7. **Dealing with fear of rejection:** Everyone fears being rejected. If you let that stop you from asking someone out, you may never have a date. Remember:

   a. The other person probably fears being rejected as much as you do. The worst thing that can happen is that they say no. Then you can ask someone else.
   b. For most people, it takes asking out many people before someone says yes. This does not mean that there is something unlikable about you; it just takes time for you to find someone you like who also likes you.

Practice

Who will I try this with? _____

When? _____

What happened? _____.

#85. ASKING SOMEONE OUT Activity Page

1. Explain the rationale and need to set reasonable expectations (that it is normal to get rejected most of the time because it is hard to find someone whom you like and who likes you). Mathematically, if person A is attracted to one out of seven people and person B is attracted to one out of seven people, the chances they both find each other attractive is one out of forty-nine! So the pickier you and the other person are, the harder it is to find a match.

2. Students should create an action plan that lists people they might want to ask out based on those they have met.

3. Any fears of rejection should be challenged (e.g., see DEALING WITH SOCIAL FEARS).

4. Discuss being prepared by addressing hygiene and appropriate attire (dress in a way that is the norm for the situation you are in).

5. Model and role-play GETTING TO KNOW THE OTHER PERSON and then ASKING IF IT IS OKAY TO EXCHANGE PHONE OR EMAIL ADDRESSES. Then role-play the transition from a shared interest to ASKING THEM OUT. Use the transition statement in the skill lesson, "Speaking of _____, would you want to get together sometime to _____?" Role-play this both when the other person seems interested and disinterested, reviewing the need to back off when the other person does not ask questions back or return calls or emails.

6. Consider getting a mentor or parent to help you interpret the other's communications to know how to respond. This is easier when using online dating platforms where you can take time to respond to someone.

#86. DO'S AND DON'TS ON A DATE

Rationale: Getting to a date is great, but having a date go well is even better. The following lists things to do and not to do to maximize the success of your date.

What to do and not to do

Skill	Do	Don't
Dress, hygiene, and grooming	**Clean your hair, teeth, and body. Wear clean clothes appropriately matched to where you are going.**	Don't wash. Wear dirty clothes that tell the other person you do not care enough to look good for them.
Listening and maintaining conversation	Listen carefully to your date. Ask about their interests and their life. Put away your phone.	Do all the talking. Tell about your life without every asking about theirs.
Show caring for others' feelings	Show that you care if they are talking about something that upset them. Say you understand, share a similar experience, or offer to help.	Ignore signs of upset or suggest that it is not that big a deal.
Compliment	Compliment them.	Insult or criticize them.
Arriving to the date	Be on time and offer to meet somewhere convenient for them.	Be late and tell them to go way out of their way to get you.
Paying for things	Offer to pay for your date (if you were the one who asked them out).	Tell them you have no money and expect them to pay.
Compromise	Find out what they want to do and offer to do some of what they like.	Insist on doing only what you want to do on the date.
Expectations (about romance and sex)	You should not expect the other person to be physical or agree to a second date yet. DO NOT BRING UP SEX unless they do. You may need to wait until after the date to see if they want to meet again.	Expect and demand that your date agree to be physical or discuss this with you or agree to meet again.

Practice

Who will I try this with? _____

When? _____

What happened? _____.

1. Explain the do's and don'ts on a date.

2. **Model and role-play** the right and wrong ways for each skill in the table.

   a. For example, you can **model** a behavior from the table and then ask "Is this a DO or a DON'T? What skill is this?"
   b. You can also ask them to **role-play** a particular skill that they have struggled with.

3. Since the table covers quite a lot of material, you may want to consider only reviewing those skills relevant to the students you are teaching. For example, if dress code is never a problem, but making small talk is, then focus on making small talk.

4. The skills most relevant to the student's needs should be primed before going on a date. They can be written on a cue card for easy review.

5. The student can get feedback about the date by calling or texting the person they saw and asking how they are and whether they enjoyed the date. Asking the person out again and getting a yes indicates a positive response. If the person says no, then it may be helpful to ask the person for feedback about what they could have done better to help learn from the experience.

#87. READING THE SIGNALS TO PURSUE A ROMANCE

Rationale: It is very important to identify the signals of when others want to be pursued for romance or physical intimacy and when they do not. Misreading the signals can sometimes have major consequences. For example, trying to touch or kiss others who do not want that can lead to legal actions.

1. **What is a romantic or intimate relationship?** When two people find each other attractive, they sometimes pursue a romantic relationship. Such a relationship may involve being physically close, holding hand hands, kissing, and possibly engaging in sexual activity.

2. **When you meet someone for the first time:** IT IS NOT OKAY TO FOLLOW THEM AROUND OR TRY TO TOUCH THEM. Before you can begin a romantic/physical relationship with someone, you must first:

   a. Get to know them (using Skill #38).
   b. Ask them out on a date.
   c. Find out if they are enjoying the date and read the signs if they might want to be physical with you.
      - While on a date, do they seek out touch with you (e.g., holding your hand, kissing you, or inching closer, putting their arm around you)?
      - Do they suggest going somewhere more private?
      - Only in the context of a date can you ask if they want to be touched. You can ask, "Is it okay to give you a hug? Hold your hand? Give you a kiss on the cheek?" If they seem to accept that, then go ahead; if they turn away from you and say no, then back off.

3. **How to know whether to pursue dating the other person?** This skill is very challenging and worth having a mentor to help you review the communications from the other person to see if they like you. The following is a checklist to assist you in this process. If you have more than three "No" answers, then you may think about backing off from pursuing a romantic relationship.

a. Do they seek you out for conversation?   Yes/No
b. Do they use sentences rather than one-word answers when you are conversing with them.   Yes/No
c. Do they inquire about your interests?   Yes/No
d. Do they share the same interest?   Yes/No
e. Do they seem excited rather than bored to see you?   Yes/No
f. Do they initiate conversations with you?   Yes/No
g. Do they call or email you?   Yes/No
h. Do they return your calls or emails?   Yes/No
i. Do they ask you to do things or activities that you both like?   Yes/No

Practice

Who will I try this with? _____

When? _____

What happened? _____.

1. **Explain** the rationale and need to follow some steps before becoming romantically involved or trying to be physical with someone.

2. Students should identify those whom they are romantically interested in and try to determine if they have gotten to know them and are receiving signals that suggest that they could go to the next step of asking the person out.

3. Model and role-play welcoming versus unwelcoming behaviors (see Skill #21). Instead of modeling and role-playing the signs of physical interest in others, which might be uncomfortable for the students, it may be better to play clips from TV shows or movies depicting the different signals of physical interest and disinterest. Soap operas, the show "Blind Date," and some of the reality shows may be good sources for such clips.

4. Students should be **reminded** of the need to sequence their approach to developing a romantic relationship rather than coming on too strong. Talking about or pushing for physical intimacy too early can scare potential dates away. Reminders to get to know others, ask someone out, read signs of interest, and ask before touching others are key.

Rationale: Sometimes students unknowingly engage in sexual harassment of others and as a result can suffer legal actions against them. It is important to know what constitutes sexual harassment and to avoid engaging in any such activity.

1. **Definition:** Sexual Harassment is any unwanted words or actions of a sexual nature. This might include:
   a. Comments or teasing about one's body, sexual behavior, or sexual orientation.
   b. Touching, pinching, grabbing, or rubbing up against someone or rubbing yourself in front of others.
   c. Graffiti, pictures, cartoons, audio, or video of a sexual nature.
   d. Threats to hurt someone or cause a problem for someone if they do not perform some act of a sexual nature.
   e. Bribes or rewards offered to someone in exchange for sexual favors.

2. **What you should know:**
   a. Sexual harassment is illegal. Schools and employment setting have a policy forbidding sexual harassment.
   b. It is illegal for anyone to punish you for telling others, so you should tell.
   c. By telling others, you may prevent the person from harassing you and others.

3. **What to do if you think you are being harassed:**
   a. Tell the person to stop. That is the best way they will know the behavior is unwanted.
   b. Tell a trusted adult, such as the principal, teacher, supervisor, human resources specialist, or a parent.
   c. Keep a record of when and where the harassment took place.
   d. If the behavior does not stop, you can file criminal charges through the police department.

4. **What to do if you were told that you were harassing others:** Immediately stop the behavior. Explain that you did not realize that it upset others, and apologize to all those involved. You may need to stay away from the people you harassed if they request that.

Practice

Who will I try this with? _____

When? _____

What happened? _____.

#88. SEXUAL HARASSMENT Activity Page

1. Explain the significance of sexual harassment and possible legal penalties. Define what it is, emphasizing that it is unwanted behavior, so it is key to ask if the other person wants or does not want the behavior.

2. Have students help you identify examples of sexual harassment (they do not need to share personal information here but can tell us general examples).

3. Model and role-play what to do if you are a victim. Practice telling others to stop and report the activity. Also practice what to do if they are a bystander or if they inadvertently harassed someone and did not realize it.

4. For students who have been harassed before, prime them on communicating to the harasser that the behavior is unwanted and to report any incident. Some students may be too afraid to report it and ask that you make the initial report for them to the proper authorities. For those who have harassed before, prime them on what is not okay to do and what are better ways to interact and get to know others.

5. Review with students any incident of sexual harassment and how they can respond as a victim or accidental perpetrator.

Rationale: Some of us do not want to hurt anyone's feelings, so we have a hard time saying no when others pressure us to date or be intimate when we do not want to. This skill is about how to say no in a nice way when you would still like to be friends.

1. **Some people do not know that you are not interested** in dating or engaging in physically intimate activities unless you tell them.

2. **If you are not interested in dating someone, but you still want to be their friend,** you can say, "I like you as a friend and hope we can remain friends, but I am not interested in dating." If they persist and ask why, you can say, "It's not that you are not attractive I just do not think you are a match for me."

3. **If you are not interested in dating or being friends** with someone, you can say, "I do not feel we are a good match for each other, so I do not want to date." If they persist and ask why, you can say, "It's not that you are not attractive; I just do not feel you are a match for me."

4. **If you are not comfortable being physical with someone, it's important to tell them.** You can say, "I like you a lot but do not feel ready to _____" or "I am not comfortable _____, but I am okay with _____."
   a. A good partner will respect your wishes.
   b. If someone says that they will leave you if you do not do something that makes you uncomfortable, then let them leave, as they are not a respectful partner. There are other more respectful partners to be found (see skill on Where to Find a Date).

Practice

Who will I try this with? _____

When? _____

What happened? _____.

1. Much of this skill is about **overcoming the fear that a partner will be mad** or that they will leave. Before practicing the words to tell a partner, one first has to address these fears. As discussed in the section of handling anxiety, we always ask two questions when handling fears:

    a. What it the probability of something bad happening?
        - Will they really be mad? Will they stop being friends? Will they really leave you? Most respectful people will not do these things.
    b. How bad would it be if it did happen?
        - So what if they got annoyed or stopped being your friend or partner? Can you get other (better) friends or partners?

2. **Model and role-play** ways to tell others politely that you:

    a. Do not want to date but want to be friends.
    b. Do not want to date or be friends.
    c. Want to date but do not want to be physical now or that there are certain things you may never want to do.

3. Some students may need to be primed just before seeing this person, and the script can be written on a cue card to help them remember it.

#90. COMMUNICATING CLEARLY TO MEET EACH OTHER'S NEEDS

Rationale: Everyone would like their needs, wishes, and wants to be met in the world. The success of a romantic relationship depends in part on each person trying to meet the other's needs. To do this, it is important for the couple to be able to positively communicate to each other instead of angrily complaining about what we did not get. The focus of this skill is on helping couples negotiate how to address each other's needs.

1. **Schedule a time to talk about ways to keep your relationship working:** Ask your partner when might be a good time to talk privately. Explain that you want to make sure you know each other's likes and dislikes so that you can continue to have a healthy, satisfying relationship.

2. You and your partner can **each make a list** of what you like when it comes to:

   a. Talking (e.g., do you get enough time to talk with them? Do they show support when you are upset?)
   b. Going out (e.g., where do you like and not like to go?)
   c. Physical intimacy (e.g., what kind of touch do you like or not like and when?)
   d. Your favorite foods, clothes, gifts, special activities
   e. What makes you laugh?
   f. What calms you when you are upset?

3. Each of you can choose to do the things your partner likes as listed as long as each of you is comfortable with those things. **Do not feel compelled to do anything on the list that makes you uncomfortable.**

   a. If you do not want to do something, you can say, "I understand why you might want me to do that, but I am not comfortable with doing that (or I do not always want to do that). Is there something else we can do together then?"

4. **State what you want your partner to do in a positive way.**

      a. For example, "I like it when you ..." or "I would love it if you would ..."

      b. Avoid complaining about what your partner does not do (e.g., "You never ..."). This will decrease their desire to please you.

Practice

Who will I try this with? _____

When? _____

What happened? _____.

#90 COMMUNICATING CLEARLY TO MEET EACH OTHER'S NEEDS Activity Page

1. Explain the importance of clearly communicating each other's needs in having a satisfying relationship. Review the steps to talking about this with their partner in a positive way without complaining.

2. Create a list of the questions they will ask their partner about their wishes and the answers they get after talking with their partner. On a separate piece of paper, have them prepare a short list of wishes they want to request of their partner.

3. Model and role-play how to request their wishes positively and how to listen to their partner's wishes with getting angry or defensive. Also model being able to say no to certain things that make them uncomfortable while still validating their partner's desire for those things.

4. Provide feedback to students when they complain about relationship difficulties with others (e.g., when they have not clearly expressed what they wanted or got information from others about what they wanted). Direct them to a way to state what they want and do not want in a positive respectful manner.

#91. HANDLING REJECTION

Rationale: When it comes to dating, we should all expect to be rejected more often than not since it is hard to find a match. Handling rejection in a positive way can help you succeed in finding a suitable partner.

1. **Expect that it will take dating many people before finding a match.** The more people you try to date, the more likely you will find a match. So do not be discouraged when you get rejected many times before finding a match.

2. **If they reject you, it does not mean there is anything wrong with you,** it just means that the two of you do not match. Getting depressed or mad about it usually comes from taking it personally or thinking that you are unattractive to others. Though there may be something you can do to improve your dating behavior, rejection does not mean that you are unattractive; it just means you are not a match for that person.

    a. If you can tolerate criticism, it may be worth asking the other person if there is anything you did that they didn't like so you can learn from it for the next time you date someone.

3. **Myth 1: Others owe me a date. No one owes you anything.** People will date you if you seem like the type they were looking for and you behave well on the date (see DOs AND DON'Ts ON A DATE).

4. **Myth 2: This was the only person for me.** If they did not like you back, they were not the right person. There are millions of people in the world and if you are persistent, you will find someone else who you like and who likes you back.

5. **Getting angry and insulting those who reject us creates a bad reputation, can get you kicked off of dating sites, and can lead to trouble with the law.**

6. **Being less picky will increase your chances** of finding a match. If you have a very narrow idea of whom you can date, you will not meet as many people. Also, seek to meet people with similar experiences since they are more likely to accept and relate to you. This could mean similar backgrounds, similar life circumstances, and even similar challenges (see WHERE TO FIND A DATE).

Practice

Who will I try this with? _____

When? _____

What happened? _____.

1. When explaining the rationale, stress the need to expect lots of rejection as part of the process of dating because of the mathematical probabilities of two people finding each other that truly like each other.

    a. You can demonstrate this with two bags of colored marbles. Pretend that a blue marble wants to find another blue marble for true love. In each bag, put one blue marble and six other colored ones. Take turns picking one marble from each bag to see if how long it takes to get a match where you pull blue from each bag on the same draw. Remember to put the marbles back in their bags after each draw.
    b. Explain how there is nothing wrong with red, yellow, green, or any non-blue colors; it's just that one blue marble wanted another blue marble. Explain how, similarly, there is nothing wrong with you if you get rejected; it's just not the right match.

2. Explore the students' ideas about Myth 1: Do people owe it to them to date them or do they have to behave the right way to get some people to like them? Similarly explore Myth 2: Are there other fish in the sea? Other blue marbles? There always are, when you look long enough.

3. Also ask them what they think would happen if they got angry and retaliated against someone who rejected them. What if the person told other potential dates? What if they call the police?

4. Explore the idea "DON'T JUDGE A BOOK BY ITS COVER." Sometimes people become more attractive over time as you get to know them. There will be more possible matches when you do not need a potential partner to look a particular way.

#92. WHEN (AND WHEN NOT) TO CALL EMERGENCY SERVICES

Rationale: It is important to know the difference between true emergencies and non-emergency problems. Calling emergency services for non-emergency problems can get you in trouble with police. Not calling emergency services when it is a true emergency can cause disasters.

1. Emergencies are situations where someone may have a life-threatening problem. Take a look at the table below for life-threatening emergencies versus non-emergency problems.

Emergency	Non-Emergency
You were robbed or assaulted (call the police)	You lost an important item like your phone (ask a trusted adult for help)
You house caught fire (call the fire department)	A family member lit a candle or made a controlled fire in a fireplace
A family member is unconscious, cannot breathe (call an ambulance), or they are complaining of intense chest pain by the heart	You twisted your ankle, stubbed your toe, and got hurt somehow, but you can breathe and are conscious (you might need to call a doctor but not an ambulance)
Someone is threatening to break into you house or physically harm you (call the police)	Someone is yelling at you or arguing with you (ask a trusted adult for help)
Your carbon monoxide or smoke detector is signaling an alarm in the middle of the night when no one is cooking (call fire department)	Smoke detector went off after you were cooking (as long as there is no fire, just reset the alarm)
You or someone you know says they want to kill or hurt themselves and they are not just joking (call 988, the suicide prevention hotline)	You or someone you know says they are really upset, sad or angry but do not want to kill or hurt themself (ask a trusted adult for help)
Someone in the house is destroying property and hurting others (may need to call police if they do not stop)	Your TV or device is not working Your food you ordered did not arrive You cannot figure out how to do your work or fix something (ask a trusted adult for help)

SOCIAL SKILLS TRAINING

2. In general, for emergencies you can access emergency services by calling 911 in the US. Or when someone is suicidal or wants to hurt themselves, call 988.

3. For non-emergencies, ask a trusted adult for help. This may be a parent when you are home, or a teacher when you are in school.

4. **If stopped by a police officer, first do what they say.** Then ask if you can give them your **Emergency Information Sheet**. This is a prepared statement to explain any behavioral differences they may observe (see sample on the following page).

Practice

Who will I try this with? _____

When? _____

What happened? _____.

(give to police or other authorized individuals during a crisis)

I have autism,

a neurobiological neurological difference. It affects my ability to communicate and interact sometimes, especially in times of stress or crisis. Individuals with autism may:

- Lack eye contact

- Be overly sensitive to sounds, touch, or light

- May not always answer questions in a way that relates to the topic

In case of an emergency, please contact:

_____ \ \ \ \ _____

(Name) \ (Cell number)

Please follow these suggestions for assisting individuals with autism:

- Be patient and calming. Individuals with autism who feel attacked may become agitated and not think about what they are saying or doing.

- If an individual is very agitated, try to distract him or her by talking about another topic until they are calm.

- Avoid abstract language, slang, or idioms, as some individuals with ASD may not understand.

1. Explain the difference between real emergencies and non-emergencies. Also explain the importance of calling emergency services for true emergencies and calling a trusted adult for non-emergencies.

2. Review the information of when to call emergency services versus a trusted adult using real situations that have occurred before or the following situations:

    a. You cannot figure out your schoolwork (ask a trusted adult)
    b. You lost your phone (ask a trusted adult)
    c. Someone stole your phone out of your hand and ran away (call the police)
    d. You are arguing with a friend about what movie to go see (ask a trusted adult)
    e. A lamp fell on your bed and caught fire (call the fire department)
    f. You fell and wonder if you broke your arm (go to Urgent Care, but you do not need police or ambulance)

3. Have them create a list of emergency service numbers and personal contacts to keep at all times (at home and on their person). Consider laminating it and putting on a card. Also keep a list of trusted adults to ask for help for all non-emergency problems.

4. Have them create a prepared statement about their challenges using the sample statement as a model. This can also be put into card form and laminated to keep with them at all times. Practice showing this to police or another authorized emergency provider.

5. Call the local police in your town to let them know you have a child/teen with challenges in case they ever get stopped by the police and are acting in unexpected ways.

REFERENCES

American Psychiatric Association, (2013). *Diagnostic and statistical manual of mental disorders. 5th ed*. Arlington, VA: American Psychiatric Association.

Anderson K.A., Sosnowy, C, Kuo A.A., Shattuck, P.T. (2018). Transition of individuals with autism to adulthood: A review of qualitative studies. *Pediatrics, 141*(Supplement_4). https://doi.org/10.1542/peds.2016-4300I. PMID: 29610413.

Baker, J. E. (2001). *Social skills picture books*. Arlington, TX: Future Horizons, Inc.

Baker, J. E. (2003). *Social skills training for children and adolescents with Aspergers syndrome and related social communication disorders*. Arlington, TX: Future Horizons, Inc.

Baker, J. E. (2005). *Preparing for life: The complete guide to transitioning to adulthood for those with Autism and Aspergers Syndrome*. Arlington, TX: Future Horizons, Inc.

Baker, J. E. (2006). *The social skills picture book for high school and beyond*. Arlington, TX: Future Horizons, Inc.

Baker, J. E. (2008). *No more meltdowns*. Arlington, TX: Future Horizons, Inc.

Baker, J. E. (2013). *No more victims: Protecting those with autism from cyber bullying, internet predators, & scams*. Arlington, TX: Future Horizons, Inc.

Baker, J.E. (2015). *Overcoming anxiety in children and teens.* Arlington, TX: Future Horizons, Inc.

Bellini, S. & Akullian, J. (2007). A meta-analysis of video modeling and video self-modeling interventions for children and adolescents with autism spectrum disorders. *Exceptional Children, 73,* 261–284.

Bellini, S., Peters, J., Berner, L., & Hopf, A. (2007) A meta-analysis of school-based social skills interventions for children with autism spectrum disorders. *Remedial and Special Education, 28*(3), 153-162.

Benson, H. (1976) *The relaxation response.* New York, NY: Avon Books

Biel, L. & Peske, N. (2009). *Raising a sensory smart child: The definitive handbook for helping your child with sensory processing issues.* New York, NY: Penguin Books.

Cannon, L., Kenworthy, L., Alexander, K.C., Werner, M.A., Anthony, L.G. (2011). *Unstuck and on target!: An executive function curriculum to improve flexibility for children with autism spectrum disorders.* Baltimore: Paul H. Brookes Pub. Co.

Canter, L. (1987). *Assertive discipline.* New York: Harper and Row.

Constantino, J.N. (2013). Social Responsiveness Scale. In: Volkmar, F.R. (eds) Encyclopedia of Autism Spectrum Disorders. New York, NY: Springer. https://doi.org/10.1007/978-1-4419-1698-3_296

Crick, N. R., & Dodge, K. A. (1994). A review and reformulation of social information-processing mechanisms in children's social adjustment. *Psychological Bulletin, 115*(1), 74–101. https://doi.org/10.1037/0033-2909.115.1.74

Deci, E. L., Koestner, R., & Ryan, R. M. (1999). A meta-analytic review of experiments examining the effects of extrinsic rewards on intrinsic motivation. *Psychological Bulletin, 125,* 627–668.

Dunn, M. (2005). *S.O.S. Social skills in our schools: A social skill program for children with pervasive developmental disorders, including high-functioning autism and asperger syndrome, and their typical peers.* Shawnee Mission, Kansas: Autism Aspergers Publishing Company.

Elliott, S.N., Gresham, F.M. (2013). Social Skills Improvement System. In: Volkmar, F.R. (eds) Encyclopedia of Autism Spectrum Disorders. New York, NY: Springer. https://doi.org/10.1007/978-1-4419-1698-3_509

Frost, L., & Bondy, A. (2006). A Common Language: Using B.F. Skinner's Verbal Behavior for Assessment and Treatment of Communication Disabilities in SLP-ABA. *The Journal of Speech-Language Pathology and Applied Behavior Analysis. 1,* 103–110.

Gates, J. A., Kang, E., & Lerner, M. D. (2017). Efficacy of group social skills interventions for youth with autism spectrum disorder: A systematic review and meta-analysis. *Clinical Psychology Review, 52,* 164–181. https://doi.org/10.1016/j.cpr.2017.01.006

Gray, C. (2004). *The sixth sense.* Arlington, TX: Future Horizons, Inc.

Greene, R. (2021). *The explosive child: A new approach for understanding and parenting easily frustrated, chronically inflexible children.* New York: Harper.

Greenspan, S.I., & Weider, S. (2009). *Engaging autism: Using the floor time approach to help children relate, communicate, and think.* Da Capo Lifelong Books.

Gresham, F.M., Sugai, G., & Horner, R. H. (2001). Interpreting outcomes of social skills training for students with high-incidence disabilities. *Exceptional Children, 67,* 331–344.

Gresham, F. M., & Elliott, S. N. (2008). *Social skills improvement system: Rating scales.* Bloomington, MN: Pearson Assessments.

Gutstein, S.E., (2009). *The RDI book: Forging new pathways for autism, Asperger's and PDD with the relationship development intervention program.* Houston, TX: Connections Center Pub.

Haimovitz, K., & Dweck, C.S. (2017). The origins of children's growth and fixed mindsets: new research and proposal. *Child Development, 88*(6), 849–1859.

Haring, T., & Breen, C. (1992). A peer mediated social network intervention to enhance the social integration of persons with moderate and severe disabilities. *Journal of Applied Behavior Analysis, 25,* 319–333.

History's Most Inspiring People On The Spectrum. (2017). Applied Behavior Analysis Programs Guide. https://appliedbehavioranalysisprograms.com/historys-30-most-inspiring-people-on-the-autism-spectrum/.

Hotton, M., & Coles, S. (2016). The effectiveness of social skills training groups for individuals with autism spectrum disorder. *Review Journal of Autism and Developmental Disorders, 3*(1), 68–81.

Kenwothy, L., Anthony, L.G., Naiman, D.O., Cannon, L., Wills, M.C., Luong-Tran, C., Werner, M.A., Alexander, K.C., Strang, J., Bal, E., Sokoloff, J.L., Wallace, G.L. (2013). Randomized controlled effectiveness trial of executive function intervention for children on the autism spectrum. *Journal of Child Psychology and Psychiatry, 55*(4), 374–83.

Koegel, R., & Koegel, L. (2018). *Pivotal response treatment for autism spectrum disorders*. Baltimore, MD: Paul H. Brookes Publishing.

Kohls, G., Schulte-Rüther, M., Nehrkorn, B., Müller, K., Fink, G. R., Kamp-Becker, I., Herpertz-Dahlmann, B., Schultz, R. T., & Konrad, K. (2012). Reward system dysfunction in autism spectrum disorders. *Social Cognitive and Affective Neuroscience, 8*(5): 565–572. https://doi.org/10.1093/scan/nss033

Koning, C., Magill-Evans, J., Volden, J., and Dick, B.(2013). Efficacy of cognitive behavior therapy-based social skills intervention for school-aged boys with autism spectrum disorders. *Research in Autism Spectrum Disorders, 7*, 1282–1290.

Kranowitz, C. S., & Miller, L.J. (2022), *The Out-of-Sync child, Third Edition: recognizing and coping with sensory processing differences*. New York, NY: Tarcher Perigee.

Laugeson, E.A. (2013). *The PEERS curriculum for school-based professionals: social skills training for adolescents with autism spectrum disorder 1st edition*, New York, N.Y: Routledge.

Mateson, J.L., Mateson, M.L., & Rivet, T.T. (2007). Social skills treatments for children with autism spectrum disorders: An overview. *Behavior Modification, 31*(5).

McGinnis, E., & Goldstein, A. (1997). *Skill streaming the elementary school child: New strategies and perspectives for teaching prosocial skills*. Champaign, IL: Research Press.

Myles, B. S., Mahler, K.J., Robbins, L.A. & Chiles, P. (2014). *Sensory issues and autism: practical solutions for making sense of the world*. Arlington, TX: Future Horizons, Inc.

Odom, S.L., & Strain, P.S. (1984). Peer-mediated approaches to promoting children's social interaction: A review. *American Journal of Orthopsychiatry, 54*, 544–557.

Odom, S.L., & Watts, E. (1991). Reducing teacher prompts in peer-mediated interventions for young children with autism. *Journal of Special Education, 25,* 26–43.

Patton, J., & Dunn, C. (1998). *Transition from school to adulthood: Basic concepts and recommended practices.* Austin, TX: Pro-Ed.

Payton, J., Weissberg, Payton, J., Weissberg, R.P., Durlak, J.A., Dymnicki, A.B., Taylor, R.D., Schellinger, K.B., & Pachan, M. (2008). *The positive impact of social and emotional learning for kindergarten to eighth-grade students: Findings from three scientific reviews.* Chicago, IL: Collaborative for Academic, Social, and Emotional Learning.

Rogers, S. J., & Dawson, G. (2010). *Early Start Denver Model for young children with autism: Promoting language, learning, and engagement.* New York: The Guilford Press.

Trimarchi, C. L. (2004). *The implementation and evaluation of a social skills training program for children with asperger syndrome.* (Unpublished doctoral dissertation), University at Albany, State University of New York.

Twemlow, S. W., Fonagy, P., Sacco, F.C. Gies, M.L., Evans, R. & Ewbank, R. (2001). Creating a peaceful school learning environment: A controlled study of elementary school intervention to reduce violence. *American Journal of Psychiatry, 158*(5), 808–810.

Wagner, S. (1998). *Inclusive programming for elementary students with autism.* Arlington, TX: Future Horizons, Inc.

Wagner, S. (2021). *Inclusive programming for elementary students with autism: A manual of social and communication skills.* Arlington, TX: Future Horizons, Inc.

About the Author

JED BAKER, Ph.D, graduated Phi Beta Kappa from SUNY-Binghamton and went on to receive the Presidential Fellowship from SUNY-Albany, where he completed his doctorate in clinical psychology. He writes, lectures, and provides training internationally on the topic of social skills training and managing challenging behaviors. He is an award winning author of numerous books, including:

- *Social Skills Training, 20th Anniversary Edition: For Children and Adolescents with Autism and Social Communication Differences*
- *Social Skills Training for Children and Adolescents with Aspergers Syndrome and Social Communication Problems*
- *Preparing for Life: The Complete Handbook for the Transition to Adulthood for Those with Autism and Aspergers Syndrome*
- *The Social Skills Picture Book*
- *The Social Skills Picture Book for High School and Beyond*
- *No More Meltdowns: Positive Strategies for Managing and Preventing Out-of-Control Behavior*
- *No More Victims: Protecting Those with Autism from Cyber Bullying, Internet Predators & Scams*
- *Overcoming Anxiety in Children and Teens*
- *School Shadow Guidelines*

His work has also been featured on *ABC World News Tonight, Nightline, The Early Show* on CBS, and the Discovery Health Channel.

OTHER TITLES
— by —
JED BAKER

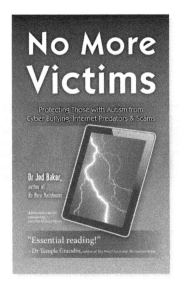

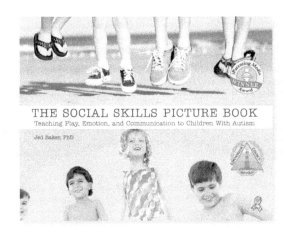

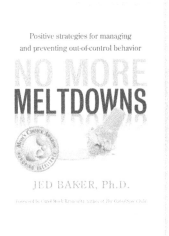

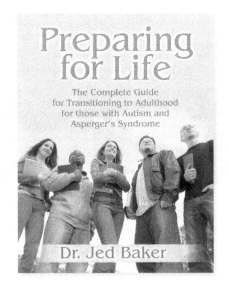

Did you like this book?

Rate it and share your opinion!

Not what you expected? Tell us!

Most negative reviews occur when the book did not reach expectation. Did the description build any expectations that were not met? Let us know how we can do better.

Please drop us a line at info@fhautism.com.
Thank you so much for your support!

FUTURE   HORIZONS

CPSIA information can be obtained
at www.ICGtesting.com
Printed in the USA
JSHW050132230723
45238JS00002B/2

9 781957 984223